Diversity Issues in Law Enforcement

THIRD EDITION

Shahé S. Kazarian

Wesley Crichlow

Simon Bradford

2007
emp Emond Montgomery Publications
Toronto, Canada

Emond Montgomery Publications Limited
60 Shaftesbury Avenue
Toronto ON M4T 1A3
http://www.emp.ca/highered

Printed in Canada.
Reprinted April 2012.

We acknowledge the financial support of the Government of Canada through the Canada Book Fund for our publishing activities.

The events and characters depicted in this book are fictitious. Any similarity to actual persons, living or dead, is purely coincidental.

Acquisitions and development editor: Peggy Buchan
Marketing manager: Christine Davidson
Director, sales and marketing, higher education: Kevin Smulan
Supervising editor: Jim Lyons
Copy editor: David Handelsman
Proofreader: Nancy Ennis
Assistant production editor: Debbie Gervais
Typesetter: Tara Wells
Indexer: Paula Pike
Cover designer: Susan Darrach, Darrach Design

Library and Archives Canada Cataloguing in Publication

Kazarian, Shahé S., 1945–
    Diversity issues in law enforcement / Shahé S. Kazarian, Wesley Crichlow, Simon Bradford. — 3rd ed.

First ed. published under title: Diversity issues in policing.
Includes index.
ISBN 978-1-55239-223-2

    1. Police — Canada — Textbooks.   2. Police–community relations — Canada — Textbooks.   3. Law enforcement — Canada — Textbooks. 4. Multiculturalism — Canada — Textbooks.   I. Crichlow, Wesley E. A. (Wesley Eddison Aylesworth), 1961–   II. Bradford, Simon, 1957–   III. Title.

HV8157.K38 2007   363.2'30971   C2007-901139-X

Contents

CHAPTER 3 Human Rights and Freedoms 63

PART II SOCIAL AND RELIGIOUS CONSIDERATIONS IN POLICING

CHAPTER 4 Host Communities and Immigration Policies 103

PART III PROCESS AND OUTCOME CONSIDERATIONS

CHAPTER 7 Policing Diversity-Motivated Beliefs and Practices

CHAPTER 8 Policing with Diversity Competency

PART IV SPECIAL DIVERSITY CONSIDERATIONS

CHAPTER 9   Policing Family Violence 253

CHAPTER 10   Policing Mental Illness 275

Introduction 276

Concept of Mental Illness 277

Mental Health Legislation 278

    Mental Health Act: Ontario 278

    Mental Health Provisions in the Criminal Code 279

Mental Disturbance and Police Response 279

    Substance-Related Disorders 279

    Mood Disorders and Suicidal Behaviour 280

Preface

This third edition of *Diversity Issues in Law Enforcement* has evolved from the previous two editions, *Diversity Issues in Policing*, published in 1998, and *Diversity Issues in Law Enforcement*, published in 2001. The third edition has retained its overall organization, pedagogy, and workbook format. The decision to retain the original structure was based on continued positive feedback from instructors who have used the previous editions in the Police Foundations Program.

The third edition is different from the previous edition in four ways. First, the third edition has benefited from collaboration with two new co-authors, Dr. Wesley Crichlow, Department of Criminal Justice and Policy Studies, University of Ontario Institute of Technology, and Simon Bradford, Staff Sergeant, Ontario Provincial Police, Central Region. Second, all 10 chapters have been updated to reflect the post-9/11 environment. The September 11, 2001 terrorist attacks on the United States had profound effects on law enforcement and the imperative of national security. In fact, most chapters have been substantially revised to describe the impact of 9/11 on Canada's pluralistic society, its laws and law enforcement practices, and police–community relations. Third, all 10 chapters have been revised so that preview scenarios and chapter contents include more Canadian examples and policing issues are discussed in a specifically Canadian context. Fourth, this edition of *Diversity Issues in Law Enforcement* is accompanied by an updated instructor's guide, PowerPoint presentations, and test bank.

Writing and revising the third edition of *Diversity Issues in Law Enforcement* has been an arduous process. My co-authors and I sincerely thank Peggy Buchan of Emond Montgomery for her support, encouragement, and guidance. We also thank the WordsWorth Communications team for their invaluable efforts in the preparation of the book for publication: Jim Lyons, managing editor; David Handelsman, copy editor; Nancy Ennis, proofreader; Tara Wells, typesetter; and Paula Pike, indexer.

Finally, I would like to thank Dean Khalil Bitar of the Faculty of Arts and Sciences at the American University of Beirut and the university for supporting my request for a sabbatical, and all my colleagues in the Department of Social and Behavioral Sciences for their encouragement, particularly Nabil Dajani, Arne Dietrich, and Sari Hanafi. I would also like to express special thanks to my son Steve and my daughter Nancy and the special people in their lives, Karri and Mark, respectively, for opening their homes temporarily for me to do my writing. Finally, I thank Levonty, my spouse and partner for 35 years, for her unconditional support and love.

Shahé S. Kazarian, PhD
London, Ontario
October 27, 2006

PART I
Conceptual and Legal Considerations

CHAPTER 1

Police Culture in a Diversity Context

CHAPTER OBJECTIVES

After completing this chapter, you should be able to:

- Explain police culture in terms of a demographic police profile, the context of policing, and core values.

- Discuss the police force approach and the police services approach to policing.

- Discuss policing within the contexts of social and cultural diversity.

- Describe how the terrorist attacks of September 11, 2001 have affected policing.

PREVIEW SCENARIO

On March 16, 1982, a Lebanese immigrant of Armenian descent saved the life of Constable F. Dionne. Constable Dionne was "seeing stars" and helpless by virtue of being kicked and choked on Mount Pleasant Road in Toronto. Constable C. Szumlinski could not assist his partner because he too was being attacked by the brother of the man on top of Constable Dionne. Peter Danayan, 28, saw it as his duty as a citizen to help an overpowered police officer. The inaction of other bystanders did not deter Danayan from grabbing Constable Dionne's nightstick and subduing the attacker. Needless to say, the immigrant saviour received a police civilian citation for bravery. (Citizen saves police from attacker, 1982)

INTRODUCTION

There are many Danayans among the culturally, religiously, and linguistically diverse people that law enforcement officers serve and protect in the global village. **Pluralistic** countries that comprise the global village include Canada, Australia, the United Kingdom, and the United States. Canada is a multicultural country with a

pluralism
state of having many cultural groups in one country

proud tradition of law enforcement. The over 61,000 police officers in Canada (Statistics Canada, 2005) attend to the law enforcement needs of a culturally and linguistically diverse population of people. Canadian society comprises more than 200 different ethnic groups, and its members speak more than 100 different tongues (Statistics Canada, 2001).

Needless to say, law enforcement is embedded in diversity. And, as Canada has changed, so has law enforcement. The changing face of the multicultural Canadian society, its demographic trends, the legislative and administrative initiatives in the justice system in response to the challenge of diversity, the emergence of new forms of crime, and the September 11, 2001 terrorist attacks in the United States have led to a rethinking of law enforcement in the country. In particular, police forces and agencies have sought to enhance existing policing skills, develop new policing skills and knowledge to serve and protect the culturally diverse Canadian population more effectively and efficiently, and create a policing agenda that has national security at the forefront (Canadian Police Association and Canadian Association of Chiefs of Police, 2001). Police services in Canada are now conducting outreach initiatives that encourage women, new Canadians, Aboriginal people, and visible minorities to join police services. These initiatives are aimed at enhancing the diversity of police services.

This chapter discusses the concept of diversity and models of policing and police culture. Diversity is viewed as an asset to policing rather than a liability.

THE CONCEPT OF DIVERSITY

diversity
socially constructed characteristics on the basis of which individuals and groups define themselves and/or are defined by others

Diversity refers to the socially constructed characteristics by which individuals and groups define themselves and/or are defined by others. A narrow view of diversity considers only gender, race, and ethnicity while a broader view of diversity encompasses age, class, cultural beliefs, values and practices, language, marital status, nationality, physical ability, religion, and sexual orientation. The most inclusive definition views diversity as

> a concept that promotes mutual respect, acceptance, teamwork and productivity among people who differ in work background, experience, education, age, gender, race, ethnic origin, physical abilities and all the other ways in which we differ. (Laws, 2005, p. 3)

It is important for police officers to recognize that individuals in Canadian society may be identified or may identify themselves on the basis of one or more of these characteristics. Thus, a Canadian woman may see herself as a Muslim Canadian woman, a Muslim Arab woman, or simply a Canadian woman.

Public–police contact is considerable by virtue of the varied and socially indispensable functions that police officers perform: preserving the peace, preventing crime, assisting crime victims, apprehending and charging offenders, executing warrants, referring people to appropriate community supports and services, and providing public education. How police interact with members of the public is guided by considerations of diversity. Of course, some communities are more or less diverse than others. The diversity profiles of various communities determine the nature and extent of diversity issues for policing. In communities in which there are very few ethnic groups, diversity issues may not be as relevant for that community and police as they are in other communities.

POLICE CULTURE

Policing in Canada is the responsibility of the federal, provincial, and municipal branches of government. Policing in the province of Ontario, which has a population of over 11 million people, is the responsibility of the Ministry of Community Safety and Correctional Services. Standards for police services delivery and training are set at the level of the province, and police services boards are responsible for the adequacy and effectiveness of police service delivery. There are a total of 61 police services in Ontario with over 22,000 police officers. The Toronto Police Service and the Ontario Provincial Police (OPP) are the two largest police agencies in the province, and the West Grey Police Service is the smallest. Chiefs of police are selected by police services boards to whom senior officers in the ranks of deputy chief, staff superintendent, superintendent, staff inspector, and inspector, and police officers in the ranks of staff sergeant, sergeant, constable, and police cadet (civilian position) all ultimately report. A first-class constable usually earns a salary of $68,000 while a chief usually earns over $165,000 (Stephens, 2005).

The OPP and the Royal Canadian Mounted Police (RCMP), Canada's national police service, are led by commissioners and they have a slightly different rank structure. Both services have deputy commissioners, chief superintendents, superintendents, inspectors, sergeants, constables, and cadets. The OPP also has sergeant majors working within the Professional Standards Bureau. All police services have civilian employees who play an integral part in each police service, both as junior and senior members.

Police Recruitment, Duties, and Training

Persons who wish to become police officers must meet certain requirements. Candidates must be Canadian citizens or permanent residents; be 18 years of age or older; possess the physical and mental ability to perform the duties of a police officer; successfully complete at least four years of secondary school education; possess a valid driver's licence; be certified in CPR and first aid (at the time of the employment offer); obtain security clearance; pass background, credit, and reference checks; and be of good character. Candidates must also demonstrate the following essential qualities and competencies: analytical thinking, self-confidence, excellent communication skills, flexibility, respect for diversity, self-control, relationship-building skills, and a desire to achieve.

The Ontario Police College, founded in 1962, is one of the largest residential police training facilities in North America. It provides training to recruits and other police service personnel in its location in Aylmer, Ontario. The college offers a range of programs: Basic Constable Program, Advanced Patrol Training, Criminal Investigation, Forensic Identification, and Race Relations and Adult Education. The Basic Constable Program offers several courses including Applied Police Learning, Defensive Tactics, Firearms Training, and Officer Safety. On July 12, 2001, the Ontario Police College expanded its facilities and opened the Dynamic Simulation Area. The new structure is a realistic "streetscape" that allows students to participate in hands-on simulations. Its function is to provide a link to the classroom, allowing students to "learn it, try it" (Stephens, 2005).

Policing is a reputable and honourable profession that requires officers to provide a broad range of services. Section 4(2) of the Ontario *Police Services Act* identifies the following as core police services: crime prevention, law enforcement, assistance to victims of crime, public order maintenance, and emergency response. Police officers preserve the peace, prevent crime, assist crime victims, apprehend and charge offenders, execute warrants, provide public education, and direct people in need to the appropriate community supports and services. Police officers work many hours keeping the peace, responding to calls for service, assisting citizens in crises, and helping to resolve a wide array of social issues. In short, police officers enhance the quality of life of the people they serve.

The plethora of functions performed by police officers makes their work anything but boring and invites a deeper exploration of the inner circle of police culture. **Police culture** is the expression of common values, beliefs, and attitudes of police within a police context (Waddington, 1999). In the next section, we explore police culture by examining the demographic police profile, the context of policing, and the core values in policing.

police culture
attitudes, values, and beliefs of police and police organizations that influence police reactions and behaviours within the police services and on the street

Demographic Police Profile

As of June 15, 2005, there were 61,050 police officers in Canada (Statistics Canada, 2005a). This figure represents a rate of 189 officers per 100,000 population. Although impressive, this rate is well below those for Australia, the United Kingdom, and the United States, whose rates range from 242 officers per 100,000 population to 262 officers per 100,000 population (Statistics Canada, 2005b). Police services have been striving to represent the diversity of the communities that they serve and protect. Nevertheless, it is a historical reality that police services in pluralistic Western societies such as Canada, Australia, the United Kingdom, and the United States have often not been representative of the public they served. For example, males tended to so overrepresent police services that the police were seen as a **male white culture**.

male white culture
culture in which whiteness, masculinity, and hierarchy are emphasized and diversity, women, and gays and lesbians are devalued

Although there continues to be evidence that in some circles law enforcement represents a male-dominant culture, there is also clear evidence that law enforcement agencies are committed to increasing the female representation in their ranks. Of the 61,050 police officers in Canada in 2005, nearly 10,600 were female, representing a gain of 7 percent from the previous year. By comparison, the number of male officers in Canada increased by only 1 percent. As of 2005, women accounted for 17 percent of police officers in Canada, compared with 10 percent a decade ago. This gender balancing of law enforcement is consistent with the positive value that women bring to policing, including a reduction in police brutality, increased efficacy in police response to violence against women, and increased emphasis on conflict resolution over the use of force.

While the face of law enforcement in Canada is changing, the gender imbalance in law enforcement still exists, as do imbalances in ethnicity, race, and sexual orientation. For example, Morris (2004) reported that of the over 7,900 police recruits from municipal police services and the Ontario Provincial Police that were trained at the Ontario Police College between September 1998 and September 2003, about 80 percent were male and only 10.7 percent identified themselves as members of a First Nations/Aboriginal group and/or visible minority. Nevertheless, there is the desire and the will within law enforcement to meet the unique needs of a diverse population. A variety of initiatives have been launched, including the adaptation of new policing methods and new training and recruitment approaches. These efforts have yielded results: of the 41 new police officer recruits to the Toronto Police Services in 2005, 44 percent were visible minorities and 29 percent were female; 27 percent were bilingual (they spoke English and an additional language) and 12 percent were multilingual (they spoke two or more languages other than English) (Powell, 2005). At a recent graduation Toronto Police had

> 160 new police officers, whom Chief Bill Blair called some of the best-educated and most diverse, to graduate at the Sept. 8 ceremony in Nathan Phillips Square. … The graduating class was representative of the city it will police, with new officers speaking 33 different languages from American Sign Language to Arabic. Of those, 63 speak two languages, 24 speak three languages, and seven speak four languages. Thirty-six hold university degrees, 77 hold college diplomas, and 46 hold the OSSD or its equivalent. The class is made up of 14% women and 30% visible minorities. (Toronto Police, 2006)

Although police services are a long way from being representative of the racial and ethnic makeup of the country, they are gradually changing the face of policing (Ewatski, 2006). Their efforts are founded on the premise that constable diversity—in contrast to a homogenous white male police service—is essential for effective community policing in multicultural societies (Coutts, Schneider, Johnson, and McLeod, 2003). At the same time, it is important to note that changing the face of law enforcement is a function of the nation's demographics and that both the police and the community must share the responsibility for recruiting people from all races and ethnicities (McCormack, 2004; Wilson, 2004). In relation to demographics, trends in Canada's population are such that future police services will face a population of new immigrants from around the world who will settle mostly in metropolitan areas (see McCormack, 2004). Immigration is expected to increase as the Canadian population decreases; this will change the fabric of Canadian society and will greatly affect policing. In order for police officers to be effective, they will have to be able to effectively communicate with immigrant communities as their populations increase. In order to achieve this, members of these communities will need to become members of Canadian police services. (For illustrations and discussion of demographic trends in Canada, see the appendix.)

Police services and communities must share the responsibility for creating diversity in police services and agencies. Too few members of minorities are joining police services and, as a result, most police services do not reflect the diversity of the communities they serve. It is likely that the absence of diverse representation in police services is due at least partly to the failure of immigrant non-white families to encourage their children to consider policing as a worthwhile and satisfying career. They may believe that policing is not a rewarding career, they may lack knowledge about the extent of professional opportunities and career advancement offered by policing, or they may prefer that their children go into other professions. The reluctance of immigrant non-white families to consider policing as a career option for their children may also be due to their experiences with corrupt and repressive police in their countries of origin. Finally, they may believe that police services will not welcome them, and that police will frustrate their efforts to penetrate the exclusive membership of the well-established male white police culture. To address these concerns, police services are developing more inclusive recruiting strategies to heighten the interest of diverse groups in policing as a career. For example, the OPP has been very resourceful in providing recruiting opportunities for specific target groups. The OPP offered the Outward Bound Program—one-week immersion opportunities for women, First Nations people, visible minorities, and other target groups. These opportunities include sessions where the participants can experience police culture and explore whether they would like to pursue a career with the OPP. Other police services have used employment fairs, cultural celebrations, college recruiting drives, and direct advertising to encourage women, visible minorities, and other underrepresented groups to apply to their police services.

Policing in the Canadian Context

No society is free of crime. Crime is not easily beaten, and public fear of crime in various parts of the world continues to be appreciable. Crime rates differ among countries and within nations. Crime fluctuates over time. In 2004, each police officer in Canada handled an average of 43 *Criminal Code* incidents, a figure lower than the rate of 51 incidents per police officer in 1991 but considerably higher than the rate of 33 incidents per police officer in the mid-1970s (Statistics Canada, 2005b). *Criminal Code* incidents include violent crimes (homicide, attempted murder, assault, sexual assault, other sexual offences, and abduction and robbery); property crimes (break-and-enter, motor vehicle theft, other theft, possession of stolen goods, fraud); and other *Criminal Code* offences (including mischief, counterfeiting currency, bail violations, disturbing the peace, prostitution and arson). Of the more than 2.5 million *Criminal Code* incidents reported by police in 2003, 12 percent were violent crimes, 51 percent were property crimes, and 37 percent were other *Criminal Code* offences (Statistics Canada, 2004). (See table 1.1.)

The policing environment in Canada today is significantly different from the policing environment 30 years ago. Police efforts to keep up with both an increase in technological crimes and an increase in time commitments for investigation have put a strain on police resources. As Malm et al. have noted,

> The patterns and requirements of police work are defined by law and are continually redefined by new judicial decisions, new legislation, and new government policy initiatives … . As a consequence, demands on police operations have increased dramatically without a proportional increase in budget or person-power. In turn, these demands have had a significant workload affect on police organizations and their ability to serve the public. (Malm, Polard, Brantingham, Tinsley, Plecas, Brantingham, Cohen, and Kinney, 2005, p. 10)

Police do their best to prevent crime and put criminals behind bars or consider alternative approaches to deal with them including community sentencing, healing circles, and suspended sentences. In fact, a police motto adopted by a variety of police services in the global village is "to serve and protect." Police take their profession to heart and sacrifice a lot. According to Deputy Director Bill Stephens of the Ontario Police College, policing as a career involves "demanding duties, shift work, working many weekends and holidays, [and it] can involve high stress and danger." But, he adds, policing is also "a job where you can make a big difference in your community" (Stephens, 2005, p. 160).

TABLE 1.1   Criminal Code Incidents Reported by Police in Canada, 2003

	Number	Rate/100,000 population
Total violent crimes	304,515	963
Assaults	236,103	746
Robbery	28,332	90
Sexual assaults	23,425	74
Other assaults	12,299	39
Attempted murder	710	2
Abduction	560	2
Homicide	548	2
Total property crimes	1,303,569	4,121
Theft $5,000 and less	702,317	2,220
Break and enter	284,496	899
Motor vehicle theft	171,017	541
Fraud	92,838	294
Possession of stolen goods	32,777	104
Theft $5,000 and over	20,124	64
Total other criminal offences	964,159	3,048
Mischief	356,143	1,126
Counterfeiting currency	138,430	438
Disturbing the peace	103,691	328
Bail violations	98, 164	310
Offensive weapons	16,940	54
Arson	13,851	44
Prostitution	5,658	18
Other	231,282	731

Source: Statistics Canada (2004).

Police officers who have to fulfill the mandates of police services have to do shift work. Although many officers cope well with shift work, it becomes more challenging as they become older. In addition to contributing to sleep disturbance, shift work raises potential issues of isolation, reduced quality time with family, and more difficult family scheduling.

Police officers who must fulfill the mandate of police services and want to advance in their careers need to devote considerable time and energy to their work. Thus, police culture demands and rewards long hours of police work. Although the achievement-oriented police culture has personal, social, and economic benefits, police officers may dedicate too much time to their job and too little to family and friends. Police absorption in the job may also manifest itself as an absence of quality time at home, to the detriment of family members and friends. In fact, in most countries, police divorce rates are higher than the divorce rates for other professions. Marriage to the profession, long hours, time away from home, shift work, and hypervigilance (discussed below) may all contribute to the high divorce rate. Police officers are wise to balance the demands of work and the pleasures of family, friends, and leisure time.

Police work can be stressful and dangerous by virtue of crises and emergency responses. Although the variety and spontaneity in police work is alluring (even addictive), it is not without its drawbacks (Kirschman, 1997). First, the unpredictability of the work may interfere with planned family activities. Second, the unpredictability is stressful on the family by virtue of the host of emotions that the officer may display when he or she returns home from a shift. The officer may be irritable, exhausted, or simply glad to be home safe.

Police officers also may have to deal with public scrutiny of their work. Consider the broad coverage of incidents involving police in the daily newspapers. The often intrusive media coverage of police, and the criticisms police receive from the media and the community, can be sources of stress for police, their partners, and their children.

As well, officers may need to use violence or the threat of violence in the presence of danger. As the preview scenario at the start of the chapter shows, officers' lives may be endangered. Sometimes, when officers are obliged to use force, people may die in the process. The vast majority of police use the least amount of force necessary to effect an arrest. An extreme few may exhibit **ego forcing**, the use of unnecessary force to boost a macho self-image.

ego forcing
use of unnecessary force to boost a macho self-image

Finally, the danger involved in police work is associated with on-the-job injuries. Police injuries range from broken shoulders to twisted knees to back pain. Physical fitness is crucial for police. They cannot afford to become lethargic and out of shape. A poster in a police gym depicts a muscle-bound inmate in a prison weight room and the caption below him reads, "This inmate has not missed a work-out, have you?" Clearly, regular physical exercise is an important protective factor against work-related stress and injuries.

Core Values

A very positive aspect of police culture is that it is a collectivist culture. Police value one another for safety, mutual support, and quality of life. A number of **core values** are associated with the collectivist police culture: self-control, cynicism, respect for authority, hypervigilance, and a code of silence (Crank, 1997, 2004; Kirschman, 1997; Stansfield, 1996; Williams and Henderson, 1997). These core values may be adaptive (healthy) for police officers but they may also be maladaptive (unhealthy)—that is, they may interfere with quality of life. The benefits and drawbacks of each core value are discussed below.

core values
values of self-control, cynicism, respect for authority, hypervigilance, and a code of silence associated with the collectivist police culture

Self-control is the first core value in police culture. Police officers overcontrol their emotions by suppressing verbal and non-verbal expressions of emotion. Police officers' overcontrol of emotions is developed by virtue of their training and their prolonged exposure to the distresses and despairs of life. Self-control serves three important functions: enhancing self-image, controlling others, and saving face. Self-control enhances police self-image by allowing officers to appear knowledgeable, fearless, and in control. Self-control enables police to maintain an emotional distance in carrying out their work and to control others who require such control—for example, calming survivors of a shootout. In the absence of self-control, officers' ability to cope with situations in which they are hit, spat on, or otherwise humiliated is likely to be compromised. Finally, self-control enables police to sustain the respect and support of their fellow officers by refraining from displaying negative emotions in their presence.

self-control
overcontrol of emotions by suppression of verbal and non-verbal expressions of emotion

Although self-control is a protective strategy for police officers, overcontrolling emotions may interfere with spontaneity and intimacy in interpersonal and family relations. In addition to causing social remoteness, emotional overcontrol may make offices feel emotionally numb and may prevent self-growth by shutting off normal and appropriate expression. Police officers need to learn not to keep everything inside all the time, and to share both their joy and distress with friends and family.

Cynicism is the second core value in police culture. **Cynicism** is the belief that everyone in the world is primarily motivated by selfishness (Kirschman, 1997; Neiderhoffer, 1967; Skolnick, 1966). Police become cynical because of their prolonged exposure to the worst in human behaviour. The four stages of cynicism are over-idealism, frustration, disenchantment, and full-blown "hardened" world view. The hardened world view can contribute to officers' denying goodness in people, assuming a behavioural pattern of overprotecting self and family, and having an isolationist ("blue wall") social style that accepts only fellow cops (Skolnick, 1966).

Respect for authority is the third core value in police culture. Police are trained to develop **respect for authority**. This core value provides simplicity, clarity, and comfort for police in fulfilling their role and executing their duties. However, because officers value respect for authority, they may overreact when others do not comply with their demands, either in the line of duty or at home. Such non-compliance is a source of frustration for police, may be perceived by them as a sign of personal incompetence, and may cause them to overreact.

Hypervigilance is the fourth core value in police culture. **Hypervigilance** entails the belief that the survival of police and of others depends on police ability to view everything in the environment as potentially life-threatening and dangerous. Officers are "urged, warned, required, and rewarded for developing a habit of scanning the environment for cues to danger" (Kirschman, 1997, p. 27). The scanning behaviour associated with hypervigilance

> becomes so finely tuned that even mild danger alerts the officer's autonomic nervous system. The cop experiences this as "buzz": a general sense of aliveness, high energy, vitality, and alertness. This state of physiological elevation becomes its own reward, like a runner's high … . [T]his is what cops mean when they talk about police work getting "into their blood" or about becoming addicted to their own adrenalin. (Kirschman, 1997, pp. 27–28)

While hypervigilance helps police execute their duties and survive real or potentially dangerous situations, their alarmist world view may interfere with their ability to discriminate lethal situations from innocuous ones. Kirschman (1997) points out that

> [t]he problem arises when cops become so hypervigilant that they actually search for an opportunity to get involved in an emergency because they need that hit of adrenalin to avoid feeling depressed or listless. Or they develop a sense of superiority to anyone—including their family members—who doesn't share their alarmist point of view. (p. 28)

The problems associated with hypervigilance are exacerbated by over-investment: "Hypervigilence coupled with over-investment leads officers to believe the only person you can really trust is another cop" (Gilmartin and Harris, 1998). Police officers are encouraged to work hard in order to qualify for developmental and promotional opportunities. This often leads to an over-investment in this one area of their lives leading to neglect in other areas of their lives:

cynicism
belief that the primary motivation behind human behaviour is selfishness

respect for authority
core value stemming from the prevailing paramilitary organizational structure of police services, which provides simplicity, clarity, and comfort for police in fulfilling their role and executing their duties

hypervigilance
belief that survival of police and of others depends on police ability to view everything in the environment as potentially life-threatening and dangerous

As the over-invested officer detaches from non-work related interests or activities, a perceived sense of victimization will increase. Peer groups, friends, co-workers and potentially their entire frame of reference of life begins to change. (Gilmartin and Harris, 1998)

code of silence
core value of withholding information from anyone who is not a member of the police culture

The **code of silence** is the fifth core value in police culture. It is consistent with the brotherhood police image—that an attack on one is an attack on all (Skolnick, 1966)—and entails the value of withholding information from anyone who is not a member of the police culture. Those who are excluded include the public, the courts, and police services management (Stansfield, 1996, p. 170). While the code of silence is both informal and unofficial, its basis, according to Stansfield, is the official police "oath of secrecy" as stated in many police services acts, including that of Ontario:

> The oath or affirmation of secrecy to be taken by a police officer, auxiliary member of a police force, special constable or First Nations Constable shall be in the following form:
>
> > I solemnly swear (affirm) that I will not disclose any information obtained by me in the course of my duties as (*insert name of office*), except as I may be authorized or required by law. (O. reg. 144/91, s. 4)

The vast majority of police officers are professional and ethical in their conduct. The code of silence, however, may exert a powerful influence on police behaviour, including potentially leading them to commit perjury. Police who break the code of silence are called various names, including rat, stool pigeon, squealer, and the one who tells. In extreme cases, those who breach the code of silence are penalized and ostracized by other police to affirm commitment to the value of police solidarity represented by the code (Stansfield, 1996). Some of the known negative consequences that have been imposed on the one who tells have included harassment, threats, and the silent treatment.

police–community interface
represented by the motto "to serve and protect," the principle that police functions are to be afforded to all community residents regardless of their culture, race, ethnic origin, religion, sex, age, sexual orientation, or physical or mental ability

police force approach
approach to policing that emphasizes a reactive, crime control mandate; measures police effectiveness by such indicators as number of random patrols to deter criminal activity, response rate to police calls, number of arrests and convictions, and citizen satisfaction surveys

POLICE–COMMUNITY INTERFACE

As mentioned previously, a motto associated with a number of police services in North America is "to serve and protect." The serving and protecting functions are extended to all community residents, regardless of their culture, race, ethnic origin, religion, sex, age, sexual orientation, or physical or mental ability. A recent international survey involving 11 Western industrial nations showed that satisfaction with police performance was highest for Canada. In fact, the study found that "Canadians love their cops far more than the English love their famed British Bobby" (Durkan, 1998, p. A9). Nevertheless, issues in policing in multicultural contexts continue to evolve. Common concerns being addressed in police departments around the world include internal organizational structure and culture, and the **police–community interface**.

Two primary approaches have dominated policing in the global village: the police force approach and the police services approach (Fleras, 1992; Stansfield, 1996; Williams and Henderson, 1997; Pruegger, 2003). The effectiveness of these approaches is measured by such indicators as number of arrests and convictions, response rate to police calls, and citizen satisfaction surveys (Fleras, 1992). A summary of both approaches is provided in table 1.2. The **police force approach**

TABLE 1.2   Police Force Approach Versus Police Services Approach

Police force	Police services
Policing as a craft/trade	Policing as a profession
Emphasis on physical attributes	Emphasis on intellect
Crime-fighting	Crime-preventing
Incident-driven	Problem-driven
Reactive	Proactive
Us versus them	Partner with community
Centralized	Decentralized
Hierarchical	Horizontal
Diversity-blind	Diversity-responsive
Inwardly focused	Outwardly focused

has assumed a management structure and culture in which a reactive, crime control mandate is emphasized so that police are seen as warrior cops and police effectiveness is measured by such indicators as number of random patrols to deter criminal activity, response rate to police calls, number of arrests and convictions, and citizen satisfaction surveys (Fleras, 1992). An underlying assumption of the crime control approach is that streets and neighbourhoods can be kept safe or reclaimed only by a strong centralized police department that promotes a police culture that is hard on crime. Potential negative consequences of the crime control approach to policing are isolation from the community and the people served and police harbouring an us-versus-them mentality.

On the other hand, the **police services approach** has assumed a structure and a culture in which new core knowledge, skills, and abilities are identified to enhance police officers' effectiveness in performing their duties. The Ministry of Solicitor General Strategic Planning Committee on Police Training and Education (1992) has listed 20 police abilities, knowledge sets, and skills (PAKS) that are of strategic importance to future police organizations. The strategic learning PAKS include the following:

police services approach approach to policing that emphasizes problem solving, crime prevention, and partnerships between police and communities

- ability to accept and work with community diversity;

- ability to service victims;

- ability to use force appropriately;

- ability to reform community policing;

- ability to act ethically and professionally;

- ability to solve problems;

- knowledge of crime prevention strategies;

- knowledge of human behaviour;

- knowledge of political systems and processes and other agencies;

- communication, interpersonal, and sensitivity skills;

- conflict avoidance, resolution, and mediation skills;

- officer safety skills; and

- personal, organizational development, and team-building skills.

A key area of strategic learning and an important aspect of the police services approach is **community policing principles** or problem-solving policing principles. An underlying assumption of this crime prevention model is that streets and neighbourhoods can be kept safe or reclaimed by promoting a police culture that is inclusive of the rank and file and that focuses on civic empowerment (Clyderman, O'Toole, and Fleras, 1992; Pruegger, 2003). Empowerment entails openness on the part of the police administration (from the chief on down), input from the rank and file, and partnerships with communities. The proactive and problem-solving orientation of the police services approach provides for identifying and solving problems, resolving the underlying causes of disputes, preventing future recurrences, and finding alternatives to arrest and conviction whenever possible (Clyderman et al., 1992). Principles that are associated with community policing as articulated by the United Nations Centre for Human Rights are listed in table 1.3. Examples of problem-solving and community policing programs are Crime Stoppers, Neighbourhood Watch, and PEACE (Police, Ethnic and Cultural Exchange) programs.

In 1989, the RCMP adopted community policing as its model of law enforcement. Many police services across Canada have also embraced the challenge of community policing within a diversity framework. Nevertheless, community policing is not universally accepted and is resisted within some law enforcement circles (Lewis, Rosenberg, and Sigler, 1999). This resistance is partly due to the perception that community policing is "feminized" policing in that it abandons the traditional

TABLE 1.3   Principles of Community Policing

- Establishing a partnership between police and law abiding members of the community.

- Adopting a community relations policy and plan of action.

- Recruiting from all sectors of the community.

- Training officers to deal with diversity.

- Establishing community outreach and public information programs.

- Liaising regularly with all groups in the community.

- Building contacts with the community through non-enforcement activities.

- Assigning officers to a permanent neighborhood beat.

- Increasing community participation in policing activities and community-based safety programs.

- Involving the community in identifying problems and concerns.

- Using a creative problem-solving approach to develop responses to specific community problems, including non-traditional tactics and strategies.

- Coordinating policies, strategies, and activities with other government agencies, and with non-governmental organizations.

Source: United Nations Centre for Human Rights (n.d., pp. 17–18).

"masculine" crime-fighting approach (Miller, 1999). This perception is false. Community policing does not betray policing history—it enhances, rather than replaces, traditional law enforcement and makes policing more responsive to a culturally diverse public.

Technological changes have had profound effects on the police–community interface. The advent of cars and computers contributed to a shift in the way that police officers interacted with members of the public—from a proactive approach to policing to a reactive approach. As described by Williams and Henderson (1997), the bond between officers who "walked the beat" and members of the community provided a natural climate for public safety and crime prevention. In contrast, the use of cars and computerized communications systems minimizes routine police contact with members of the public, reduces police problem-solving opportunities, and allows for reactive and prioritized police responses to calls. Furthermore, these technologies violate the fundamental principle articulated by Sir Robert Peel, a British politician credited with founding modern policing, in 1829—namely, that "the public are the police and the police the public."

The Law Enforcement–Community Interface and Alternative Approaches to Justice

Increasingly, the effectiveness of the conventional justice system is being questioned. Critics point to its grounding in crime and punishment, the limited success of the punishment-centred, quick-fix approach in offender community reintegration, and the tension that **recidivism** (relapse into criminal activity) creates between the community and law enforcement in their role as gatekeepers in the criminal justice system. Alternative, less court-based and adversarial and more effective and restorative approaches are being considered (Cooper and Chatterjee, not dated). For example, in the **restorative justice approach**, the offender, the victim, and the affected community work together to deal with the harm caused by the offender. This approach has four aspects: redemption, accountability, repair, and prevention. The offender, in addition to being shamed and showing remorse in a caring and a supportive context for the ultimate purpose of community reintegration, is expected to assume responsibility for causing the harm and make himself or herself accountable to the victim and the community by repairing or minimizing both material and psychological damages to the victim. The restorative justice approach to policing is exemplified by the RCMP's Community Justice Forum initiative and is deemed more effective than the conventional incarceration-oriented approach, particularly with young offenders (Cooper and Chatterjee, not dated).

recidivism
relapse into criminal activity

restorative justice approach
involvement of offender, victim, and community to repair material and psychological damage to victim and community reintegration of offender by use of shaming and invoking remorse for wrongful action

The Law Enforcement–Community Interface: Post 9/11

The September 11, 2001 terrorist attacks in the United States and Canada's full commitment to participate in the war against terrorism have had profound effects on police–community relations in Canada. In particular, Canada's efforts to combat terrorism have brought to the forefront new concerns about racism and other forms of discrimination in the country generally, and in local communities in particular. They have also raised important issues regarding the process by which law enforcement has adapted to the diversity and national security realities in the post-9/11 environment, and have underlined the need for law enforcement agencies to balance heightened security requirements with civil liberties, both in Canada and abroad. As Jean Augustine, former Canadian Secretary of State (Multiculturalism) (Status of Women), has said (2003, June 5),

> As we all know, the world changed on September 11, 2001. The events of that day have led to heightened national security around the globe and brought new pressures and concerns about racism and other forms of discrimination in our communities and in our country.
>
> Individuals here were made to feel uncomfortable, even in communities in which they may have lived for many years or many generations, because of their racial and cultural backgrounds, faith or traditions.
>
> The fact is, some communities and individuals in Canada have felt targeted by virtue of the colour of their skin, the place where they worship, their clothing and traditions, even by their gender.
>
> These experiences were felt despite the fact that the vast majority of Canadians condemn racism and discrimination.
>
> Some Police Services have been criticized for their treatment of Aboriginal people, African Canadians, and members of the Arab and Muslim communities.
>
> Under the law every Canadian is equal. Nevertheless, it is clear we have some barriers to overcome before every citizen of Canada can feel truly accepted and truly included; and before we reach equality of outcome or substantive equality.

Similarly, Chief Jack Ewatski (2006, April 20) identified the post 9/11 "stresses and strains that are testing our community policing model." He described the tension associated with the principle of information sharing to combat terrorism and the principle of privacy rights and protection of personal information, and the high cost of compromising either of them. As an illustration, he cited the case of Maher Arar, a Muslim Canadian man who was intercepted in the United States while en route to Canada from a family visit abroad and subsequently detained in Syria, where he alleges that he was tortured on suspicion of having terrorist ties. A judicial inquiry has looked into the actions of Canadian officials and has determined that Mr. Arar's rights as a Canadian were violated in the process of international information and intelligence sharing. Chief Ewatski argues that trust is essential to effective law enforcement and counter-terrorism. He suggests that cross-cultural understanding leads to trust and he advocates the right and responsibility of the public to participate in policing. He describes a number of initiatives to build trust: recruitment from diverse linguistic and cultural groups, education of police in the best practices of policing with cultural competency, and establishment of the Law Enforcement Aboriginal and Diversity (LEAD) network for the purpose of improving police capacity to serve Aboriginal, ethno-cultural and ethno-racial communities serving in national, provincial, regional, and local roles.

POLICE CULTURE IN A DIVERSITY CONTEXT: POLICE ABILITIES, KNOWLEDGE, AND SKILLS

Police serve and protect a diverse public. In their day-to-day lives, police encounter individuals from a variety of cultural groups, languages, genders, ages, socio-economic classes, religions, sexual orientations, and physical and mental abilities, and with different levels of psychological well-being. This diversity dictates a diversity-oriented policing structure and function that focuses on multiculturalism, human rights and freedoms, community orientation, and restorative justice.

The diversity face of law enforcement is challenging and changing. The vast majority of police see diversity as positive evidence of their challenging and rewarding police lifestyle. As in any profession, a minority may see diversity as a negative influence on policing. People of diversity are not the orphans of the communities served and protected by police but vital and contributing members of those communities. Principle 5 of the Ontario *Police Services Act* envisions a police service that is sensitive to the "pluralistic, multiracial and multicultural character of Ontario society" (s. 1). The actual practice of this principle requires that the diversity of the communities be reflected within the police services from the highest to the lowest rank, and that police services develop a **diversity policing framework**. This is not just for the benefit of those communities but for the benefit of the police as well. There is more than suggestive evidence that diversity within police departments and the provision of diversity-appropriate services *enhance* police safety and respect from diverse communities.

A number of specific benefits to adopting a diversity policing framework have been identified (for example, Burstein, 2004; Multilingual Orientation Service Association for Immigrant Communities, 2003). These include:

- reduction in the frequency of injuries to law enforcement officers and citizens;

- decrease in the number of citizen complaints and lawsuits against police;

- improvement in police–community relations;

- recognition and appreciation of the value of diversity to police services and its use as an asset rather than a liability; and

- effective response to major demographic changes in communities served.

Four core values are identified with diversity policing: affirming and valuing diverse modes of being and relating; assuming a police–community climate that validates diverse perspectives; empowering diverse voices within and outside the police service in goal setting, problem solving, and decision making; and promoting a police culture that respects the rights of people of diversity and police safety and personhood.

A paradigm shift toward diversity policing is evident in the development and enhancement of community policing in seven areas: organizational support and culture; training and education; policy development; recruitment, selection, retention, and promotion practices; staff development; community relations and development; and evaluation (Pruegger, 2003). Table 1.4 lists a number of initiatives in

diversity policing framework
policing framework that affirms and values people of diversity; assumes a police–community climate that validates diversity; empowers voices of diversity within and outside the police force in goal setting, problem solving, and decision making; and promotes a police–community culture that is respectful of police safety and police personhood

TABLE 1.4   Diversity Initiatives in Policing

- Police recruitment, selection, retention, and promotion practices within a diversity framework.

- Establishment of police-relevant diversity training programs that focus on anti-racism and that provide on-the-job training and mentoring for diversity competency.

- Hiring of human rights officers to respond to complaints related to discrimination and harassment.

- Involvement of leaders of diverse communities in criminal investigations.

- Increased citizen participation in crime prevention initiatives.

- Increased community involvement in review of police activity (for example, civilian review boards).

- Establishment of hate crime units in police services in the wake of 9/11 terrorist attacks in the United States.

- Creation of Aboriginal policing programs to improve Aboriginal–police relations and quality of policing services to Aboriginal people.

- Inclusion of courses on diversity issues in policing as part of Police Foundations programs.

support of efforts to diversify policing and to address diversity issues in policing generally and in community policing in particular.

The remaining chapters of this book address a variety of diversity principles in policing with a view to rethinking policing in a diversity context, grounding law enforcement in the frameworks of multiculturalism, human rights and freedoms, community orientation, and restorative justice, and engendering seven diversity-based policing competencies: analytical thinking, valuing diversity, effective communication, flexibility, self-confidence, self-control, and relationship building. The chapters also focus on the need for students in policing programs to adopt an achievement orientation and to develop their mental and physical skills and abilities. The process of rethinking policing in this way can evoke highly charged emotions when one is exposed to controversial and politically correct or incorrect diversity issues and positions. Although this process can lead to better personal understanding and growth, interpersonal relations, and policing effectiveness, it can also be confusing and painful at times. However, gains can be made in personal and interpersonal growth, and the process can be made easier by construing diversity as a positive energy and engendering a climate of self-respect, respect for others, dialogue, patience, hard work, and willingness to grow. A list of related dos and don'ts for police officers is provided in table 1.5.

TABLE 1.5 Dos and Don'ts of Police Culture

Dos	Don'ts
Respect yourself, your superiors, and the public.	Don't blame the ills of the world on people of diversity.
Embrace a diversity policing framework.	Don't overcontrol (or undercontrol) your emotions.
Be professional and ethical.	
Take care of your body and psyche.	Don't be cynical—life is beautiful.
Be physically fit.	Don't sweat the small or the big stuff—be happy.
Live to work and work to live.	
Nurture your feminine and masculine traits.	Don't be hypervigilant around family and friends.
Develop good coping skills to deal with stress.	Don't consider yourself a hero
	Don't assume an us-versus-them attitude.
Recognize the merits of the restorative justice approach to law enforcement.	

CHAPTER SUMMARY

Police serve and protect people of diversity in the global village. Police culture and organization affect police services' approach to policing and thus police–community relations. The September 11, 2001 terrorist attacks have created new challenges for law enforcement in Canada and around the world. Because the public is culturally and socially pluralistic and because diversity pervades all aspects of policing, a diversity policing framework is required. The diversification of policing promotes a police–community interface that respects diversity and enhances police safety and effectiveness, and promotes trust and public safety.

APPENDIX: DEMOGRAPHIC TRENDS

FIGURE 1.1   Canada's Population Growth, 1921 to 2031

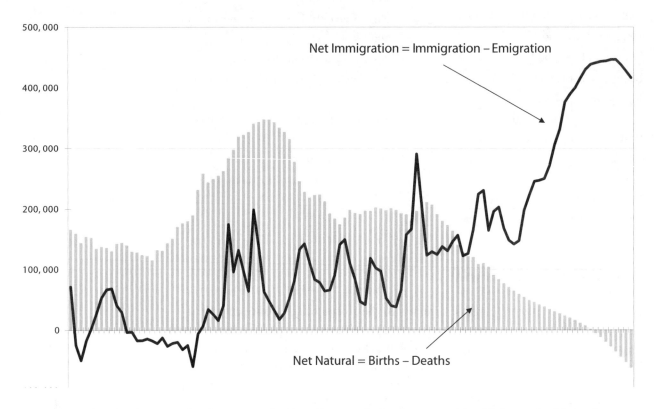

Notes: Immigration is expected to increase as the Canadian population decreases; this will change the fabric of
Canadian society and will greatly affect policing both internally and externally. In order for police officers to be
effective, they will have to be able to effectively communicate with immigrant communities as their populations
increase. In order to achieve this, members of these communities will need to become members of Canadian police
services.

Source: The Centre for Spatial Economics.

FIGURE 1.2   Ontario's Births and Deaths, 1971 to 2031

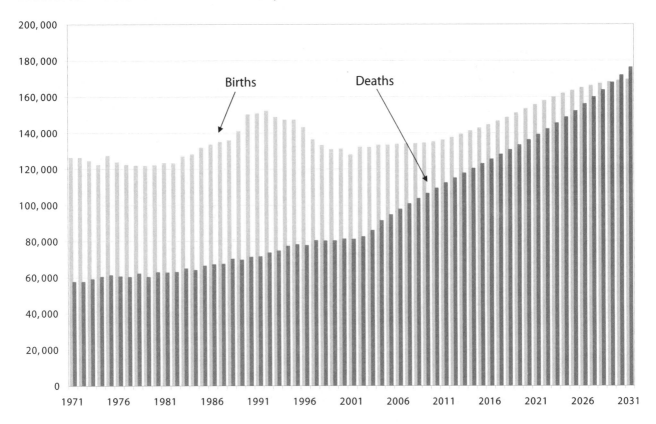

Notes: Birth rates in Canada are declining, and as Canadian birth rates fall, the needs of an aging population are increasing. By 2030 the death rate in Canada is projected to exceed the birth rate. Canada will need to increase immigration to combat this decline.

Source: The Centre for Spatial Economics.

FIGURE 1.3   Ontario's Population Growth Sources, 1971 to 2031

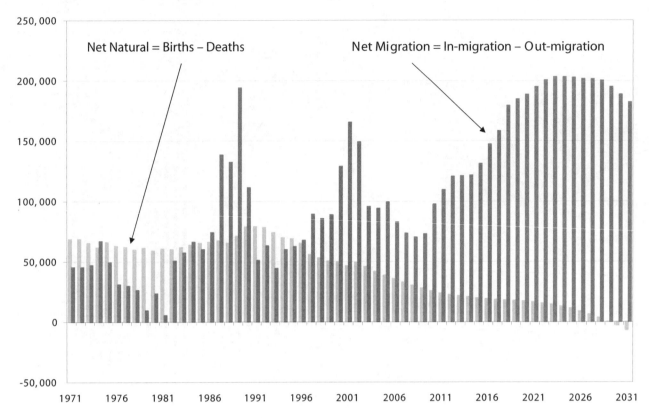

Notes: Projected immigration targets are increasing over the next 20 years as the Canadian population declines. This will have an impact on Canadian policing.

Source: The Centre for Spatial Economics.

FIGURE 1.4   Canada's Immigration by Source, 1956 to 2001

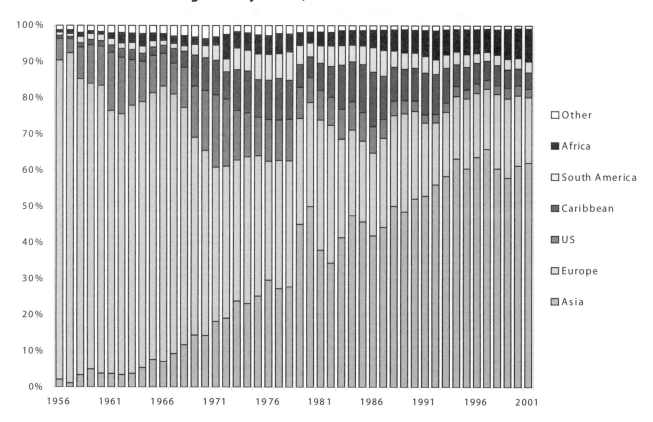

Notes: Traditional immigration patterns are projected to change and we are seeing an increase in immigration from continents such as Africa, South America, and Asia. These changes in population makeup will influence approaches to policing as Canadian police services attempt to attract people from these diverse cultures.

Source: The Centre for Spatial Economics.

TABLE 1.6   Visible Minority Shares of the Population, Ontario Metropolitan Areas from 2005 to 2030

	2005	2015	2030
Canada.	15.2	19.2	29.2
Ontario	21.2	25.6	35.6
Toronto	38.7	42.0	50.2
Ottawa-Gatineau	15.7	21.1	33.1
Windsor.	14.8	18.8	28.7
Kitchener.	12.6	16.4	26.7
Hamilton.	12.2	17.7	28.9
Oshawa	11.6	23.6	39.7
London	10.3	13.4	22.5
Kingston	6.8	10.6	20.4
St. Catharines-Niagara	5.4	8.5	15.4
Thunder Bay	2.3	2.5	3.1
Sudbury.	2.1	2.2	3.0
All Other Ontario	3.3	6.4	13.0

Notes: Settlement patterns and visible minority shares of the population will shift from 15.2 percent of the Canadian population in 2005 to almost 30 percent of the population in 2030. Toronto will see an 11.5 percent increase in visible minorities. Cities such as Oshawa will see up to a 28 percent increase in visible minority population. These increases may present challenges for police services in Ontario, including the challenge of attracting members of these diverse minorities to policing organizations.

Source: The Centre for Spatial Economics.

KEY TERMS

pluralism	code of silence
diversity	police–community interface
police culture	police force approach
male white culture	police services approach
ego forcing	community policing principles
core values	recidivism
self-control	diversity policing framework
cynicism	restorative justice approach
respect for authority	diversity policing framework
hypervigilance	

REFERENCES

Augustine, J. (2003, June 5). Speaking notes for the Honourable Jean Augustine, Secretary of State (Multiculturalism) (Status of Women) on the occasion of the Conference on Aboriginal and Diversity Law Enforcement Respect in Service, Winnipeg, Manitoba. http://www.canadianheritage.gc.ca/progs/ multi/pubs/speeches/17_e.cfm.

Burstein, M. (2004). *Developing the business cases for multiculturalism.* Outreach and Promotion Directorate, Multiculturalism and Human Rights Branch, Department of Canadian Heritage. http://www.canadianheritage.gc.ca.

Canadian Police Association and Canadian Association of Chiefs of Police (2001). Strategic Human Resource Analysis of Public Policing in Canada.

Chan, J.B.L. (1997). *Changing police culture: Policing in a multicultural society.* Boston: Cambridge University Press.

Chan, J.B.L. (2004). *Changing police culture: Policing in a multicultural society.* Second edition. Boston: Cambridge University Press.

Citizen saves police from attacker. (1982, March 17). *The Toronto Star,* p. D19.

Clyderman, B.K., C.N. O'Toole, and A. Fleras (Eds.). (1992). *Police, race and ethnicity.* Toronto: Butterworths.

Cooper, C., and J. Chatterjee. (n.d.). *Punishment at the turn of the century: The RCMP perspective.* Canadian Institute for the Administration of Justice Conference. http://www.ciaj-icaj.ca.

Coutts, L.M., F.M. Schneider, A. Johnson, and P. McLeod. (2003). Recruitment and selection of community policing officers. *The Canadian Journal of Police and Security Services: Practice, Police and Management* 1.

Crank, J.P. (1997). *Understanding police culture.* Cincinnati, OH: Anderson.

Crank, J.P. (2004). *Understanding police culture.* (2nd ed.). Cincinnati, OH: Anderson.

Criminal Code, RSC 1985, c. C-46, as amended.

Durkan, S. (1998, March 24). Canadian cops top the list in most-popular survey. *The London Free Press,* p. A9.

Ewatski, J. (2006, April 20). Trust as counter-terrorism. Lecture presented as part of the Global Information and Intelligence Sharing Panel Session. Fifth Annual 2006 International Counterterrorism Conference: Public and Private Partnership, Washington, DC.

Fleras, A. (1992). From enforcement to service: Community policing in a multicultural society. In B.K. Clyderman, C.N. O'Toole, and A. Fleras (Eds.), *Police, race and ethnicity* (pp. 69–126). Toronto: Butterworths.

Gash, N. (1972). *Sir Robert Peel: The Life of Sir Robert Peel after 1830.* Totowa, NJ: Rowman & Littlefield.

Gilmartin, K.M., and J.J. Harris. (1998, January). Law enforcement ethics: The continuum of compromise. *Police Magazine.* 25–28.

Kirschman, E. (1997). *I love a cop: What police families need to know.* New York: The Guilford Press.

Laws, L. (2005, February 4). *Durham Regional Police Service (DRPS): 2001-2010 Diversity Strategic Plan.* Ottawa: Graybridge Malkam.

Lewis, S., H. Rosenberg, and R.T. Sigler. (1999). Acceptance of community policing among police officers and police administrators. *Policing: An International Journal of Police Strategies and Management* 22: 5670–88.

Malm, A., N. Polard, P. Brantingham, P. Tinsley, D. Plecas, P. Brantingham, I. Cohen, and B. Kinney. (2005). *A 30 year analysis of police service delivery and costing: "E" Division-Research Summary.* Burnaby, BC: Institute for Canadian Urban Research Studies.

McCormack, T. (2004, Fall). The key impacts of immigration on Canada's population. *Canadian Police Chief Magazine,* pp. 29–30.

Miller, S.L. (1999). *Gender and community policing: Walking the talk.* Boston: Northeastern University Press.

Ministry of Solicitor General Strategic Planning Committee on Police Training and Education. (1992). *PAKS.* Toronto: Ministry of Solicitor General.

Morris, R. (2004). Ontario Police College recruit profile: September 1998 to September 2003. http://crpr.icaap.org/issues/issue1/morris.html. Retrieved 14/7/2006.

Multilingual Orientation Service Association for Immigrant Communities (2003). *Diverse cultures, responsive policing: A policy framework.* Vancouver. www.mosaicbc.com.

Neiderhoffer, A. (1967). *Behind the shield.* New York: Anchor.

Police Services Act, RSO 1990, c. P.15, as amended.

Powell, B. (2005, May 12) The new faces of policing: The class of '05. *The Toronto Star.*

Pruegger, V. (2003, February). Community and policing in partnership. Paper developed for Policing in a Multicultural Society Conference, Ottawa.

Reiner, R. (2000). *The Politics of the Police, Third Edition.* New York: Oxford University Press.

Skolnick, J.H. (1966). *Justice without trial.* New York: Wiley.

Skolnick, J.H. (2000). Code blue. *The American Prospect* 11.

Stansfield, R.T. (1996). *Issues in policing: A Canadian perspective.* Toronto: Thompson Educational Publishing.

Statistics Canada. (2001). Ethnic origin in the 2001 census.www12.statcan.ca/
    English/census01/products/references/tech_rep/ethnic.cfm#ethnic2001.

Statistics Canada. (2004, July 28). Crime statistics: 2003. *The Daily*.
    http://www.statcan.ca/Daily/English/040728/d040728a.htm.

Statistics Canada. (2005a). Police personnel. Table 254-0002. Product no. 85-225-X.
    http://www40.statcan.ca/l01/cst01/legal15.htm.

Statistics Canada. (2005b). Police personnel and expenditures: 2005. *The Daily*,
    December 15, 2005. http://www.statcan.ca/Daily/English/051215/
    d051215d.htm.

Stephens, B. (2005, February 27). Policing as a career in Ontario. Lecture presented
    to Hong Kong University Alumni Association. Aylmer, ON: Ontario Police
    College.

Toronto Police. (2006, September 8). Largest grad class parades at City Hall.
    http://www.torontopolice.on.ca.

United Nations Centre for Human Rights. (n.d.). *International Human Rights
    Standards for Law Enforcement.* Geneva: United Nations High Commissioner
    for Human Rights.

Waddington, P.A.J. (1999). Police (canteen) sub-culture. *British Journal of
    Criminology* 39: 287–309.

Williams, W.L., and B.B. Henderson. (1997). *Taking back our streets: Fighting crime
    in America.* New York: Lisa Drew/Scribner.

Wilson, S. (2004, Fall). Policing in changing demographics. *Canadian Chiefs of
    Police Magazine*, pp. 25–28.

EXERCISES AND REVIEW

Personal Reflections

Read each statement below and circle whether you agree or disagree with it.

1. A good police department is willing to listen to what the public has to say and welcomes input from all its staff—from the chief of police to the newest rookie on the beat.

    AGREE   DISAGREE

2. Police know what is best for the public; they don't need the public to tell them what to do or what not to do.

    AGREE   DISAGREE

3. The most effective police departments are those that recruit the "Rambos" of the world rather than those that are people-oriented.

    AGREE   DISAGREE

4. Police services and agencies should consider civil liberties in their pursuit of national security.

    AGREE   DISAGREE

5. The best-trained officer is the one who makes the most arrests.

    AGREE   DISAGREE

6. Police services are more effective when sexual harassment is rampant within the ranks.

    AGREE   DISAGREE

7. Police officers are more likely to treat the public fairly if they are treated fairly by police management.

    AGREE   DISAGREE

8. Police should focus more on working with residents, schools, and community groups to address issues that are meaningful to the communities they serve.

    AGREE   DISAGREE

9. Police departments should reflect the values and diversities of the communities they serve and protect.

    AGREE   DISAGREE

10. Crime control rather than crime prevention should be the main role of police.

   AGREE   DISAGREE

SCORING: Give yourself one point each for agreeing with the following statements: 1, 4, 7, 8, and 9. Give yourself one point each for disagreeing with the remaining statements. The higher your score, the more favourable your attitude toward community policing.

Diversity IQ: Multiple Choice

Circle the best answer.

1. Which of the following is true about the demographic police profile?

   a. Most police services are what they were 50 years ago.

   b. People of diversity may be reluctant to join police services.

   c. Most police are chauvinistic pigs.

   d. all of the above

2. Which of the following dimensions of police work is relevant to police culture?

   a. unpredictability

   b. public scrutiny

   c. long hours of work

   d. all of the above

3. Which of the following is a core value in policing?

   a. cynicism

   b. self-control

   c. code of silence

   d. all of the above

4. Which of the following is a primary dimension of diversity?

   a. gender

   b. ethnicity

   c. sexual orientation

   d. all of the above

5. Which of the following terms best characterizes a police force?

    a. crime-focused

    b. incident-driven

    c. centralized

    d. all of the above

6. Which of the following issues has preoccupied law enforcement post-9/11?

    a. personal security

    b. civil liberty

    c. national security

    d. all of the above

7. Which of the following is a community policing principle?

    a. disempowerment of police and the community

    b. acceptance of sexual harassment, discrimination, and bias

    c. cultural diversity in policing

    d. all of the above

8. Which of the following is true about policing?

    a. most police are corrupt

    b. most police do their best to serve and protect the public

    c. most police are unprofessional in their conduct

    d. all of the above

9. Which of the following is true about the restorative justice approach to dealing with young offenders?

    a. it aims at community reintegration of the young offender

    b. it is incarceration-oriented

    c. it is incompatible with community policing principles

    d. all of the above

10. The best approach to addressing diversity issues in policing is

    a. engaging in the practice of white male bashing

    b. learning skills that promote harmonious police–community relations

    c. adopting a diversity policing framework

    d. b and c

Diversity IQ: True or False?

_____   1. Police culture is a meaningful concept.

_____   2. Police effectiveness is diminished by recruiting people of diversity.

_____   3. It is best to leave some social issues in policing alone.

_____   4. Historically, police officers in pluralistic Western societies have been male.

_____   5. An advantage of police work is that it is very predictable.

_____   6. Physical fitness is important for preventing on-the-job police injuries.

_____   7. Community policing means ensuring that the men and women of a police service reflect the diversity of the community they serve.

_____   8. Community policing is feminized policing.

_____   9. Law enforcement legislation is silent on the issue of policing multicultural and multiracial communities.

_____ 10. Cultural diversity in policing enhances police safety and respect for police.

Application Now

1. Develop an understanding of your culture by tracing your cultural roots as far back as possible. In addition, you may want to identify your family's cultural values and your own values. You may also want to compare your cultural values with those of police culture. How compatible are they? How incompatible are they? Consider sharing your culture with your classmates.

2. A widely used police slogan is "to serve and protect." What does the slogan really mean? As a class, discuss the meaning of the slogan in the contexts of diversity and the 9/11 terrorist attacks.

3. List the advantages and disadvantages of the police services (community policing) approach.

    Advantages and disadvantages to people of diversity:

    Advantages and disadvantages to police:

4. List the advantages and disadvantages of having a police service whose members reflect the diversity of the communities they serve.

5. List the advantages and disadvantages of the restorative justice approach to law enforcement.

Food for Thought

1. Have you ever been a minority? Think of a time when you were in the numerical minority—for example, by virtue of your opinion, age, sex, religion, occupation, sexual orientation, socioeconomic status, or skin colour. If you have been in this situation, how did you feel? How did you cope with your feelings? Share your feelings and thoughts with the class.

2. There have been questions raised about citizenship and what citizenship means post-9/11. More recent events in the Middle East, such as the 2006 conflict between Israel and Hezbollah in Lebanon, which precipitated the evacuation of thousands of Lebanese Canadians from Lebanon at the expense of the Canadian government, have also raised questions concerning the rights and responsibilities of Canadian citizens who have chosen to live abroad.

    Discuss what makes a person a good Canadian citizen.

3. What aspects of police culture do you like, and what aspects do you not like?

From Thought to Action

1. A definition of diversity that is universal to policing in Canada is lacking. Policing services that have the mandate to recognize and embrace diversity and work toward developing policing structures and strategies that reflect and embrace the diverse communities that they serve and protect must be guided by a universally accepted definition of diversity in the context of policing to achieve their ideals. The absence of a clear understanding of the meaning of diversity and its parameters is limiting. For example, is the OPP's definition of diversity inclusive of sexual orientation, and does the OPP openly reach out to the gay and lesbian communities to encourage their members to apply to their ranks? In groups of three or four, develop a definition of diversity that you think police services should adopt, and compare your results with those of the rest of the class.

2. Using the Internet and other resources, list diversity initiatives in law enforcement and report them to the class.

Lessons from History

Invite members of your local police service to your class to talk about the history of policing in your community or country, and the relevance of that history to contemporary policing.

The Great Debate

Two approaches have been considered for police efforts to preserve and protect the safety of streets and neighbourhoods. The first is a police force approach for the purpose of crime control. The second is a police services approach for the purpose of crime prevention. Debate the merits of these approaches by dividing the class into two groups. One group supports the crime-control approach. The second group supports the crime-prevention approach. Follow the debate with a general class discussion.

CHAPTER 2

Diversity Ideologies and Policies

CHAPTER OBJECTIVES

After completing this chapter, you should be able to:

- Describe four prevailing state ideologies that apply to diversity.
- Understand the history and current status of Canada's multiculturalism policy.
- Discuss federal and provincial policy and legislation on diversity.
- Discuss the human rights imperatives of law enforcement.

PREVIEW SCENARIO

In the early '70s, a young man in his mid-twenties immigrated to Canada. He married a young woman from his country of origin. They started a family and had twins, a boy and a girl. After the birth of his children, he decided to enter university, where he attained a Ph.D. in psychology. He developed a close attachment to what he called "this wonderful country, Canada" and, upon completion of his education, applied for and obtained citizenship. He considered himself Canadian first and ethnic Armenian second, and participated as fully as he could in the life of his community and adopted country. He presented himself as Canadian when travelling to different countries and represented his nation and people proudly to others overseas, particularly when it came to tipping. He identified strongly with the scientist-practitioner lens of his profession, and he grounded his career and personal thinking in multicultural democracy. He firmly believed in addressing the root causes of national and international problems rather than focusing on their symptoms. The roots of poverty, marginalization, discrimination, and perceived injustice and their consequences to the physical, psychological, social, and spiritual well-being of individuals, groups, and national and global communities were his primary preoccupations, as were national identity and protection of civil order. There were minor issues that irritated him. These included the continued misspelling and mispronouncing of his name. When he applied for citizenship, he was subjected to interrogations to determine where he came from and where he was born after a customs officer commented that his accent was not Canadian. It was at times difficult to discern whether the background questions asked of him were of genuine interest or a conscious or unconscious effort to communicate to him that he could not be a "real" Canadian because he was not born in Canada. The young man is now in his early sixties, a healthy Canadian citizen still attached to a nation called Canada and Canadian people.

INTRODUCTION

ideology
belief system or world view of an individual, a group, or a society

Nations adopt different **ideologies** that shape their legal, economic, cultural, and political policies, and their approach to national security, international relations, and thus their criminal justice systems. A state ideology and a criminal justice system that support integration and promote mutual understanding and respect for diversity breed a harmonious, contented, and secure civil society. Such a society is good for its people, good for its government, good for its police officers, and good for the rest of the world. This chapter discusses state ideologies and policies, how they influenced policing before the September 11, 2001 terrorist attacks in the United States, and their implications for policing in a diversity context post-9/11.

FOUR STATE IDEOLOGIES

The four prevailing ideologies of host cultures as they apply to their own members and to people they accept as immigrants and refugees are the multiculturalism ideology, civic ideology, assimilation ideology, and ethnist ideology (Bourhis et al., 1997; Kymlicka, 1995).

multiculturalism ideology
ideology that recognizes and supports people of diversity in maintaining or promoting their diversity, provided that their practices do not clash with the laws of the nation

public values
democratic ideals, constitutional and human rights provisions, and civil and criminal codes of the state

private values
personal attitudes and activities of individuals in the domains of domestic and interpersonal relations

Multiculturalism Ideology

Multiculturalism is an ideology of ethnic integration. It represents a fairly recent outgrowth of the constitutionally entrenched ideal of cultural dualism, a concept that recognizes the French and English roots of Canadian society (Kallen, 1982). However, multiculturalism as an ideal does not replace the dominant ideology of Canada as a bilingual and bicultural society, entrenched in the *Constitution Act, 1982*, the supreme law of our nation. The **multiculturalism ideology** recognizes and supports people of diverse cultural and linguistic backgrounds, allowing them to maintain and promote their diversity, provided that their practices do not clash with the civil and criminal laws of the host nation.

Four main principles are associated with the multiculturalism ideology. First, people of diverse backgrounds are expected to adopt the public values of the nation. **Public values** are embodied in the democratic ideals, constitutional and human rights provisions, and civil and criminal codes of the state. Second, the multiculturalism ideology protects the private values of individual citizens. **Private values** are the personal attitudes and activities of individuals in the domains of domestic and interpersonal relations. Third, this ideology disallows state interference with the private values of people of diversity. Thus, the state values the efforts of immigrants to maintain their cultural and linguistic distinctiveness, provided that their conduct is within the boundaries of the laws of the state. Fourth, the multiculturalism ideology endorses state funding for the ethnocultural activities of both citizens and newcomers. The state legitimizes this support on the ground that both groups contribute to the state through taxation.

Canada and Australia are prototypes of states that espouse this ideology. Canada is also the first nation in the world to enshrine a multiculturalism policy in its *Charter of Rights and Freedoms* (discussed in detail below). The European Multicultural Foundation endorses the multiculturalism ideology as a means of ensuring the development of a successful civil society (Australian Multicultural Foundation, 2001).

Civic Ideology

The **civic ideology** shares the principles of the multiculturalism ideology but does not support state funding to maintain and promote ethnocultural diversity. Great Britain is an example of a state that supports the civic ideology.

civic ideology
ideology that shares the principles of multiculturalism ideology but does not support state funding to maintain and promote ethnocultural diversity

Assimilation Ideology

Assimilation refers to the social processes whereby members of different ethnic and cultural groups interact and participate in ethnocultural institutions other than those of the ethnic community to which they belong (Kallen, 2003). The **assimilation ideology** is a homogenization or melting pot ideology. This ideology expects people of diverse backgrounds to relinquish or forget their cultural and linguistic identity and adopt the culture of the host state. In return, the state promises to protect the private values of individual citizens but reserves the right to limit expression of some domains of private values, particularly those that pertain to immigrant minorities—for example, one immigrant group wilfully promoting hatred against another group. The United States is a nation that has espoused the melting pot ideology and assumed that all cultures can be assimilated. Homogenization in the United States has its roots in World War I, when this ideology was seen as critical for the success of the United States in the war. However, the United States is shifting gradually to a civic ideology. A significant contributor to this shift is the tendency of recent immigrants not to "melt" as readily as earlier immigrants to the country.

assimilation ideology
ideology that expects people of diversity to relinquish their cultural and linguistic identity and adopt the culture of the host state

Ethnist Ideology

The **ethnist ideology** is similar to the assimilation ideology except that the state defines which groups should or should not assimilate. Germany is one state that espouses ethnist ideology. Those who are not allowed to assimilate on the grounds of blood, religion, or culture—for example, Turks—are not accorded the same rights as other German citizens.

ethnist ideology
ideology that expects people of diversity to assimilate, but the state defines which groups should assimilate and thus which ones will not enjoy the same legal rights as other members of the state

DIVERSITY POLICIES: CULTURAL HERITAGE AND LANGUAGE

The global village can benefit from the experiences of various nations in terms of nation building and policing. Because Canada is the only country in the world with an official state *policy* of multiculturalism, this policy, its historical roots, and its effectiveness are described in some detail here.

Concept of Multiculturalism

The term "multiculturalism" has assumed different meanings and evokes different attitudes and emotions. Multiculturalism may be interpreted simply as a *celebration* of cultural diversity. It may also be interpreted as a *factual descriptor* of the actual cultural diversity of a population. Multiculturalism as a celebration of diversity and as a fact is characteristic of many countries, including Australia, the United Kingdom, and the United States. As mentioned earlier, multiculturalism may also be a national ideology and a state policy. The adoption of multiculturalism as a national ideology and a state policy is a more recent phenomenon and is unique to Canada.

Canada's Multiculturalism Policy

multiculturalism policy
Canadian policy that recognizes, values, and promotes the cultural and racial diversity of its people by allowing them the freedom to preserve, enhance, and share their cultural heritage

Canada's **multiculturalism policy** evolved over time. From its inception as an innocuous symbolic gesture, multiculturalism grew into a nation-building public philosophy (Paquet, 1994). Why Canada has a public policy of multiculturalism is a complex question that continues to be the subject of debate.

Canada's first official multiculturalism policy was adopted on October 8, 1971 by Prime Minister Pierre Elliott Trudeau. The new policy was described as "multiculturalism within a bilingual framework." This policy addressed two aspects of diversity: cultural (racial) heritage and language. Diversities other than those related to culture and language (for example, gender and sexual orientation) were protected by a variety of other federal and provincial statutes, which are discussed in detail in the next chapter.

The four broad objectives of the multiculturalism policy were to assist cultural groups to retain and foster their ethnic identity, to assist cultural groups to overcome barriers to full participation in Canadian society, to promote creative exchanges and interchanges among cultural groups in the Canadian context, and to assist immigrants in acquiring at least one of the two official languages (Multiculturalism and Citizenship Canada, 1991). The intent of the policy was to encourage members of *all* cultural groups to maintain and share their language and cultural heritage with a view to reducing assimilation policies and promoting tolerance of diversity and positive intergroup attitudes, thus reducing levels of prejudice within society and avoiding ethnic group isolation and **ghettoization**. The policy was meant to apply to everyone in Canada, not just newcomers, immigrants, select ethnic groups, or visible minorities. This view, however, is not universally supported. For example, Harding (1992) asserts that the notion of ethnic pluralism obscures the fundamental difference between Aboriginal peoples and immigrants in that it reduces both groups to an outsider identity by "totally ignor[ing] the problems of self-determination peculiar to colonized peoples" (p. 630).

ghettoization
process in which members of a particular ethnic, religious, or national group live in high concentration in poverty stricken areas either by choice or by force

The Canadian Multiculturalism Act

The passage of the *Canadian Charter of Rights and Freedoms* in 1982 enshrined in law fundamental rights and freedoms for all peoples of Canada and paved the way for the *Canadian Multiculturalism Act*. Section 27 of the 1982 *Canadian Charter of Rights and Freedoms* provides protection for the multicultural character of Canadian society:

> **27.** This Charter shall be interpreted in a manner consistent with the preservation and enhancement of the multicultural heritage of Canadians.

Jean Chrétien, as minister of justice, commented on the importance of the Charter in protecting the rights of a multicultural and ethnically diverse population:

> In a free and democratic society, it is important that citizens know exactly what their rights and freedoms are, and where to turn for help and advice in the event that those freedoms are denied or those rights infringed. In a country like Canada— vast and diverse, with 11 governments, 2 official languages, and a variety of ethnic origins—the only way to provide equal protection for everyone is to enshrine those basic rights and freedoms in the Constitution. (1982, p. v)

The *Canadian Multiculturalism Act* was proclaimed in 1988, making Canada the first nation to adopt multiculturalism as a national policy. The objectives of the Act are listed in table 2.1. As the Act makes clear, multiculturalism is not just ornamental or folkloric, but the full acceptance of cultural and linguistic diversity, inclusiveness, and equality.

In addition to the stated objectives, the Act sets out specific policy requirements for federal institutions. These requirements are listed in table 2.2.

Provincial Diversity Policies

Provincial multiculturalism policies and legislation support federal multiculturalism legislation. As an example, section 3 of the British Columbia *Multiculturalism Act* sets out the province's multiculturalism policy, which requires the government of British Columbia to

> (a) recognize and promote the understanding that multiculturalism reflects the racial and cultural diversity of British Columbians,
>
> (b) promote cross cultural understanding and respect and attitudes and perceptions that lead to harmony among British Columbians of every race, cultural heritage, religion, ethnicity, ancestry and place of origin,
>
> (c) promote the full and free participation of all individuals in the society of British Columbia,
>
> (d) foster the ability of each British Columbian, regardless of race, cultural heritage, religion, ethnicity, ancestry or place of origin, to share in the economic, social, cultural and political life of British Columbia in a manner that is consistent with the rights and responsibilities of that individual as a member of the society of British Columbia,
>
> (e) reaffirm that violence, hatred and discrimination on the basis of race, cultural heritage, religion, ethnicity, ancestry or place of origin have no place in the society of British Columbia,
>
> (f) work towards building a society in British Columbia free from all forms of racism and from conflict and discrimination based on race, cultural heritage, religion, ethnicity, ancestry and place of origin,

(g) recognize the inherent right of each British Columbian, regardless of race, cultural heritage, religion, ethnicity, ancestry or place of origin, to be treated with dignity, and

(h) generally, carry on government services and programs in a manner that is sensitive and responsive to the multicultural reality of British Columbia.

Diversity and Police

Diversity is incorporated in two of the six principles of the Ontario *Police Services Act* (Hamilton & Shilton, 1992): the principle of sensitivity to the pluralistic, multi-racial, and multicultural character of Ontario society, and the principle of ensuring that police services are representative of the communities they serve (see table 2.3).

DIVERSITY POLICIES CRITIQUED

Diversity policies have not been without their critics, even though their value in enriching people's quality of life is universally recognized (Bibby, 1994).

TABLE 2.1   Objectives of the Canadian Multiculturalism Act

3(1) It is hereby declared to be the policy of the Government of Canada to

(a) recognize and promote the understanding that multiculturalism reflects the cultural and racial diversity of Canadian society and acknowledges the freedom of all members of Canadian society to preserve, enhance and share their cultural heritage;

(b) recognize and promote the understanding that multiculturalism is a fundamental characteristic of the Canadian heritage and identity and that it provides an invaluable resource in the shaping of Canada's future;

(c) promote the full and equitable participation of individuals and communities of all origins in the continuing evolution and shaping of all aspects of Canadian society and assist them in the elimination of any barrier to that participation;

(d) recognize the existence of communities whose members share a common origin and their historic contribution to Canadian society, and enhance their development;

(e) ensure that all individuals receive equal treatment and equal protection under the law, while respecting and valuing their diversity;

(f) encourage and assist the social, cultural, economic and political institutions of Canada to be both respectful and inclusive of Canada's multicultural character;

(g) promote the understanding and creativity that arise from the interaction between individuals and communities of different origins;

(h) foster the recognition and appreciation of the diverse cultures of Canadian society and promote the reflection and the evolving expressions of those cultures;

(i) preserve and enhance the use of languages other than English and French, while strengthening the status and use of the official languages of Canada; and

(j) advance multiculturalism throughout Canada with the national commitment to the official languages of Canada.

Source: *Canadian Multiculturalism Act*, RSC 1985, c. 24 (4th Supp.), as amended.

Multiculturalism Policy on Trial

Three main themes can be discerned from issues associated with cultural and linguistic policies. The first theme is the belief in the *subversiveness* of the multiculturalism policy. The few who subscribe to this view see multiculturalism as a deliberate plot to challenge the legitimacy of the mainstream culture.

The second theme is *national disunity*. Critics see multiculturalism as inadvertently causing national and political disunity and preventing the development of a metaculture (an all-encompassing and inclusive identity). Terms that reflect the national disunity sentiment include ethnicization, fetishization of ethnic groups,

TABLE 2.2   Requirements of Federal Institutions Under the Canadian Multiculturalism Act

3(2) It is ... declared to be the policy of the Government of Canada that all federal institutions shall

(a) ensure that Canadians of all origins have an equal opportunity to obtain employment and advancement in those institutions;

(b) promote policies, programs and practices that enhance the ability of individuals and communities of all origins to contribute to the continuing evolution of Canada;

(c) promote policies, programs and practices that enhance the understanding of and respect for the diversity of the members of Canadian society;

(d) collect statistical data in order to enable the development of policies, programs and practices that are sensitive and responsive to the multicultural reality of Canada;

(e) make use, as appropriate, of the language skills and cultural understanding of individuals of all origins; and

(f) generally, carry on their activities in a manner that is sensitive and responsive to the multicultural reality of Canada.

Source: *Canadian Multiculturalism Act*, RSC 1985, c. 24 (4th Supp.), as amended.

TABLE 2.3   Principles of the Ontario Police Services Act

Declaration of principles

Police services shall be provided throughout Ontario in accordance with the following principles:

1. The need to ensure the safety and security of all persons and property in Ontario.
2. The importance of safeguarding the fundamental rights guaranteed by the *Canadian Charter of Rights and Freedoms* and the *Human Rights Code.*
3. The need for co-operation between the providers of police services and the communities they serve.
4. The importance of respect for victims of crime and understanding of their needs.
5. The need for sensitivity to the pluralistic, multiracial and multicultural character of Ontario society.
6. The need to ensure that police forces are representative of the communities they serve.

Source: *Police Services Act*, RSO 1990, c. P.15, as amended.

fragmentation, ghettoization, mosaic madness, tribalization, balkanization, and babelization. Evidence of national disunity is seen in the greater demand for adjustment imposed on members of the host culture relative to immigrants, the "prostitution of ethnic groups" by virtue of the funding of ethnic institutions (for example, community centres), the erosion of national symbols, and the threat to "national interest" by virtue of ethnic groups importing their old-world conflicts into the host country (Weinfeld, 1994).

The third theme is the belief that multiculturalism is an *instrument of racism.* Godfrey Brandt, a British radical anti-racist, for example, argues that multiculturalism in the United Kingdom and the United States "is none other than a more sophisticated form of social control and it has the effect of containing black resistance" (Brandt, 1986, cited in Bonnett, 2000, p. 107). Brandt asserts that multiculturalism is "an instrument of oppression, a way for the state to co-opt racialized groups and subvert their rebellion" (cited in Bonnett, 2000, p. 108). Similarly, Canadian critics view Canada's multiculturalism policy as supporting dualism, or a two-tier political culture, by assigning the charter cultures—that is, the British and the French—a superior position in Canadian society and relegating the "other," non-charter cultures to an inferior position. Terms that are used to reflect the two-tier system sentiment include vertical mosaic (Porter, 1965), cultural separatism, ethnicization, and divided loyalty. Evidence of a two-tier political culture is seen in intolerant attitudes toward immigrants and newcomers, and members of non-charter cultures.

Supporters of the multiculturalism policy argue that it is not about ethnic separatism or divided loyalty but about transforming a fragmented society into a harmonious nation (Fleras, 1994); it remains a social ideal as yet to be fulfilled (Day, 2000). Similarly, Kymlicka suggests that cultural diversity needs to be acknowledged and the option of a multination state needs to be considered. He suggests that Canada should not fear recognizing the demands of Aboriginal people or Quebec for nation status, arguing that the confidence and security afforded to minority nations unleashes their desire to "become more willing cooperators in the flourishing of the larger state" (cited in Reich, 2000, p. F4).

Evaluation of Multiculturalism Policy

Although critiquing multiculturalism policy is a legitimate process and the associated issues deserve serious consideration and resolution, it is equally important to evaluate and debate the policy in a rational, systematic, and politically neutral way.

ATTITUDES TOWARD MULTICULTURALISM

Surveys conducted on attitudes toward multiculturalism since the 1970s indicate that Canadians generally support the policy. For example, a 1974 survey (Berry, Kalin, & Taylor, 1977) indicated that 63.9 percent of Canadians were in favour of the idea of Canada as a diverse society and 32.9 percent were not. A similar survey conducted in 1991 (Berry & Kalin, 1995) showed that support for the multiculturalism policy had increased over time—that is, 69.3 percent were in favour and 27.3 percent were not. Berry and Kalin concluded that "[m]ulticulturalism is generally accepted by the Canadian population, both as an ideal and in practice" (p. 316).

Cultural groups differ in their support for multiculturalism. British and other ethnic groups view this ideology and its practice more positively than those with a

French background, particularly those of French origin living in Quebec. A likely explanation is the perceived threat to the French language and culture that francophones in Quebec associate with multiculturalism (Berry, Kalin, & Taylor, 1977).

The survey approach to evaluating the effectiveness of Canada's multiculturalism policy has been criticized on the ground that survey questions can be asked or worded in such a way that they elicit favourably biased responses. This is not an unreasonable criticism. However, there is other evidence that Canada supports the multicultural idea. For example, Canada's mourning of the death of former prime minister Pierre Elliott Trudeau on September 28, 2000 provides indirect support for the validity of the survey findings. The tributes and outpouring of emotion from coast to coast for a man who championed multiculturalism were unprecedented. Old and young, men and women, gay and straight, the penniless and the affluent, all paid tribute to the statesman for fathering the bilingual-multicultural Canada. The people paid tribute to Mr. Trudeau for his instrumental role in envisioning a just society, for patriating the constitution, and for adding the *Canadian Charter of Rights and Freedoms* to the constitution.

ACCEPTANCE OF CULTURAL GROUPS

A number of studies have surveyed the extent to which people are willing to accept individuals or groups of various cultures or races. A national survey was carried out by the Angus Reid Group in June and July 1991 for the Canadian Department of Multiculturalism and Citizenship. A total of 3,325 individuals, consisting of a national sample of 2,500 adults (18 years and older), with oversamples in Montreal, Toronto, and Vancouver to ensure a sample of 500 in each of the three cities, participated in the survey. Respondents rated on a 7-point scale (1 = not at all comfortable, 7 = completely comfortable) their level of comfort in being around people from 14 different groups: British, French, Ukrainians, Sikhs, South Asians (Indo-Pakistanis), Germans, Chinese, West Indian blacks, Jews, Arabs, Italians, Portuguese, Native Canadian Indians, and Muslims. Three main findings are relevant here. First, *all cultural groups were rated relatively highly*—that is, no group received a rating lower than 4.8 on the 7-point scale. Second, each rated group received the highest ratings from its own members (Kalin & Berry, 1996, p. 257). This finding was considered evidence of **ethnocentrism** in intercultural relations—"the tendency to view one's in-group more positively than others, and to view other groups as inferior" (Kalin & Berry, 1996, p. 254). Third, the results indicated that a **preference hierarchy for cultural groups** exists, with British at the top, followed by Italians, French, Ukrainians, Germans, Jews and Portuguese, Chinese, Native Canadian Indians, West Indian blacks, Arabs, Muslims, South Asians, and Sikhs (Kalin and Berry, 1996). In general, these results suggest that Aboriginal peoples and European cultural groups evoke feelings of comfort more so than groups of non-European origin, particularly those considered visible minorities—that is, Arabs and South Asians.

VIABILITY OF THE CULTURAL GROUPS

The survival of cultural groups without ghettoization or compromise to **Canadianism** is an important indicator of the success of Canada's multiculturalism policy. Two lines of research, on ghettoization and ethnic identity, have examined the effects of multiculturalism on cultural groups.

ethnocentrism
tendency to view one's ethnocultural group more positively than others, and to view other groups as inferior

preference hierarchy for cultural groups
expressed feeling of comfort with particular cultures, suggesting that Aboriginal peoples and European cultural groups evoke feelings of comfort more so than groups of non-European origin, particularly those considered visible minorities

Canadianism
national Canadian identity that cuts across age, income, and gender differences and goes beyond regional, ethnic, and linguistic lines

Two economic studies were conducted by the Economic Council of Canada in the early 1990s on the effects of Canada's multiculturalism policy (Economic Council of Canada, 1991). The Economic Council concluded that integration leads to greater immigrant participation in the host society, strengthens people's confidence in their own individual identity and place in the Canadian mosaic, and facilitates their acceptance of the rights of members of other groups. An additional economic advantage of multiculturalism policy is the establishment of international communication and trade links (Laczko, 1994).

Kymlicka (1997) examined the questions of whether multiculturalism policy breeds "ghettoization" or isolation of ethnic groups and to what degree cultural groups integrate socially and politically. He compared domestic and international data on four indicators of citizenship and integration: naturalization rates, political participation, official language competencies, and exogamy (marriage outside one's ethnic group). The following represent Kymlicka's domestic findings:

- Naturalization rates: The naturalization (adoption of citizenship) rate of immigrants has been on the increase since 1971 (the year that Canada officially adopted a multiculturalism policy). This increase is particularly significant given that the economic incentives to naturalize have lessened over the last several years (that is, landed immigrants and citizens have similar labour market access, social benefits rights, and so on). Immigrants from non-traditional source countries or "multicultural" groups show the highest naturalization rates in the country.

- Political participation of cultural groups: Minority ethnic group participation in mainstream politics has been on the increase. First, ethnic groups have had greater representation in Parliament after the institution of the multicultural policy than before. Second, ethnic groups have been joining established political parties rather than forming individual political parties. Third, members of ethnic groups tend to vote for traditional national parties since such parties uphold Canada's basic liberal democratic principles.

- Official language competencies: Immigrant eagerness to learn an official language has been sustained. The majority of Canadians (97 percent) speak either English or French. Demand for English and French as a second language classes is at its highest, and existing classes in some cities fall short of meeting people's needs.

- Exogamy: The endogamy (marriage within one's ethnic group) rates have been falling since 1971 for both immigrants and native-born people, and the intermarriage rates have been rising. Approval for ethnic friendships and mixed marriages is at its highest. In 1968, 52 percent of Canadians approved of ethnic marriages; in 1995, the approval rate was about 81 percent.

Studies on ethnic identity have also revealed the effects of multiculturalism on cultural groups. **Ethnic identity** refers to a "positive personal attitude and attachment to a group with whom the individual believes he has a common ancestry based on shared characteristics and shared socio-cultural experiences" (Driedger,

ethnic identity
attachment to, or feeling of pride in, one's cultural heritage

1989, p. 162). Because measures of ethnic identity range from positive to neutral to negative, people may have ethnic origins but not ethnic identities—that is, they may not have attachments to or feelings of pride in their cultural heritage.

According to Kalin and Berry (1996), ethnic identification may be symbolic (knowledge of and pride in one's cultural heritage) and behavioural (outward expressions of one's ethnic origin). *Symbolic ethnic identity* is reflected in the way that individuals think of themselves—that is, Canadian versus hyphenated Canadian (for example, Portuguese-Canadian) versus ethnic (for example, Portuguese). *Behavioural ethnic identity* is reflected in such indicators as fluency in and use of heritage language, friendships (all Canadian versus all ethnic versus mixed), and club membership. Individuals may show weak symbolic and behavioural ethnic identity, strong symbolic and behavioural ethnic identity, strong symbolic ethnic identity but weak behavioural ethnic identity, and weak symbolic ethnic identity but strong behavioural ethnic identity.

While the strength and feeling of ethnic identity are still not well understood, research on behavioural and symbolic ethnic identity indicates that ethnic communities in many segments of Canadian society are vibrant and that Canadians, generally, see themselves as Canadian rather than ethnic (Kalin & Berry, 1996). In the 1991 Angus Reid Group survey, 89 percent of those interviewed identified themselves as Canadian, and only 6 percent reported any other form of identification. The majority asserted that Canadians share many values in common (78 percent) and that these values are important in binding people together as a nation (91 percent). Of significance was the majority belief (73 percent) that Canada's multiculturalism policy was instrumental in ensuring that culturally diverse people had a sense of belonging to Canada without feeling shame or embarrassment regarding their cultural heritage. In fact, about 95 percent of respondents expressed simultaneous pride in their Canadianness and their ancestry.

Taken together, these findings indicate that the multiculturalism policy is achieving its goal of sustaining the vitality of cultural groups while simultaneously engendering a national Canadian identity. This conclusion is consistent with results from a telephone poll of 1,200 Canadians between the ages of 18 and 29, including 200 in-depth interviews conducted by *Maclean's* magazine and CBC Television's *The National* in 1997. The findings showed that "across age, income and gender differences, beyond regional and linguistic lines exists a 'remarkably' cohesive Canadian society—despite the population's growing diversity" (Ayed, 1997, p. A1). The findings also provided a "consistent picture of a people who are tolerant, generous, surprisingly optimistic and committed to the same moral values and beliefs, regardless of their generational and regional differences" (Ayed, 1997, p. A1). In an editorial, *The London Free Press* ("Tolerance needs," 1997, p. A12) commented that "while Canadians celebrate diversity, we also share common values and distinct traditions, suggesting that we are forming a national identity that may not be as easily definable as the hot-dog-and-apple-pie image of Americans, but is a unifying image nonetheless." The consolidation of a national identity is evident in census data showing a significant increase in the number of Canadians reporting Canadian as their ethnic origin in the past two decades (0.5 percent in 1986, 3.8 percent in 1991, 31 percent in 1996, and 39 percent in 2001; Census Canada, 2001).

Comparative Evaluation of Multiculturalism

The finding of a positive relationship between cultural pluralism and national attachment is not specific to Canada. A study of ethnic identification and national attachment in England showed similar results (Modood, 1997). The English study of over 5,000 individuals of ethnic origins as diverse as Caribbean, African black, South Asian, and Chinese showed that ethnic identity is not antithetical to a sense of Britishness. Over 50 percent of the Chinese and more than 75 percent of the other groups said that they felt British. National attachment was even higher among young people and those born in Britain.

Kymlicka (1997) compared Canada, the United States, and Australia on citizenship and integration indicators and found that Canada fared much better than the other countries. He concluded that there is no real evidence that policies on cultural and linguistic diversity breed ethnic group ghettoization; in fact, the opposite is likely to be true.

MULTICULTURALISM POST-9/11

Following the terrorist attacks on the United States on September 11, 2001, there was considerable hostility and discrimination toward Arabs, South Asians, and Muslims in North America and Europe (Biles & Ibrahim, 2002a; Helly, 2004). In addition, the immigration and multiculturalism policies of many governments came under attack. Critics asserted that these policies undermined national security even though a fundamental aim of pluralism is building a peaceful society where no one's identity or cultural heritage should have to be compromised. In the aftermath of 9/11, faith in diversity and its intrinsic value to a citizen's sense of self-worth, identity, and attachment to country was shaken. Thus, the very immigrants who were welcomed to Canada under the multiculturalism philosophy to enrich the traditional Canadian mosaic, to solve the country's demographic and economic ills, and to remedy the declining birth rate and labour shortages arising from an aging population were now seen by critics as potential threats to national security. Issues regarding citizenry were raised and a view of citizenry that dichotomized citizens as monocitizens and dual citizens emerged. The monocitizens were viewed as real citizens by virtue of being born in Canada and being loyal to the nation state, and the dual citizens, particularly from certain ethnic or religious groups were deemed inferior by virtue of their being "hyphenated Canadians" and holding more than one citizenship and more than one passport. Hyphenated Canadians were characterized as paper citizens, citizens of convenience, and most importantly, as less than loyal to the nation state and a threat to civil order. In Canada, security measures and legislation such as the *Anti-terrorism Act* were introduced by the federal government in October 2001, and the national security policy issued in April 2004, to address the threat of terrorism both internally and externally. The national security policy focused on three core national security interests: protecting Canadians at home and abroad, ensuring that Canada is not a base for threats to its allies, and contributing to international security. The security measures that were introduced by the federal government included surveillance by federal law enforcement agents.

Tolerance and Harmony

As a multicultural society, Canada has embraced the "globe within its borders" and has fostered the values of peace, justice, and mutual respect. The 9/11 events tested Canada's commitment to these values. In the month following the 9/11 attacks, increased acts of discrimination and violence against Canadian visible minorities and religious groups (Muslims, Jews, Hindus, and Sikhs) and increased surveillance of individuals of Muslim and Arab descent by Canadian law enforcement and intelligence officials were reported by Arabs and Muslims; the charitable donations of Canadians of Muslim and Arab descent were also scrutinized and individuals under suspicion were restricted from travelling to or from the United States (Biles & Ibrahim, 2002b).

A public opinion poll taken two weeks after the 9/11 attacks showed 50 percent of Canadians favouring increased police and customs security of individuals of Arab origin, but 82 percent reporting worry that people of Arab descent or Muslims may become the target of unwarranted racism or personal attacks because of terrorist acts (Ipsos News Centre, 2001). A repeat of the poll two months after 9/11 saw public support for increased police and customs security drop to 32 percent, suggesting diminution in public fear and concern over security. As important, Canadian acceptance of their own was reflected in a separate survey showing many Canadians offering empathic support and understanding to their Muslim and Arab neighbours (Abu-Laban & Abu-Laban, 2004).

While national security continues to be a national and a global preoccupation, and regulatory mechanisms to limit surveillance are on the increase, Frank (2004) suggests that the Canadian public view is such that it condemns extremism while simultaneously promoting a "live and let live" approach to radical groups. Frank attributes Canadians' attitude of tolerance to 30 years of multiculturalism during which an implicit non-interference pact among different ethnic groups living in Canada had prevailed.

DIVERSITY IDEOLOGIES AND POLICIES: POLICE ABILITIES, KNOWLEDGE, AND SKILLS

Nations around the world are increasingly experiencing diversity but holding different attitudes toward people of diversity. Canada is unique in having a constitutionally enshrined multiculturalism policy that is inspired by a diversity framework.

Police in pluralistic societies are part of, rather than apart from, the diversity mosaic. For example, the more than 22,000-person police force in Ontario is a cultural community within a community of over 12 million people of diversity. Multiculturalism and human rights legislation provide the legal foundation for a diversity policing framework and a core infrastructure for protecting individual and collective rights for diversity sustenance and enhancement. Regardless of their culture, everyone has the right to democratic citizenry, to full and equal participation in society, and to the preservation of their diversity. Police have a responsibility to promote these rights by honouring both the letter and the spirit of diversity policies. A list of dos and don'ts for policing people of diversity is provided in table 2.4.

Table 2.4   Dos and Don'ts of Policing People of Diversity

Dos

- Recognize the diversity of society and the right of all people to preserve, enhance, and share their diversity.

- Recognize, accept, and nurture your own diversity.

- Recognize that people of diversity are an asset to society rather than a liability.

- Support the integration of people of diversity into society.

- Help remove barriers to the full participation of people of diversity in society.

- Abide by the motto "equal treatment and equal protection under the law."

- Be sensitive and responsive to the public, including people of diversity.

- Balance concerns for national security with respect for all people of diversity

Don'ts

- Don't contribute to the alienation or ghettoization of people of diversity.

- Don't be unfair to people because of their diversity.

- Don't be overcritical and intolerant of people of diversity.

- Don't blame all the country's ills on multiculturalism.

CHAPTER SUMMARY

Four state ideologies that have profound effects on citizenry and policing are the multiculturalism ideology, civic ideology, assimilation ideology, and ethnist ideology. As a state with a multiculturalism ideology, Canada has enshrined its cultural and linguistic diversity in law. Its multicultural character has been endorsed by provincial legislation in the form of multiculturalism policies and is evidenced in the inclusion of diversity in Ontario's *Police Services Act*. A fundamental principle of policies on cultural and linguistic diversity is the equal treatment under the law of all citizens, regardless of their cultural heritage, racial group, or religion. Research indicates that Canada's multiculturalism policy is evolving into the social ideal of sustaining the vitality of cultural groups and, simultaneously, engendering a national identity and a peaceful society. As the embodiment of law and social justice, policing structures, values, and functions need to mirror Canada's goals of equal treatment and equal protection under the law and be consistent with standards of respect and acceptance for cultural and linguistic diversity and national safety.

KEY TERMS

ideology

multiculturalism ideology

public values

private values

civic ideology

assimilation ideology

ethnist ideology

multiculturalism policy

ghettoization

ethnocentrism

preference hierarchy for cultural groups

Canadianism

ethnic identity

REFERENCES

Abu-Laban, B., & S. Abu-Laban (2004). The Canadian Arab/Muslim community and public opinion two years after 9/11. Paper presented at the 7th Metropolis National Conference, Montreal, Quebec, February 25–March 8, 2004.

Ayed, N. (1997, December 22). We're different, but the same. *The London Free Press*, pp. A1–A2.

Berry, J.W., & R. Kalin. (1995). Multicultural and ethnic attitudes in Canada: An overview of the 1991 national survey. *Canadian Journal of Behavioural Science* 27: 301–20.

Berry, J.W., R. Kalin, & D. Taylor. (1977). *Multiculturalism and ethnic attitudes in Canada*. Ottawa: Supply and Services Canada.

Bibby, R.W. (1994). Is multiculturalism tearing us apart? In M. Charlton and P. Barker (Eds.), *Contemporary political issues* (pp. 20–24). Scarborough, ON: Nelson.

Biles, J., & H. Ibrahim. (2002a). After September 11, 2001: A tale of two Canadas. Paper presented at the 7th International Metropolis Conference, Oslo, Norway.

Biles, J., & H. Ibrahim. (2002b). Testing the Canadian diversity model: Hate, bias and fear after September 11. *Canadian Issues*, 54–60.

Bonnett, A. (2000). *Anti-racism*. London: Routledge.

Bourhis, R.Y., L.C. Moïse, S. Perreault, & S. Senécal. (1997). Towards an interactive acculturation model: A social psychological perspective. *International Journal of Psychology* 32: 369–86.

Brandt, G. (1986). *The realization of anti-racist teaching*. Lewes, UK: The Falmer Press.

Canadian Charter of Rights and Freedoms, part I of the *Constitution Act, 1982*, RSC 1985, app. II, no. 44.

Canadian Multiculturalism Act, RSC 1985, c. 24 (4th Supp.), as amended.

Census Canada. (2001). Ethnic origin. http://www12.statcan.ca/English/census01/ products/reference/techrep/ethnic.cfm#ethni2001.

Chrétien, J. (1982). *Canadian Charter of Rights and Freedoms: A guide for Canadians.* Ottawa: Minister of Supply and Services.

Constitution Act, 1982, RSC 1985, app. II, no. 44.

Day, R.J.F. (2000). *Multiculturalism and the history of Canadian diversity.* Toronto: University of Toronto Press.

Driedger, L. (1989). *The ethnic factor: Identity in diversity.* Toronto: McGraw-Hill Ryerson.

Economic Council of Canada. (1991, May). New faces in the crowd: Economic and social impacts of immigration. Cited in Canadian Heritage, *Ethnic identity reinforces attachment to Canada.* Vol. 1. May 21, 1998. http://www.pch.gc.ca/ progs/multi/evidence/series1_e.cfm.

Fleras, A. (1994). Multiculturalism as society-building: Doing what is necessary, workable and fair. In M. Charlton and P. Barker (Eds.), *Contemporary political issues* (pp. 25–40). Scarborough, ON: Nelson.

Frank, S. (2004, May 3). Islam in Canada. *Time,* 34.

Hamilton, J.F., & B.R. Shilton. (1992). *Police Services Act, 1993.* Toronto: Carswell.

Harding, J. (1992). Policing and aboriginal justice. In K.R.E. McCormick & L.A. Visano (Eds.), *Policing in Canada* (pp. 625–46). Toronto: Canadian Scholars' Press.

Harney, R.F. (1988). "So great a heritage as ours": Immigration and the survival of the Canadian polity. *Daedalus* 117: 51–97.

Helly, D. (2004). Are Muslims discriminated against in Canada since September 2001? *Canadian Ethnic Studies* 36: 24–47.

Ipsos News Centre. (2001). Research, opinions and insight. http://www.ipsos-na. com/news/pressrelease.cfm?id=1309.

Kallen, E. (1982). Ethnicity and human rights in Canada. Agincourt, ON: Gage.

Kallen, E. (2003). Ethnicity and human rights in Canada. Agincourt, ON: Gage.

Kalin, R., & J.W. Berry. (1996). Interethnic attitudes in Canada: Ethnocentrism, consensual hierarchy and reciprocity. *Canadian Journal of Behavioural Science* 28: 253–61.

Kymlicka, W. (1995). *Multicultural citizenship: A liberal theory of minority rights.* New York: Oxford University Press.

Kymlicka, W. (1997, November). Immigrants, multiculturalism, and Canadian citizenship. Department of Philosophy, University of Ottawa. Paper presented at the symposium on Social Cohesion Through Social Justice organized by the Canadian Jewish Congress, Ottawa. Cited in Canadian Heritage, *Multiculturalism promotes integration and citizenship.* Vol. 3. September 21, 1998. http://www.pch.gc.ca/progs/multi/evidence/series3_e.cfm.

Laczko, L.S. (1994, February). Civic experience and feelings of fraternity in Canada: An empirical exploration. Paper prepared for the Round Table on Ethnicity and Citizenship. Royal Society conference, Ottawa. Cited in Canadian Heritage, *Ethnic identity reinforces attachment to Canada.* Vol. 1. May 21, 1998. http://www.pch.gc.ca/progs/multi/evidence/series1_e.cfm.

Modood, T. (1997, October). Antiessentialism, multiculturalism and the recognition of religious groups. Policy Studies Institute, London, UK. Paper presented for the Conference on Citizenship in Diverse Societies, Toronto. Cited in Canadian Heritage, *Ethnic identity reinforces attachment to Canada.* Vol. 1. May 21, 1998. http://www.pch.gc.ca/progs/multi/evidence/series1_e.cfm.

Multiculturalism and Citizenship Canada (1991). *The Canadian Multiculturalism Act: A guide for Canadians.* Ottawa: Ministry of Supply and Services.

Multiculturalism Act, RSBC 1996, c. 321, as amended.

Paquet, G. (1994). Political philosophy of multiculturalism. In J.W. Berry and J.A. Laponce (Eds.), *Ethnicity and culture in Canada* (pp. 60–80). Toronto: University of Toronto Press.

Police Services Act, RSO 1990, c. P.15, as amended.

Porter, J. (1965). *The vertical mosaic: An analysis of social class and power in Canada.* Toronto: University of Toronto Press.

Reich, D. (2000, July 8). Peace builder. *The London Free Press*, p. F4.

Tolerance needs constant vigil. (1997, December 23). *The London Free Press*, p. A12.

Weinfeld, M. (1994). Ethnic assimilation and the retention of ethnic cultures. In J.W. Berry and J.A. Laponce (Eds.), *Ethnicity and culture in Canada* (pp. 238–66). Toronto: University of Toronto Press.

EXERCISES AND REVIEW

Personal Reflections

Read each statement below and circle whether you agree or disagree with it.

1. I believe that we should encourage individuals from diverse cultures to maintain their cultural heritage.

   AGREE   DISAGREE

2. It pleases me when I see people from different cultures in my country.

   AGREE   DISAGREE

3. I think my country would be a better place if more people from various ethnic groups came to live here.

   AGREE   DISAGREE

4. All of us would be happier if all immigrants valued their heritage cultures and the host state culture.

   AGREE   DISAGREE

5. People who come to my country make my country a better place to live.

   AGREE   DISAGREE

6. It is nice to have radio or TV programs in heritage languages.

   AGREE   DISAGREE

7. My country should accept immigrants from all over the world.

   AGREE   DISAGREE

8. Multiculturalism is the main source of my country's political, economic, and social wealth.

   AGREE   DISAGREE

9. My country should encourage multiple languages because they help with worldwide trade.

   AGREE   DISAGREE

10. Newcomers should combine the best of their heritage culture with the best of the host culture.

    AGREE   DISAGREE

11. Encouraging children to learn languages other than French or English is of great benefit to my country.

    AGREE   DISAGREE

12. Multiculturalism is anything but "mosaic madness."

    AGREE   DISAGREE

13. Funding programs and services for newcomers and refugees—for example, teaching English as a second language—is of benefit to them and my country.

    AGREE   DISAGREE

14. The host state should do everything to integrate newcomers as quickly as possible.

    AGREE   DISAGREE

15. The quality of life in countries with a multiculturalism ideology is far superior to the quality of life in countries with a melting pot ideology.

AGREE   DISAGREE

SCORING: Give yourself one point for each statement you agreed with. The higher your score, the more positive your attitude toward cultural pluralism, or the greater your inclination toward a multiculturalism ideology. Compare your score with a classmate's.

Diversity IQ: Multiple Choice

Circle the best answer.

1. Which of the following is true about the concept of multiculturalism?

   a. it may refer to a fact

   b. it may refer to a state policy

   c. it may refer to the celebration of diversity

   d. all of the above

2. Which of the following is a state ideology?

   a. civic

   b. ethnist

   c. assimilation

   d. all of the above

3. Which of the following is a public value?

   a. civil code

   b. criminal code

   c. constitution

   d. all of the above

4. The civic ideology

   a. does not support state funding to promote diversity

   b. endorses state interference in the private values of citizens

   c. embraces the reality of funding ethnocultural activities

   d. all of the above

5. Which of the following state ideologies relies on blood citizenship?

   a. ethnist

   b. assimilation

   c. pluralism

   d. civic

6. Those who support the policy and practice of multiculturalism

   a. do not feel nationalistic at all

   b. are as patriotic as any other citizen

   c. wish to destroy the host society

   d. do so for their own benefit rather than the benefit of the nation

7. The *Canadian Multiculturalism Act* dictates that police policies, procedures, and practices

   a. recognize and promote the understanding that cultural pluralism is a fundamental characteristic of the communities served by police

   b. support the full participation of citizens in policing, regardless of their diversity

   c. recognize and promote the understanding that police forces should reflect the diversity of the communities served

   d. all of the above

8. Diversity policies on cultural heritage and language

   a. are meant only for immigrants and minority groups

   b. apply to policing

   c. promote discrimination against the mainstream culture

   d. all of the above

9. Police officers who are inspired by a multiculturalism ideology are likely to

   a. ensure that all citizens receive equal treatment and protection under the law

   b. disrespect and devalue the diversity of the communities they serve

   c. hinder the full and equitable participation of cultural groups in policing

   d. all of the above

10. Cultural and linguistic diversity in policing has the benefit of

    a. accepting others and supporting an inclusive and a just civil society

    b. promoting disharmonious police–community relations

    c. muddying the image of the police in the community

    d. all of the above

Diversity IQ: True or False?

_____ 1. France is the first nation in the world to enact a policy on cultural and linguistic diversity.

_____ 2. A multiculturalism ideology contributes to the ghettoization of ethnic groups.

_____ 3. At present, the United States is shifting to a civic ideology from an assimilation ideology.

_____ 4. Australia is best described as a state with a multiculturalism ideology.

_____ 5. Great Britain is a state with a civic ideology.

_____ 6. Weakening the minority cultures strengthens the state.

_____ 7. Ethnocentrism does not exist in culturally pluralistic societies.

_____ 8. Germany is a country with an ethnist ideology.

_____ 9. The political participation of immigrant groups in Canada is best described as inactive.

_____ 10. A state with an ethnist ideology defines citizenship exclusively in biological, ethnic, or religious terms.

Application Now

1. List the benefits of a multiculturalism policy to a culturally pluralistic society in general and to policing in particular.

    a. Benefits to a culturally pluralistic society

    b. Benefits to policing

2. Identify at least three core values for policing that would be consistent with the spirit of the policy of multiculturalism.

Food for Thought

Write down the cultural group you identify yourself with most—for example, Chinese-Canadian, Hispanic, or American.

1. Rate your level of comfort in interacting with individuals from the cultures listed below, including your own. Use the following scale for your ratings:

    1 = not comfortable at all

    2 = somewhat uncomfortable

    3 = neither comfortable nor uncomfortable

    4 = somewhat comfortable

    5 = very comfortable

    _____ Your culture (if different from any of those listed below)

    _____ British heritage

    _____ French heritage

    _____ Arab heritage

    _____ Sikh heritage

    _____ South Asian heritage

    _____ African heritage

    _____ Chinese heritage

2. Answer the following questions:

   a. Did you rate your own group the highest (very comfortable)? If so, does your rating support the notion of ethnocentrism? Why or why not?

   b. Did you rate the remaining groups differently? If so, do your ratings support the notion of a preference hierarchy for cultural groups?

   c. List your reasons for rating some cultural groups as 1 (not comfortable at all) or 2 (somewhat uncomfortable).

   d. Now list your reasons for rating some cultures as 4 (somewhat comfortable) or 5 (very comfortable).

From Thought to Action

What do each of the following core values of Canada's multiculturalism policy mean in terms of police conduct or behaviour?

1. Respect

2. Acceptance

3. Equal treatment under the law

4. Equal protection under the law

5. Full and equitable participation

Lessons from History

1. Invite individuals or groups from the mainstream French or English culture and people of diversity to your class to discuss state ideologies from a historical perspective. What lessons have been learned? What are the implications of past experiences for contemporary society and policing?

   Some individuals argue that historical reminders of ill treatment of people (for example, Aboriginal people) are nothing but "country bashing," and that the newer generations are sick and tired of being reminded of their country's sins every day. What is your response to such reactions? Is there any benefit to knowing about the wrongs of the past? Should we tell historians to bag their histories and sell them somewhere else? Explain.

2. What can we learn from these past events? How can these events help us now in terms of our human relations in a culturally diverse context?

3. What lessons can police learn from past maltreatment of cultural groups?

The Great Debates

1. As a class, debate the four state ideologies from social and policing perspectives.

2. In dealing with individuals from diverse cultures, the criminal justice system has considered the cultural values and norms of some offenders before sentencing them. Courts have given these offenders lighter sentences than others who have committed the same offence. An alternative view is that the law applies to all people equally and that culture should not enter into the criminal justice system. Discuss this controversial issue and its implications for law enforcement.

CHAPTER 3

Human Rights and Freedoms

CHAPTER OBJECTIVES

After completing this chapter, you should be able to:

- Explain how human rights legislation influences people's individual and collective rights and freedoms.

- Discuss the impact of policy and legislation on the recognition of rights of people of diversity.

- Discuss policing in the context of human rights and freedoms.

- Discuss how the September 11, 2001 terrorist attacks on the United States have led to changes in Canadian legislation and created new challenges for law enforcement agencies.

PREVIEW SCENARIO

Benamar Benatta, a 32-year-old former Algerian Air Force lieutenant, sought political asylum in Canada, beginning his refugee claim at the Peace Bridge days before the September 11, 2001 terrorist attacks on the United States. On September 12, 2001, Canadian immigration officials handed Benatta over to American customs officials on the ground that he was a terror suspect. On September 12, 2001, there was no Canadian law stipulating that Canadian government officials should return refugee claimants suspected of terrorism to the United States. Benatta's transfer to the United States marked the beginning of a five-year nightmare in US jails. Benatta, whose case had some parallels to that of Canadian Maher Arar, a dual citizen deported to Syria under the controversial practice of rendition, found himself in solitary confinement under abusive conditions south of the border.

Benatta had arrived in the United States on a six-month visitor's visa in late December 2000 and engaged in military surveillance and anti-terrorism training with other Algerian Air Force personnel with a Virginia-based defence contractor. However, he became a conscientious objector with no plans to return to Syria, and by the end of the summer of 2001 had decided to file a refugee claim in Canada. Benatta "expected difficulties with his claim when he arrived at the Peace Bridge, on September 5, 2001, because he was carrying false US identification cards, including the social security card he had used to get work as a busboy in New York City after his visa expired." His documents prompted Canadian immigration officials to detain him for "identification checking." Benatta first learned about the 9/11 terrorist attacks from FBI agents on September 12, 2001 when they questioned him on the subject. Even though Benatta was cleared of terrorist links in November 2001 following intensive interrogations, he was "left to languish at the Brooklyn jail [a facility normally used to house crime suspects rather than immigration detainees] until the following April." According to a federal magistrate, Benatta had been "held in custody under harsh conditions which can be said to be 'oppressive'" and "undeniably deprived of his liberty." Attorneys from the American Civil Liberties Union later alleged that he had been subjected to a "high security prison regime ... that could be described as torture." As well, jail guards wrote the letters "WTC" on his cell door to signify his connection to the World Trade Center investigation. At no time during his detention and interrogation was Benatta given access to a lawyer. Benatta was eventually allowed to leave a US immigration lockup after being in custody for 58 months when his lawyers brokered a deal with Canadian immigration authorities to let him pursue the refugee claim he originally began at the Peace Bridge before 9/11. Benatta ran from his country because of persecution and threats against his life, and because of his desire to forget what happened to him back home, and because of his expectation that Canada or the United States would open their arms to him so he could get on with his life. As of this writing, Benatta is staying at a Toronto refugee shelter. He is likely to wait for more than a year to learn about the outcome of his refugee claim. Benatta is believed to be "the last of about 1,200 Muslim men swept up in post-9/11 investigations to be released." (Leeder, 2006)

INTRODUCTION

The evolution of civil rights has influenced political and civil structures and processes around the world and has inspired the character of nations and the quality of life of their people. Human rights and freedoms are discussed in this chapter for four main reasons. First, they form an important part of the collective conscience of nations. Second, they provide the international community with basic standards by which nations can identify and measure equality and fairness. Third, understanding human rights and freedoms is paramount to the ability of police to fulfill their mandate. Fourth, in the wake of 9/11, law enforcement agencies and police officers face the added challenge of respecting the human rights and freedoms of all Canadians while fighting terrorism.

INTERNATIONAL HUMAN RIGHTS AND FREEDOMS

The idea of human rights has been traced back to the ancient Greeks and Romans. However, the concept as understood today seems to have been nurtured at the beginning of the 13th century. In 1215, the signing of England's Magna Carta, or Great Charter, symbolized a cry against oppression. This document, a response to the misuse of power by the monarchy and royal officials, addressed such issues as unfair and arbitrary taxes imposed on the people, their inability to get a fair hearing of their complaints, and other problems. The Magna Carta inspired future instruments on human rights and freedoms. Liberty and equality were at the core of these documents, which declared the right of people not to be imprisoned arbitrarily, to pursue happiness, to own property, and to enjoy free speech.

In 1948 the General Assembly of the United Nations set down the Universal Declaration of Human Rights (Office of the United Nations High Commissioner for Human Rights, 1948), whose 30 articles recognize the equality and dignity of all people, and their fundamental rights, including the right to freedom, security, personal expression, an adequate standard of living, and education. Recently, a UN Human Rights Council replaced the UN Human Rights Commission. Even though the 47-member council has been criticized for showing bias and for failing to confront human rights abuses, in the words of Kofi Annan, the Secretary General of the UN, "This council represents a great chance for the UN, and for humanity, to renew the struggle for human rights" (Editorial, *International Herald Tribune*, June 24-25, 2006, p. 6).

HUMAN RIGHTS IN CANADA: FEDERAL

Canadian Human Rights Act

The road to the *Canadian Human Rights Act* began with the *Royal Proclamation of 1763*, which conferred on provincial legislatures in Canada the power to pass laws in relation to property and civil rights and local private matters. This Royal Proclamation was a forerunner of the *British North America Act, 1867* (BNA Act). This Act also granted Quebec the power to retain a civil-law tradition. The *Canadian Bill of Rights* was introduced in 1960 to protect individual rights and freedoms. In 1977, the federal government passed the **Canadian Human Rights Act**, in which discrimination based on "race, national or ethnic origin, colour, age, sex, marital status, disability or conviction for an offence for which a pardon has been granted" was prohibited. The Act was amended in 1996 to include sexual orientation as a prohibited ground of discrimination. The Act has recently undergone a comprehensive review by the Canadian Human Rights Act Review Panel (2000).

In section 40(1), the Act stipulates that

> any individual or group of individuals having reasonable grounds for believing that a person is engaging or has engaged in a discriminatory practice may file with the [Canadian Human Rights] Commission a complaint in a form acceptable to the Commission.

Canadian Human Rights Act
law that prohibits discrimination based on race, national or ethnic origin, colour, age, sex, marital status, disability, sexual orientation, or conviction for an offence for which a pardon has been granted

Canadian Human Rights Commission
federal body responsible for investigating and adjudicating complaints of violations of the *Canadian Human Rights Act*

The **Canadian Human Rights Commission** is a government agency with the mandate to investigate human rights complaints and to develop policies and address issues pertaining to discrimination based on disability, race, religion, sex, and sexual orientation; employment and pay equity; and aboriginal peoples. For example, the commission has developed policies on drug testing in the workplace (1999), HIV/AIDS (2000), harassment in the workplace (1998), and the *Employment Equity Act* (1995).

Canadian Charter of Rights and Freedoms

Canadian Charter of Rights and Freedoms
part of the Canadian constitution that establishes the protection of nine basic rights and freedoms deemed essential to the maintenance of a free democratic society and a united country

fundamental freedoms
freedom of conscience and religion; freedom of thought, belief, opinion, and expression, including freedom of the press and other media of communication; freedom of peaceful assembly; and freedom of association

The *Canadian Charter of Rights and Freedoms* was introduced in the *Constitution Act, 1982*. The Charter entrenches *minimum* rights for Canadian citizens. It defines 10 basic rights and freedoms, which apply to all governments—federal, provincial, and territorial. These are summarized in table 3.1.

GUARANTEE OF RIGHTS AND FREEDOMS AND FUNDAMENTAL FREEDOMS

Section 1 of the Charter guarantees rights and freedoms to all Canadians subject to reasonable and legal limits, and section 2 lists the **fundamental freedoms** (see the box on p. 67). The Charter guarantees freedom of speech and freedom of the press and other media. Consequently, past laws that (1) required newspapers to reveal their sources of news; (2) banned the propagation of certain political ideologies by closing down any premises used for that purpose; (3) prohibited the distribution of any book, pamphlet, or tract without permission of a chief of police; and (4) restricted a religious group from its right to free expression and religious practice are contrary to the spirit of the Charter and may be struck down by the courts or sent back to Parliament for revision. Finally, the Charter ensures the right of Canadians to gather in peaceful groups and protects their freedom of association. However, these freedoms are not absolute. For example, freedom of speech is subject to laws governing libel and slander in recognition of the fact that an absolute right to freedom of speech fails to protect the rights of others. We can see the wisdom of such a

TABLE 3.1   Basic Rights and Freedoms Enshrined in the Canadian Charter of Rights and Freedoms

1. Guarantee of rights and freedoms
2. Fundamental freedoms
3. Democratic rights
4. Mobility rights
5. Legal rights
6. Equality rights
7. Official languages of Canada
8. Minority language educational rights
9. Enforcement
10. General: Rights of Aboriginal peoples, multiculturalism, and rights of women

Source: *Canadian Charter of Rights and Freedoms*, part I of the *Constitution Act, 1982*, RSC 1985, app. II, no. 44.

qualification when faced with hate literature against particular groups in Canadian society.

GUARANTEE OF RIGHTS AND FREEDOMS AND FUNDAMENTAL FREEDOMS

Guarantee of Rights and Freedoms

1. The *Canadian Charter of Rights and Freedoms* guarantees the rights and freedoms set out in it subject only to such reasonable limits prescribed by law as can be demonstrably justified in a free and democratic society.

Fundamental Freedoms

2. Everyone has the following fundamental freedoms:

a. freedom of conscience and religion;

b. freedom of thought, belief, opinion and expression, including freedom of the press and other media of communication;

c. freedom of peaceful assembly; and

d. freedom of association.

Source: *Canadian Charter of Rights and Freedoms*, part I of the *Constitution Act, 1982*, RSC 1985, app. II, no. 44.

DEMOCRATIC RIGHTS

In addition to enshrining certain fundamental freedoms for everyone in Canada, the Charter gives all Canadian citizens **democratic rights** to vote or run in an election (section 3) and the assurance that no government has the right to continue to hold power indefinitely without seeking a new mandate from the electorate (section 4). However, special rules apply for police officers. Section 46 of the Ontario *Police Services Act* states, "No municipal police officer shall engage in political activity, except as the regulations [to the Act] permit." The regulations state that a serving police officer may only run for office if he or she is granted a leave of absence.

democratic rights
rights to vote or run in an election and the assurance that no government has the right to continue to hold power indefinitely without seeking a new mandate from the electorate

MOBILITY RIGHTS

The **mobility rights** granted to Canadian citizens and permanent residents in section 6 of the Charter assure them the freedom to enter, remain in, or leave the country. This section also allows them to live and seek employment anywhere in Canada. Nevertheless, provinces have the right to set residence requirements that residents must meet in order to qualify for certain provincial social and welfare benefits. Provinces also have the right to apply employment requirements to both newcomers and long-time residents.

mobility rights
freedom to enter, remain in, or leave the country, and to live and seek employment anywhere in Canada

LEGAL RIGHTS

The **legal rights** provisions of the Charter (sections 7–14), known as the lawyers' section, provide basic legal protection to safeguard Canadian citizens in their dealings

legal rights
basic legal protection to safeguard Canadian citizens in their dealings with the state and the justice system

with the state and the justice system (see the box below). More specifically, Canadian citizens' right to life, liberty, and security prohibit the use not only of unreasonable search or seizure but also of unreasonable manner of executing these functions—for example, police cannot use unnecessary force in apprehending a suspect. The legal rights also guarantee that no one will be detained or held arbitrarily. Thus, a police officer has to show reasonable cause for detaining an individual.

LEGAL RIGHTS

7. Everyone has the right to life, liberty and security of the person and the right not to be deprived thereof except in accordance with the principles of fundamental justice.

8. Everyone has the right to be secure against unreasonable search or seizure.

9. Everyone has the right not to be arbitrarily detained or imprisoned.

10. Everyone has the right on arrest or detention

(a) to be informed promptly of the reasons therefor;

(b) to retain and instruct counsel without delay and to be informed of that right; and

(c) to have the validity of the detention determined by way of *habeas corpus* and to be released if the detention is not lawful.

11. Any person charged with an offence has the right

(a) to be informed without unreasonable delay of the specific offence;

(b) to be tried within a reasonable time; …

(d) to be presumed innocent until proven guilty … ;

12. Everyone has the right not to be subjected to any cruel and unusual treatment or punishment.

13. A witness who testifies in any proceedings has the right not to have any incriminating evidence so given used to incriminate that witness in any other proceedings, except in a prosecution for perjury or for the giving of contradictory evidence.

14. A party or witness in any proceedings who does not understand or speak the language in which the proceedings are conducted or who is deaf has the right to the assistance of an interpreter.

Source: *Canadian Charter of Rights and Freedoms*, part I of the *Constitution Act, 1982*, RSC 1985, app. II, no. 44.

The legal rights on arrest and detention also protect members of the public from arbitrary or unlawful actions by law enforcement agencies. In being held or arrested by any authority, people have the right to be informed of the reasons for their being taken into custody, the right to be instructed of their right to contact and consult a lawyer without delay, and the right to have a court determine quickly whether the detention is lawful. Finally, these legal rights ensure that no individual is subjected to cruel and unusual treatment or punishment.

EQUALITY RIGHTS

Section 15, **equality rights**, states categorically that all Canadians, regardless of their race, national or ethnic origin, colour, religion, sex, age, or mental or physical disability, are equal before the law and are to enjoy equal protection and benefit of the law (see the box below). When put into practice, this equality right may be compromised by a citizen's inability to fund a defence in a court case. For example, a successful defence against an impaired driving charge can easily cost $10,000 and not all people can afford to mount such a costly defence. If someone were to defend himself, the likelihood of a successful outcome would be considerably diminished.

equality rights
rights of all Canadians, regardless of race, national or ethnic origin, colour, sex, age, or mental or physical disability, to be equal before the law and to enjoy equal protection and benefit of the law

EQUALITY RIGHTS

15(1) Every individual is equal before and under the law and has the right to the equal protection and equal benefit of the law without discrimination and, in particular, without discrimination based on race, national or ethnic origin, colour, religion, sex, age or mental or physical disability.

(2) Subsection (1) does not preclude any law, program or activity that has as its object the amelioration of conditions of disadvantaged individuals or groups including those that are disadvantaged because of race, national or ethnic origin, colour, religion, sex, age or mental or physical disability.

Source: *Canadian Charter of Rights and Freedoms*, part I of the *Constitution Act, 1982*, RSC 1985, app. II, no. 44.

...t a Supreme ...scrimination.

...cial languages ...ome bilingual ...communicate ...vernment ser- ...uage in Parlia-

official languages
English and French as confirmed by the Charter, which guarantees that the federal government can serve members of the public in the official language of their choice

...hts of Canadian ...rovince to allow ...p. 71). The first ...ipulates that in- ...ch and who live ...ght to have their ...h and who live in ...hildren educated ...*the parents were*

OFFICIAL LANGUAGES OF CANADA

16(1) English and French are the official languages of Canada and have equality of status and equal rights and privileges as to their use in all institutions of the Parliament and government of Canada.

(2) English and French are the official languages of New Brunswick and have equality of status and equal rights and privileges as to their use in all institutions of the legislature and government of New Brunswick. ...

17(1) Everyone has the right to use English or French in any debates and other proceedings of Parliament.

(2) Everyone has the right to use English or French in any debates and other proceedings of the legislature of New Brunswick. ...

19(1) Either English or French may be used by any person in, or in any pleading in or process issuing from, any court established by Parliament.

(2) Either English or French may be used by any person in, or in any pleading in or process issuing from, any court of New Brunswick.

20(1) Any member of the public in Canada has the right to communicate with, and to receive available services from, any head or central office of an institution of the Parliament or government of Canada in English or French, and has the same right with respect to any other office of any such institution where

(a) there is a significant demand for communication with and services from that office in such language; or

(b) due to the nature of the office, it is reasonable that communications with and services from that office be available in both English and French.

(2) Any member of the public in New Brunswick has the right to communicate with, and to receive available services from, any office of an institution of the legislature or government of New Brunswick in English or French.

21. Nothing in sections 16 to 20 abrogates or derogates from any right, privilege or obligation with respect to the English or French languages, or either of them, that exists or is continued by virtue of any other provision of the Constitution of Canada.

22. Nothing in sections 16 to 20 abrogates or derogates from any legal or customary right or privilege acquired or enjoyed either before or after the coming into force of this Charter with respect to any language that is not English or French.

Source: *Canadian Charter of Rights and Freedoms*, part I of the *Constitution Act, 1982*, RSC 1985, app. II, no. 44.

educated in Canada. The Charter stipulates that individuals who were educated in English or French and live in a province where that language is in the linguistic minority have the right to send their children to a school that uses that minority language. The third criterion relates to the *language in which other children in the family are receiving or have received their education*. The Charter protects the right of children whose siblings have received primary or secondary school instruction in either official language to be educated in the same language. In a separate section

MINORITY LANGUAGE EDUCATIONAL RIGHTS

23(1) Citizens of Canada

(a) whose first language learned and still understood is that of the English or French linguistic minority population of the province in which they reside, or

(b) who have received their primary school instruction in Canada in English or French and reside in a province where the language in which they received that instruction is the language of the English or French linguistic minority population of the province,

have the right to have their children receive primary and secondary school instruction in that language in that province.

(2) Citizens of Canada of whom any child has received or is receiving primary or secondary school instruction in English or French in Canada, have the right to have all their children receive primary and secondary school instruction in the same language. ….

Source: *Canadian Charter of Rights and Freedoms*, part I of the *Constitution Act, 1982*, RSC 1985, app. II, no. 44.

(section 29), the Charter guarantees the establishment and operation of religious schools and provides them immunity from other provisions. Thus, the Charter ensures that neither the freedom of conscience and religion provision nor the equality rights provision can override existing constitutional rights with respect to the establishment and state financing of religious schools.

ENFORCEMENT

Section 24 allows a person or group whose rights have been denied or infringed upon by law or by action taken by the state to apply to a court for a remedy (see the box on p. 72). An example of a potential infringement is police breaking into and searching a person's premises and discovering incriminating evidence. In such a circumstance, the courts could exclude the evidence in a subsequent trial in which it is alleged that a right under the Charter was infringed, or the courts could rule that admission of the illegally obtained evidence brings the administration of justice into disrepute.

GENERAL RIGHTS OF ABORIGINAL PEOPLES, MULTICULTURALISM, AND RIGHTS OF WOMEN

The rights of Canada's aboriginal peoples (First Nations, Inuit, and Métis), enshrinement of Canada's multicultural character, and the rights of women are contained in sections 25, 27, and 28 of the Charter, respectively (see the box on p. 73).

Section 25 recognizes and affirms **aboriginal peoples' rights** to preserve their culture, identity, customs, traditions, and languages, and any special rights that they have currently or rights that they may acquire in the future (section 35 of the constitution recognizes and affirms existing aboriginal and treaty rights. This section

aboriginal peoples' rights
rights of Canada's aboriginal peoples to preserve their culture, identity, customs, traditions, and languages, and any special rights that they have currently or may acquire in the future

ENFORCEMENT

24(1) Anyone whose rights or freedoms, as guaranteed by this Charter, have been infringed or denied may apply to a court of competent jurisdiction to obtain such remedy as the court considers appropriate and just in the circumstances.

(2) Where, in proceedings under subsection (1), a court concludes that evidence was obtained in a manner that infringed or denied any rights or freedoms guaranteed by this Charter, the evidence shall be excluded if it is established that, having regard to all the circumstances, the admission of it in the proceedings would bring the administration of justice into disrepute.

Source: *Canadian Charter of Rights and Freedoms*, part I of the *Constitution Act, 1982*, RSC 1985, app. II, no. 44.

---

multicultural heritage
the unique and constitutionally enshrined multicultural character of Canadian society

Ontario *Human Rights Code*
Ontario statute that protects the dignity and worth of every person and provides for "equal rights and opportunities without discrimination that is contrary to law"

freedom from discrimination
under part I of the Ontario *Human Rights Code*, freedom from discrimination with respect to services, goods, facilities, accommodation, contracts, employment, and occupational associations, and freedom from sexual solicitation in the workplace and by those in a position of power

Ontario Human Rights Commission
provincial body responsible for investigating and adjudicating complaints of violations of the Ontario *Human Rights Code*

also ensures that any new benefits that the aboriginal peoples may gain from a settlement of land claims "would not run afoul of the general equality rights as set out in the Charter."

Section 27 provides a constitutionally unique provision by enshrining the multicultural character of Canadian society—that is, the maintenance and enhancement of Canada's **multicultural heritage**.

Finally, section 28 ensures that all rights in the Charter are guaranteed equally to both sexes. Including this provision in the Charter ensures that it cannot be overridden by a provincial legislature or by Parliament.

HUMAN RIGHTS IN ONTARIO

Human Rights Code

At the time that the *Canadian Bill of Rights* was enacted, the provinces developed their own human rights codes. Due to space limitations, the focus in this section is on the Ontario *Human Rights Code*, which was enacted in 1962.

The preamble to the **Ontario *Human Rights Code*** states that "recognition of the inherent dignity and the equal and inalienable rights of all members of the human family is the foundation of freedom, justice and peace in the world and is in accord with the *Universal Declaration of Human Rights* as proclaimed by the United Nations." Part I of the Code, which deals with **freedom from discrimination**, is provided on pp. 74-75. Individuals who believe that their rights have been infringed under the Code can file a complaint with the **Ontario Human Rights Commission**. Part IV of the Code outlines the complaint process. The commission investigates complaints of discrimination and harassment with a view to settlement of the complaints between the parties or litigation of the cases at the Human Rights Tribunal of Ontario and higher courts. In 2005-6, the Ontario Human Rights Commission investigated, mediated, or otherwise completed a total of 2,117 individual complaints of discrimination, and referred a total of 170 cases to the Human Rights Tribunal of Ontario for a hearing (Ontario Human Rights Commission, 2006). The commission also saw the Legislature of Ontario pass a bill to end mandatory retirement and allow as

GENERAL: RIGHTS OF ABORIGINAL PEOPLES, MULTICULTURALISM, AND RIGHTS OF WOMEN

25. The guarantee in this Charter of certain rights and freedoms shall not be construed so as to abrogate or derogate from any aboriginal, treaty or other rights or freedoms that pertain to the aboriginal peoples of Canada including

(a) any rights or freedoms that have been recognized by the Royal Proclamation of October 7, 1763; and

(b) any rights or freedoms that may be acquired by the aboriginal peoples of Canada by way of land claims settlement. ...

27. This Charter shall be interpreted in a manner consistent with the preservation and enhancement of the multicultural heritage of Canadians.

28. Notwithstanding anything in this Charter, the rights and freedoms referred to in it are guaranteed equally to male and female persons. ...

Source: *Canadian Charter of Rights and Freedoms*, part I of the *Constitution Act, 1982*, RSC 1985, app. II, no. 44.

of December 2006 employees the choice to continue working past age 65. Complaints may now be brought against employers on this basis.

Ontario Human Rights Commission Policies and Initiatives

The Ontario Human Rights Commission has issued a number of policies that clarify or complement the Ontario *Human Rights Code*, some of which are described below. In advancing its various policies, the commission makes reference to harassment, a poisoned environment, and constructive discrimination. As defined in the Code (part II, section 10(1)(e)), **harassment** is a "course of vexatious comment or conduct that is known or ought reasonably to be known to be unwelcome." A poisoned environment is one in which a person or a group of people are treated differently for reasons related to prohibitory grounds, such as gender, race, and sexual orientation. According to the Code (part II, section 11(1)), **constructive discrimination** refers to a "requirement, qualification or factor ... that is not discrimination on a prohibited ground but that results in the exclusion, restriction or preference of a group of persons who are identified by a prohibited ground of discrimination." A requirement, qualification, or factor is not discriminatory if it can be established that it is reasonable and bona fide (in good faith) in the circumstances. Two conditions are required to establish that it is bona fide: first, it must be demonstrated that there is an objective relationship between the selection criteria and the job in question, and, second, it must be shown that the standards required for the job are imposed in good faith.

The following sections describe some Ontario Human Rights Commission policies. Table 3.2 lists all the policies at time of publication and the date on which each policy was instituted.

harassment
comments or conduct toward another person that is unwelcome

constructive discrimination
discrimination that results from a requirement, qualification, or factor that seems reasonable but effectively excludes, restricts, or favours some people contrary to human rights laws

ONTARIO HUMAN RIGHTS CODE, PART I: FREEDOM FROM DISCRIMINATION

Services

1. Every person has a right to equal treatment with respect to services, goods and facilities, without discrimination because of race, ancestry, place of origin, colour, ethnic origin, citizenship, creed, sex, sexual orientation, age, marital status, same-sex partnership status, family status or handicap.

Accommodation

2(1) Every person has a right to equal treatment with respect to occupancy of accommodation, without discrimination because of race, ancestry, place of origin, colour, ethnic origin, citizenship, creed, sex, sexual orientation, age, marital status, same-sex partnership status, family status, handicap or the receipt of public assistance.

Harassment in Accommodation

(2) Every person who occupies accommodation has a right to freedom from harassment by the landlord or agent of the landlord or by an occupant of the same building because of race, ancestry, place of origin, colour, ethnic origin, citizenship, creed, age, marital status, same-sex partnership status, family status, handicap or the receipt of public assistance.

Contracts

3. Every person having legal capacity has a right to contract on equal terms without discrimination because of race, ancestry, place of origin, colour, ethnic origin, citizenship, creed, sex, sexual orientation, age, marital status, same-sex partnership status, family status or handicap.

Accommodation of Person Under Eighteen

4(1) Every sixteen or seventeen year old person who has withdrawn from parental control has a right to equal treatment with respect to occupancy of and contracting for accommodation without discrimination because the person is less than eighteen years old.

Idem

(2) A contract for accommodation entered into by a sixteen or seventeen year old person who has withdrawn from parental control is enforceable against that person as if the person were eighteen years old.

Employment

5(1) Every person has a right to equal treatment with respect to employment without discrimination because of race, ancestry, place of origin, colour, ethnic origin, citizenship, creed, sex, sexual orientation, age, record of offences, marital status, same-sex partnership status, family status or handicap.

(Concluded on next page)

Harassment in Employment

(2) Every person who is an employee has a right to freedom from harassment in the workplace by the employer or agent of the employer or by another employee because of race, ancestry, place of origin, colour, ethnic origin, citizenship, creed, age, record of offence, marital status, same-sex partnership status, family status or handicap.

Vocational Associations

6. Every person has a right to equal treatment with respect to membership in any trade union, trade or occupational association or self-governing profession without discrimination because of race, ancestry, place of origin, colour, ethnic origin, citizenship, creed, sex, sexual orientation, age, marital status, same-sex partnership status, family status or handicap.

Harassment Because of Sex in Accommodation

7(1) Every person who occupies accommodation has a right to freedom from harassment because of sex by the landlord or agent of the landlord or by an occupant of the same building.

Harassment Because of Sex in Workplaces

(2) Every person who is an employee has a right to freedom from harassment in the workplace because of sex by his or her employer or agent of the employer or by another employee.

Sexual Solicitation by a Person in Position to Confer Benefit, etc.

(3) Every person has a right to be free from,

(a) a sexual solicitation or advance made by a person in a position to confer, grant or deny a benefit or advancement to the person where the person making the solicitation or advance knows or ought reasonably to know that it is unwelcome; or

(b) a reprisal or a threat of reprisal for the rejection of a sexual solicitation or advance where the reprisal is made or threatened by a person in a position to confer, grant or deny a benefit or advancement to the person.

Reprisals

8. Every person has a right to claim and enforce his or her rights under this Act, to institute and participate in proceeding under this Act and to refuse to infringe a right of another person under this Act, without reprisal or threat of reprisal for so doing.

Infringement Prohibited

9. No person shall infringe or do, directly or indirectly, anything that infringes a right under this Part.

Source: *Human Rights Code*, RSO 1990, c. H.19, as amended.

TABLE 3.2　Timeline of Ontario Human Rights Commission Policies

April 9, 1996	Policy on Female Genital Mutilation (FGM)
June 19, 1996	Policy on Discrimination and Language
June 19, 1996	Policy on Height and Weight Requirements
June 19, 1996	Policy on Racial Slurs and Harassment and Racial Jokes
June 19, 1996	Policy on Requiring a Driver's Licence as a Condition of Employment
September 10, 1996	Policy on Sexual Harassment and Inappropriate Gender Related Comments and Conduct
September 11, 1996	Policy on Discrimination Because of Pregnancy
October 20, 1996	Policy on Creed and the Accommodation of Religious Observances
November 27, 1996	Policy on Drug and Alcohol Testing
November 27, 1996	Policy on Employment-Related Medical Information
November 27, 1996	Policy on HIV/AIDS-Related Discrimination
July 8, 1997	Policy on Scholarships and Awards
January 11, 2000	Policy on Discrimination and Harassment Because of Sexual Orientation
March 30, 2000	Policy on Discrimination and Harassment Because of Gender Identity
June 2005	Policy and Guidelines on Racism and Racial Discrimination

Source: Ontario Human Rights Commission (1996, 2000, 2006).

POLICY ON FEMALE GENITAL MUTILATION (FGM)

Female genital mutilation (FGM), sometimes called female circumcision, is the ritualistic or traditional practice of some cultures of cutting and removing a female's external sexual organs for the purposes of preservation of virginity, control over her sexuality, class distinction, and other possible reasons. The Ontario Human Rights Commission now recognizes FGM as a practice that not only violates human rights but endangers the health of women and can have adverse obstetric outcomes including maternal death and infant mortality (Rosenthal, 2006).

The commission's (OHRC, 1996a) view of the practice as a violation of human rights is consistent with the international community's view of FGM as a gender-specific violation of the rights of girls and women to physical integrity and health. FGM also falls within the definition of aggravated assault under the *Criminal Code*. In October 1994, the Ontario Ministry of the Solicitor General and Correctional Services advised all chiefs of police and the commissioner of the Ontario Provincial Police that FGM is a criminal offence. Licensed physicians in Ontario who perform FGM may be charged with assault, in addition to professional misconduct.

POLICY ON DISCRIMINATION AND HARASSMENT BECAUSE OF SEXUAL ORIENTATION

Discrimination on the grounds of sexual orientation and same-sex partnership status is prohibited. *Sexual orientation* is "more than simply a 'status' that an individual possesses; it is an immutable personal characteristic that forms part of an individual's core identity. Sexual orientation encompasses the range of human sexuality from gay and lesbian to bisexual and heterosexual orientations" (OHRC, 2000a). This policy was updated to include the March 2005 amendments to the Code in which marital status was redefined to include same-sex conjugal relationships, to reflect the rights of same-sex marriage partners, to improve understanding of discrimination experienced by lesbian, gay, and bisexual individuals, and to assist organizational development of harassment-free environments (OHRC, 2006).

On May 20, 1999, the Supreme Court of Canada found the "opposite sex" definition of "spouse" in part III of Ontario's *Family Law Act* to be unconstitutional. In response to the Supreme Court's decision, Ontario introduced Bill 5, which received royal assent on October 28, 1999. This Bill amended the *Family Law Act* to allow its provisions governing support obligations to apply to same-sex partners. Bill 5 also amended the Ontario *Human Rights Code* by defining the term "marital status" to include "same-sex partnership status" and the term "spouse" to include "same-sex partner." "Same-sex partner" is further defined to mean the individual with whom a person of the same sex is living in a conjugal relationship outside marriage. Similarly, same-sex partnership status is defined to mean the status of living with an individual of the same sex in a conjugal relationship outside marriage.

The federal *Civil Marriage Act* has extended the "legal capacity to marry for civil purposes to same-sex couples while respecting religious freedom" (Department of Justice, 2005). The *Civil Marriage Act* augments those rights stated in the amended Ontario *Human Rights Code*.

POLICY ON DISCRIMINATION AND HARASSMENT BECAUSE OF GENDER IDENTITY

In this policy, the term "sex" under the *Human Rights Code* is interpreted to include *gender identity* (OHRC, 2000b). Gender identity is not the same as sexual orientation, but diverges from a person's birth-assigned identity (almost exclusively transgenderists and transsexuals). The personal attributes associated with gender identity include self-image, physical and biological appearance, behaviour, and gender-related conduct. The term "transgendered" refers to "people who are not comfortable with or who reject, in whole or in part, their birth-assigned gender identities" (OHRC, 2000b). Transgendered people include transsexuals, cross-dressers, and intersexed individuals.

POLICY ON SEXUAL HARASSMENT AND INAPPROPRIATE GENDER-RELATED COMMENTS AND CONDUCT

This policy provides the fundamental human right to freedom from sexual harassment and other forms of unequal treatment expressed through demeaning comments and actions based on gender (OHRC, 1996c). The policy clearly distinguishes between accepted social interaction or consensual relations and behaviour that is known or ought reasonably to be known to be unwelcome. Also, the policy provides a framework for educational initiatives (for example, the development of training materials and anti-harassment policies) by employers and others.

There are two views of sexual harassment. In a narrow context, *sexual harassment* is defined as the making of an objectionable comment or objectionable conduct of a sexual nature. In a broader context, sexual harassment includes conduct that is not overtly sexual in nature but is related to the person's gender, and demeans or causes personal humiliation or embarrassment to the recipient. In most cases men are the harassers of women. However, there are women harassers of men, and sexual harassment between members of the same sex is known to occur.

A person can be guilty of sexual harassment or discrimination without making explicit reference to gender or sex. Sex discrimination may involve gender-based harassing comments or conduct. The comments or actions do not have to be made with the intention to discriminate for them to be considered violations of human rights. For example, an employer may indirectly harass a female employee, with the intent to discourage her from continuing her employment in a particular position, because of her gender.

Specific examples of sexual harassment and inappropriate gender-related comments and conduct include the following (OHRC, 1996c, section 6):

    i)   gender-related comments about an individual's physical characteristics or mannerisms;

    ii)   unwelcome physical contact;

    iii)   suggestive or offensive remarks or innuendoes about members of a specific gender;

    iv)   propositions of physical intimacy;

    v)   gender-related verbal abuse, threats, or taunting;

    vi)   leering or inappropriate staring;

    vii)   bragging about sexual prowess;

    viii)   demands for dates or sexual favours;

    ix)   offensive jokes or comments of a sexual nature about an employee, client, or tenant;

    x)   display of sexually offensive pictures, graffiti, or other materials;

    xi)   questions or discussions about sexual activities;

    xii)   paternalism based on gender which a person feels undermines his or her self-respect or position of responsibility;

    xiii)   rough and vulgar humour or language related to gender.

This policy is consistent with laws in several countries on workplace discrimination and harassment. A harassment-free work environment is one that does not tolerate a hostile or abusive atmosphere where an employee is subjected to offensive remarks, behaviour, or surroundings that create intimidating, hostile, or humiliating working conditions.

POLICY ON RACIAL SLURS, RACIAL HARASSMENT, AND RACIAL JOKES

This policy endorses the right of every individual to live and work in an environment that is free of race-related demeaning comments and actions (OHRC, 1996b). The policy defines as discriminatory those acts or expressions that are manifested through slurs, jokes, or behaviour intended to demean a person because of his or her race. *Racial harassment* involves offensive, humiliating, derogatory, or hostile acts or expressions that are racially based. A comment or conduct need not be explicitly racial in order to constitute racial harassment. The term "race" in the policy refers to all of the race-related grounds (that is, race, ancestry, colour, and ethnic origin) and to citizenship, place of origin, and creed.

POLICY AND GUIDELINES ON RACISM
AND RACIAL DISCRIMINATION

This policy updates and significantly expands on the policy on racial slurs and racial jokes (OHRC, 2006). The policy describes a number of considerations for the
determination of racial discrimination, and stresses the importance of the development of organizational cultures that respect human rights and prevent racial
discrimination. Main ways in which racial discrimination can occur include stereotyping and prejudice, racial profiling, subtle racial discrimination, racial harassment, poisoned environment, language-related discrimination, and association
with a racialized person or persons.

HUMAN RIGHTS AND LAW ENFORCEMENT

The United Nations Centre for Human Rights (UNCHR) has published a reference
for law enforcement agencies called *International Human Rights Standards for Law
Enforcement*. The standards developed by the Centre relate to policing ethics and
legal conduct, policing in democracies, non-discrimination in law enforcement,
police investigations, arrest, detention, the use of force and firearms, civil disorder,
states of emergency, armed conflict, protection of juveniles, the human rights of
women, refugees, non-nationals, victims, police command and management, community policing, and police violations of human rights.

Police legislation in Canada is consistent with international standards and with
federal and provincial laws regarding human rights and freedoms. In its declaration of principles, the **Ontario *Police Services Act*** stipulates that police services shall
be provided at the provincial level in accordance with the safeguards that guarantee
the fundamental rights enshrined in the *Canadian Charter of Rights and Freedoms*
and the Ontario *Human Rights Code* (principle 2).

Ontario *Police Services Act*
law that stipulates that police services shall be provided throughout Ontario in accordance with the safeguards that guarantee the fundamental rights enshrined in the Charter and the Ontario *Human Rights Code*

HUMAN RIGHTS AND FREEDOMS: POST 9/11

In the aftermath of 9/11, the Canadian government increased its focus on national
and international security issues. It sought to strengthen its partnership with its
neighbour to the south and law enforcement agencies for the purpose of preventing
domestic and international terrorist acts. The Canadian government's heightened
sensitivity to security threats and its legislative changes related to law enforcement
created a tension between civil liberties and police powers. The government faced a
dilemma: it was being asked to preserve important civil liberties but at the same
time give police the powers they needed to fight terrorism. It wanted to treat all its
citizens fairly while taking strong action to fight terrorism and reassuring the public
that it was tough on terror. Critics of the government's approach asserted that the
symptoms of terrorism were being tackled rather than the cause. However, Canadians
disagreed over what the cause was. Several candidates were considered: the alleged
violent nature of the Muslim religion, poverty, marginalization of Muslim and Arab
immigrants and their communities by democratic Western countries that racialize
immigrants from particular ethnic and religious groups, cynicism invoked by perceived violations of democratic principles and values preached by democratic

countries and their support of dictatorial regimes, and differential application of human rights standards to nations construed as friendly allies and those that were deemed unfriendly.

HUMAN RIGHTS AND FREEDOMS: POLICE ABILITIES, KNOWLEDGE, AND SKILLS

In Canada, and around the world, the importance of human rights and freedoms to people's quality of life is increasingly being recognized. Many countries are actively involved in preserving and protecting the human rights and freedoms of their citizens, and law enforcement is assuming a significant role in these initiatives. Police services operate in accordance with international, national, and provincial human rights provisions that enshrine basic individual and collective rights and freedoms at social and institutional levels. The intent of these provisions is to create a collective conscience for the protection of democratic citizenship and societal justice. The human rights and freedoms acts, codes, and policies are more than just principles and goals—they are tools designed to change a culture that is plagued by human rights violations, complaints, inquiries, court actions, disciplinary hearings, and penalties into a culture that treasures and preserves equal treatment and protection under the law.

A police culture in which all police officers uphold the letter and the spirit of human rights laws and are committed to the fundamental values of justice, respect, acceptance, and harmonious coexistence is a police community that befits the dignity of the profession

Nevertheless, the focus of law enforcement on counterterrorism and national security is challenging from both the perspectives of human rights and community policing. More specifically, terrorist threats and acts in Western countries such as Canada, Great Britain, Spain, and the United States have challenged the role of law enforcement and invoked a tension between human rights and freedoms and the imperative of law and order. On the one hand, law enforcement agents are expected to honour human rights standards, respect the civil rights of citizens, and establish a trusting relationship with the communities they serve and protect. On the other hand, law enforcement agencies that are also expected to maintain law and order may go overboard in their zeal to prevent threats to national security, show muscle, and, possibly, turn a blind eye to due process. After all, the end does justify the means, and national security cannot be achieved with good intentions alone.

The imperative of law and order is also challenging to law enforcement because it may conflict with community policing. The dilemma for law enforcement agents, who are empowered to protect national security and civil order and participate in the war against terrorism, is that they are expected to partner with the very people and communities that they serve and protect but they deem as possible threats to national security.

Thus, law enforcement in the 21st century is challenged by two fundamentally antagonistic approaches to policing: democratic community policing and democratic dictatorship policing. Democratic community policing honours the imperatives of law and order and due process while democratic dictatorship policing honours the imperative of law and order over the imperative of civil liberties. Mansur has argued

TABLE 3.3   Dos and Don'ts of Policing Human Rights and Freedoms

Dos

- Respect the dignity, rights, and freedoms of all people.

- Exercise absolute impartiality in serving the law.

- Preserve the tradition that the police are the people and the people are the police.

- Treat all people equally and fairly.

- Serve and protect all people equally.

- Inform those you apprehend of their rights under the law.

- Promote a police culture that actively supports and enhances diversity.

Don'ts

- Don't deny any person his or her rights and freedoms.

- Don't discriminate on the ground of any diversity characteristic.

- Don't subject anyone to cruel or inhumane treatment.

- Don't abuse your authority.

- Don't subject anyone to arbitrary arrest or detention.

- Don't conduct unreasonable searches and seizures.

- Don't execute any police function that is contrary to the letter or the spirit of the law.

that civilized and democratic nations and their law enforcement services cannot and should not make "any allowance for those who seek to profit by terror … a lesson when ignored or forgotten, leads to the ruin of civilized living" (Mansur, 2006). A list of dos and don'ts of policing human rights and freedoms is provided in table 3.3.

CHAPTER SUMMARY

Human rights laws and policies enshrine basic rights and freedoms and provide protection for democratic citizenry and social justice. They place a responsibility on law enforcement agencies and police officers to treat all citizens equally and with respect, regardless of their culture, race, religion, gender, age, sexual orientation, gender identity, socioeconomic status, or physical or mental ability. The events of 9/11 have created a challenge for law enforcement agencies and police officers. Police must balance the responsibilities of protecting the civil liberties of all Canadians.

KEY TERMS

Canadian Human Rights Act

Canadian Human Rights Commission

Canadian Charter of Rights and Freedoms

fundamental freedoms

democratic rights

mobility rights

legal rights

equality rights

official languages

aboriginal peoples' rights

multicultural heritage

Ontario *Human Rights Code*

freedom from discrimination

Ontario Human Rights Commission

harassment

constructive discrimination

Ontario *Police Services Act*

REFERENCES

Canadian Bill of Rights, RSC 1960, c. 44.

Canadian Charter of Rights and Freedoms, part I of the *Constitution Act, 1982*, RSC 1985, app. II, no. 44.

Canadian Human Rights Act, RSC 1985, c. H-6, as amended.

Canadian Human Rights Act Review Panel. (2000). *Promoting equality: A new vision*. http://www/chrareview.org/frp/frp-toce.html.

Canadian Human Rights Commission (CHRC). (1999). Policy on drug testing. http://www.chrc-ccdp.ca/legis&poli/drgpol-poldrg.asp.

Canadian Human Rights Commission (CHRC). (2000). Policy on HIV/AIDS. http://www.chrc-ccdp.ca/ee. See Publications & Policies, Employment Equity Branch.

Canadian Human Rights Commission (CHRC) in cooperation with Human Resources Development Canada and Status of Women Canada. (1998). *Anti-harassment policies for the workplace: An employer's guide*. http://www.chrc-ccdp.ca/publications.

Centre for Human Rights. (n.d.). *International Human Rights Standards for Law Enforcement*. Geneva: United Nations High Commissioner for Human Rights.

Commission on Systemic Racism in the Ontario Criminal Justice System. (1994). *Report on youth and street harassment: The police and investigative detention*. Toronto: Queen's Printer for Ontario.

Constitution Act, 1982, RSC 1985, app. II, no. 44.

Criminal Code, RSC 1985, c. C-46, as amended.

Family Law Act, RSO 1990, c. F.3, as amended.

Human Rights Code, RSO 1990, c. H.19, as amended.

Justice Department. (2005). http://www.justice.gc.ca/en/news/nr/2005/doc_ 31578.html.

Leeder, J. (2006, July 27). His nightmare began on 9/12. *The Toronto Star*, pp. A1, A13.

Mansur, S. (2006, August 19). Trudeau right to crush terror. *The London Free Press*, p. F6.

Office of the United Nations High Commissioner for Human Rights. (1948). *Universal Declaration of Human Rights.* http://www.ohchr.org/english.

Ontario Human Rights Commission (OHRC). (1996a, April 9). Policy on female genital mutilation (FGM). http://www.ohrc.on.ca/en/resources/Policies.

Ontario Human Rights Commission (OHRC). (1996b, June 19). Policy on racial slurs and harassment and racial jokes. http://www.ohrc.on.ca/en/resources/ Policies.

Ontario Human Rights Commission (OHRC). (1996c, September 10). Policy on sexual harassment and inappropriate gender related comments and conduct. http://www.ohrc.on.ca/en/resources/Policies.

Ontario Human Rights Commission (OHRC). (2000a, January 11). Policy on discrimination and harassment because of sexual orientation. http://www.ohrc.on.ca/en/resources/Policies.

Ontario Human Rights Commission (OHRC). (2000b, March 30). Policy on discrimination and harassment because of gender identity. http://www.ohrc.on.ca/en/resources/Policies.

Ontario Human Rights Commission (OHRC). (2006). Ontario *Human Rights Commission annual report 2005–2006.* Toronto: Author.

Police Services Act, RSO 1990, c. P.15, as amended.

Rosenthal, E. (2006, June 2). Study tracks genital cutting's deadly legacy. *International Herald Tribune*, p. 4.

EXERCISES AND REVIEW

Personal Reflections

Read each statement below and circle whether you agree or disagree with it.

1. As a society, we should restrict the definition of "spouse" to opposite-sex couples.

   AGREE   DISAGREE

2. If women want to breast-feed their infants, they should do so in the privacy of their homes rather than in public.

   AGREE   DISAGREE

3. A Christian country should demand that all of its public school students say the Lord's Prayer in the morning before starting classes.

   AGREE   DISAGREE

4. Adoption agencies with policies that permit adoption of a child by parents with similar religious beliefs or cultural backgrounds are discriminatory.

   AGREE   DISAGREE

5. Gay or lesbian couples should not have the same rights or benefits as heterosexual married couples.

   AGREE   DISAGREE

6. Human rights provisions in many countries are nothing but efforts to "window dress" diversity.

   AGREE   DISAGREE

7. Criminals are getting away with murder by relying on human rights and freedoms provisions in Canadian laws.

   AGREE   DISAGREE

8. Like the right to decide on abortion, each woman has the right to decide to circumcise her daughter.

   AGREE   DISAGREE

9. Employers should have the right to do drug testing of all potential employees.

   AGREE   DISAGREE

10. The law should protect police officers more so that they can do their job without constant fear of reprisal.

    AGREE   DISAGREE

SCORING: This exercise does not require scoring. Nevertheless, compare your responses with a classmate's, and try to reconcile any differences of opinion.

Diversity IQ: Multiple Choice

Circle the best answer.

1. What is at the core of human rights and freedoms?
   a. equality
   b. liberty
   c. a and b
   d. none of the above

2. Which of the following fundamental freedoms are specifically mentioned in the *Canadian Charter of Rights and Freedoms*?
   a. freedom of conscience and religion
   b. freedom of peaceful assembly
   c. freedom of thought, belief, opinion, and expression
   d. all of the above

3. Which of the following is the subject of an Ontario human rights policy?
   a. gender identity
   b. sexual orientation
   c. drug testing
   d. all of the above

4. Human rights and freedoms are important because they
   a. prohibit police use of unnecessary force
   b. allow police to detain an individual without reasonable cause
   c. condone arbitrary or unlawful actions by law enforcement agencies
   d. none of the above

5. The Charter

   a. fails to recognize the equality rights of women

   b. prohibits the promotion of equal employment opportunities for women

   c. supports affirmative action programs to improve the lot of those who are disadvantaged by virtue of past discriminatory practices

   d. all of the above

6. The Ontario *Police Services Act*

   a. stipulates that police services shall be provided in accordance with federal and provincial human rights provisions

   b. denies police officers' rights and freedoms

   c. takes lightly occurrences of serious injury and death that may result from criminal offences committed by police officers

   d. none of the above

7. A harassment-free work environment means an employment climate that is

   a. free from intimidating, hostile, or humiliating conditions that arise from offensive remarks, behaviour, or surroundings

   b. free from discrimination or harassment because of race, colour, ancestry, place of origin, ethnic origin, language or dialect spoken, citizenship, religion, sex, sexual orientation, age, marital status, family status, actual or perceived disability, criminal charges, or criminal record

   c. free from unequal treatment of persons on the basis of their membership in a specific group—for example, women

   d. all of the above

8. Which of the following are basic rights or freedoms under the Charter?

   a. equality rights

   b. minority language educational rights

   c. legal rights

   d. all of the above

9. Sexual harassment includes

   a. welcome attention

   b. threat of reprisal for non-compliance with sexual demands

   c. comments or conduct that is genuinely complimentary

   d. all of the above

10. Which of the following examples of police misconduct are actionable?

    a. diversity slurs

    b. racial jokes

    c. use of unnecessary force because of a suspect's race, cultural origin, sex, age, sexual orientation, socioeconomic status, or physical disability

    d. all of the above

Diversity IQ: True or False?

_____ 1. The concept of human rights and freedoms influences political structures and processes.

_____ 2. Police have the right to harass citizens on the basis of their gender or sexual orientation.

_____ 3. Supervisors in the police force are not liable if the police officers they supervise sexually harass female employees.

_____ 4. A police officer can be charged for harassing another police officer.

_____ 5. The relocation and internment of Japanese-Canadians by the Canadian government in World War II is an example of violation of the right to mobility.

_____ 6. Police who execute their duties in an unreasonable manner are violating the legal rights of citizens.

_____ 7. In being charged with an offence, a citizen does not have to be informed of the specific offence.

_____ 8. In being detained or arrested, a citizen has the right to be informed promptly of the reasons for the detention or arrest.

_____ 9. A deaf person, or a party or witness who does not understand or speak the language of any proceedings, has the right to the assistance of an interpreter.

_____ 10. The Charter rejects laws, programs, or activities that have as their object the improvement of conditions of disadvantaged individuals or groups because of race, national or ethnic origin, colour, religion, sex, age, or mental or physical disability.

Application Now

What are the implications of human rights and freedoms to the following duties of police?

1. Preserving the peace

2. Preventing crimes and other offences and providing assistance and encouragement to other persons in their prevention

3. Assisting victims of crime

4. Apprehending criminals, other offenders, and others who may lawfully be taken into custody

5. Laying charges and participating in prosecutions

6. Executing warrants and performing related duties

7. Performing the lawful duties assigned by the chief of police

8. Completing prescribed training

Food for Thought

The vast majority of police officers protect the rights and freedoms of citizens. In rare cases, police abuse their authority. Three types of police abuse of authority have been identified:

- *Physical abuse/excessive force.* Police use of more force than is necessary to affect an arrest or search.

- *Verbal/psychological abuse.* Police reliance on their authority to verbally assail, ridicule, harass and/or diminish an individual's self-esteem or self-image, or instilling fear by psychological coercion and verbal threats of physical harm.

- *Violation of civil rights.* Police violation of an individual's federal and provincial rights without the individual showing any apparent psychological or physical damage.

1. Read each police action below and indicate the nature of abuse: write "PA" in the blank space if it is physical abuse/excessive force, "VPA" if it is verbal/psychological abuse, or "VCR" if it is a violation of civil rights.

    _____ a. stopping cars without justifiable reasons

    _____ b. punching a citizen

    _____ c. kicking a suspect

    _____ d. spraying concentrated tear gas (mace or Capstun)

    _____ e. hitting a citizen with a flashlight

    _____ f. using deadly force

    _____ g. hitting a citizen with a baton

    _____ h. overtightening handcuffs

    _____ i. intentionally bumping a citizen's head on the door frame while pushing him into the back seat of a police car

    _____ j. holding someone incommunicado for interrogation

    _____ k. conducting a search without justifiable reason

    _____ l. calling a citizen derogatory names such as "asshole" or "punk"

    _____ m. not allowing a person held for interrogation to contact an attorney

    _____ n. imposing a police-dominated atmosphere during interrogation

    _____ o. sexually harassing a female citizen in custody

    _____ p. taking someone into custody because of his or her race

    _____ q. booking a lesbian or gay citizen because of the person's sexual orientation

_____ r. taking someone into custody without legal grounds

_____ s. harassing a citizen because of the colour of his or her skin

2. Divide the class into small groups of three to five students. Have each student in each group independently read the two stories below ("Citizen of Chinese heritage" and "Citizen of Jamaican heritage") and identify possible violations of human rights and freedoms. Have students compare their analyses of the stories with the other members of their group. Appoint a spokesperson for each group to report the group's findings to the class for general discussion.

Citizen of Chinese Heritage

I had a very traumatic experience with police about three years ago. At about 9:30 one evening, I heard someone banging on my door. When I opened the door, three very big white officers in their thirties stood in front of me. They barged in and started accusing me of drug smuggling and being a member of the Chinese mafia. When I told them that I really did not know what they were talking about but that they were welcome to search the house if they wanted to, they started harassing my 12-year-old younger brother. I told the officer who was harassing my brother to leave him alone. The cop hit me. I went flying into the wall and then fell unconscious. The next thing I remember is waking up in a hospital to a police officer telling me that if I helped him by giving him the names of gang members, he would drop all charges against me. It so happened that my father walked into my room and, knowing from my brother what had happened, told the cop in a fury to "get the fuck out" as "my son is not saying anything; he is in no condition to be harassed." My father also told the officer that he would be hearing from our lawyer. When I saw our lawyer the next morning, he asked whether the police had a warrant to search the house. I told him that the police did not state that they had a warrant and did not show me one. I told my lawyer that I wanted to press charges against the police officers involved.

A year and a half later, the court ruled that two of the three police officers were guilty, and the judge described the event as an "unfortunate incident." One of the officers was fired from his job and the other one was suspended. I was awarded compensation for my legal fees. I don't feel that justice was served. That night I was so angry that I almost wanted to join a gang to get back at the cops. A friend of mine stopped me.

Source: Adapted from Commission on Systemic Racism in the Ontario Criminal Justice System (1994), p. 55.

Violations of human rights and freedoms:

Citizen of Jamaican Heritage

I am a 27-year-old single male of Jamaican heritage. My friend and I were travelling in a rented car at about 9 p.m. en route to Montreal. We noticed a police car behind us and, a few minutes later, another car tailing us. My friend and I were not concerned because we had nothing illegal with us. Soon we heard a siren and noticed that the car closer on our tail was flashing its lights. We pulled over. Almost immediately another police car pulled up from the opposite direction. Four white officers jumped out with guns drawn and yelled at us to get out of our car. My friend started protesting but as soon as we got out we were both flung violently against our car and told, "Shut your fucking mouths." We were searched roughly by two police officers while the other two stood some distance away with their guns aimed at us. When the cops could not find anything, they told us gruffly to turn around. My friend was again told to shut up when he protested. We found out that the police were searching for guns because they had received a report about shots being fired at a party not far from where we were and that the gunmen had driven off. My friend asked whether they had a description of the gunmen since he and I had no guns and had not been at a party. The police ignored us and started going through the car. They looked disappointed when they did not find anything, and asked us for our IDs. We both gave our driver's licences. One of the cops told my friend that if he did not shut up, he was going to make him shut up.

The police officer checked our licences on the computer. He came back and told the other officers that I had served time in jail for drug trafficking. He asked that the car be checked again thoroughly for signs of drugs. My friend complained that first we were stopped for guns and now we were being stopped for drugs. The police came up to him, pushed him back roughly against the car, and told him to keep quiet. They found nothing again but quizzed me about drugs and whether I was still involved in drugs. I answered their questions calmly. They asked me to empty my pockets, and they searched our wallets. Nothing turned up. Reluctantly, they told us to leave.

Source: Adapted from Commission on Systemic Racism in the Ontario Criminal Justice System (1994), pp. 63–64.

Violations of human rights and freedoms:

From Thought to Action

1. Critique the list of dos and don'ts in table 3.3 (on p. 81). What should be deleted from the list, and what should be added?

2. You apprehend a citizen with limited command of English and French. You do not speak her language yourself, but as an officer it is your duty to inform her of her right to know the reasons for taking her into custody, her right to contact and consult a lawyer forthwith to obtain legal advice.

    What human rights and freedoms provisions would guide your decisions in handling this situation?

    What action would you take in this situation?

3. You take a Sikh man into custody. From your course on diversity issues in policing, you remember that a Sikh religious practice entails carrying a kirpan (a small ceremonial dagger).

   What human rights and freedoms provisions would guide your decisions in dealing with this man and his kirpan?

   What action would you take in this situation?

4. As a supervisor, which of the following complaints from a police officer would you consider a verbal or physical sexual harassment complaint? Write "V" for verbal and "P" for physical.

_____ a. inappropriate comments on physical appearance

_____ b. requests for sex

_____ c. sex-oriented jibes

_____ d. leers

_____ e. staring at genitals

_____ f. pinches

_____ g. pats

_____ h. grabs

_____ i. deliberate physical contact

_____ j. "goosing" another person

_____ k. telling "off-colour" jokes

5. What are the implications of sexual harassment for the harasser?

6. What are the implications of sexual harassment for the victim?

7. How can sexual harassment be prevented?

8. How can harassment on the Internet be prevented? Is online harassment of people on the basis of age, gender, sexual orientation, or other grounds protected through legislation? What about the right to freedom of speech?

Lessons from History

1. A police service permits a Sikh to wear his turban on duty, and allows Aboriginal officers to continue their practice of wearing braids down to the top of the armpit to connect with Mother Earth.

   a. Is the police service justified in its decisions? Explain.

b. Do you consider these practices examples of the erosion of national symbols in Canadian culture? Why or why not?

c. Do you consider the actions of the police service as "kowtowing to the whims of human rights activists"? Why or why not?

d. Do you think these decisions could lead nudists to challenge the dress code policy? Why or why not?

e. Can you think of other practices or events that you consider evidence of the erosion of national symbols? Justify your thoughts and feelings.

f. What relevance, if any, do human rights and freedoms provisions in Canadian laws have in influencing the decisions of a police service? What relevance, if any, do human rights and freedoms codes have on other potential challenges to traditional Canadian culture—for example, a woman's right to walk topless in the streets?

2. E.M. was arrested by police and interrogated for several hours about a rape. He was held incommunicado and not permitted access to an attorney during repeated questioning by police. E.M. finally confessed and was convicted. However, the Supreme Court overturned the conviction. Which of the following factors do you think formed the court's basis for overturning the conviction? Explain your answer in the space provided.

   a. physical coercion—that is, use of excessive force

   b. psychological coercion—that is, an atmosphere as coercive from a psychological perspective as it would have been if the officers had used physical coercion

   c. violation of legal rights under the Charter

The Great Debate

In the aftermath of 9/11, the Canadian government passed legislation giving law enforcement agencies sweeping powers to fight terrorism. The government's actions brought the issue of civil liberty versus national security to a head. Have one group take the position that civil liberties should take precedence over national security. Have the second group take the position that national security should take precedence over civil liberties. Include in the debate situations in which police confront the dilemma of having to balance the rights of individuals against a need to preserve law and order.

PART II

Social and Religious Considerations in Policing

CHAPTER 4

Host Communities and Immigration Policies

CHAPTER OBJECTIVES

After completing this chapter, you should be able to:

- Explain how host community orientations influence immigration and the settlement and adaptation patterns of citizens, permanent residents, and foreign nationals.

- Understand the varied adaptation patterns of citizens and newcomers.

- Explain how historical immigration trends influenced current immigration and refugee policy.

- Understand the effects of 9/11 on national security, immigrants, and immigration policy.

PREVIEW SCENARIO

On June 2 and 3, 2006, Canadian authorities arrested 17 male Canadian residents in a massive counterterrorism sweep. The arrests were made after the group accepted delivery of three tons of ammonium nitrate, the same type of fertilizer that was used in the 1995 Oklahoma City bombing in which 168 people were killed. The arrests of the 12 men and 5 teenage suspects foiled a series of planned terrorist attacks. The men faced a court hearing and each was charged with one count of participating in a terrorist group. In addition, 3 of the suspects were charged with importing weapons and ammunition for the purpose of terrorist activity, 9 with receiving training from a terrorist group, and 4 with providing training in terrorism. Six of the suspects were also charged with intent to cause an explosion that could cause serious bodily harm or death. The charges against one of the suspects alleged that the suspect plotted to storm the Parliament of Canada, take politicians hostage, and demand the release of Muslim prisoners. There was also an allegation that the same suspect wanted to behead Prime Minister Stephen Harper. Although Canadian police indicated that there was no evidence to tie the suspect group to al-Qaida, they described the group as sympathetic to jihadist ideology, and expressed concern that many of the 17 members were youth and had been radicalized in a short amount of time. (DePalma, 2006; Associated Press, 2006)

INTRODUCTION

In Canada, police assume the fundamental role of serving and protecting all people, whether they are Canadian citizens, permanent residents, or foreign nationals (people other than Canadian citizens or permanent residents). It is therefore important that police gain an understanding of the many cultures and traditions of the people they are mandated to serve.

Police can develop this understanding by learning about the history of the people, their role in nation building, and their cultural and religious values, and, above all, by being committed to treating them as people first—that is, as individuals worthy of acceptance and respect regardless of the way they look, talk, or think, and regardless of the group they belong to. This chapter discusses the concept of the host community and people of diversity. The chapter also provides a historical overview of the evolution of immigration practices, the varied orientations that host communities display toward people of diversity, and the influence of these orientations on immigration, settlement and adaptation of newcomers, and national security.

Today, Canada and the United States are host countries for people of diverse linguistic and cultural backgrounds. However, in the 17th-century, American colonial entrepreneurs actively recruited European settlers, who spoke primarily English. The arrival of waves of German settlers in the 18th century was a source of alarm and resentment for the mainstream Anglo-Americans. Over time, however, both groups learned to live together peacefully. Similarly, the arrival of Irish Catholics who escaped the potato famine in 1841 was at first a source of worry and resentment for the predominantly Anglo-Protestant community, who feared that the Irish Catholics would destroy the prevailing American culture. Of course, the American culture did not crumble, and American anti-immigrant sentiment subsided. In fact, in the 1880s, America found itself in need of cheap immigrant labour to staff assembly lines and build bridges and skyscrapers. The United States called on Germany, Ireland, and the southern and eastern European states to encourage their people to enter the American golden gate of immigration. Over the years, America has opened and closed its gate many times, but it has never forgotten that it is a nation of immigrants in pursuit of the American dream (Axelrod, 2000).

The history of immigration to Canada is similar, but while both countries valued immigrants for their ambition and vitality, the United States favoured a melting pot approach to immigration whereas Canada favoured the creation of a cultural mosaic. The melting pot concept assumes that immigrants of different ethnicities and races can assimilate and that both minority and majority cultures can succeed equally. It is built on the idea of one nation, one people, and one culture. By contrast, in a cultural mosaic, immigrants are encouraged to retain their cultural and ethnic identities. According to Kallen, in contemporary parlance, the melting pot and the cultural mosaic models of ethnic integration have come to assume the status of national myths in the United States and Canada (2003). But on neither side of the Canadian–American border have these egalitarian ideals ever closely represented social reality. Neither in Canada nor the United States have all citizens enjoyed full equality of opportunity, regardless of ethnic classification.

CONCEPT OF THE HOST COMMUNITY

A host community is sometimes called the host culture, dominant culture or society, host nation, or majority culture. **Host communities** comprise groups of people who have the power and influence to shape societal attitudes toward the remaining groups in society. The host community sets the tone for how the rest of society views and deals with the less powerful *other*. For example, a host culture such as that in the United States may view marriage as a sacred heterosexual institution, may be reluctant to change its views to appease a minority gay and lesbian community, and may be opposed to legislative initiatives to legalize gay and lesbian marriages. Host communities also determine immigration policies—that is, who is a desirable addition to the host culture and who is undesirable. Finally, host communities affect the settlement and adaptation patterns of the people they accept as newcomers.

host community
comprises groups of people who have the power and influence to shape societal attitudes toward the remaining groups in society

CULTURAL PLURALISM OF HOST COMMUNITIES

A host community consists of people with different **settlement patterns**. The people may have either lived on the land or come from other parts of the world to live together and to form the culturally diverse character of the host nation. In the case of colonized countries such as Canada, the United States, and Australia, indigenous people lived on the land before it was colonized. The first inhabitants of Canada were the aboriginal peoples, and they are believed to have immigrated from East Asia (Kelley & Trebilcock, 1998). They were scattered across the whole country; showed great diversity in language, culture, and economic pursuits; and possessed a rich social life, a strong social structure, and highly sophisticated art forms.

settlement patterns
the variety of ways that people establish themselves in a country, whether born there or as immigrants

Contrary to popular belief, the cultural pluralism that characterizes many Western host states in the global village is not a recent phenomenon. In Canada's case, cultural diversity predated Confederation (Agnew, 1967). The first population census following Confederation was conducted in 1871. It showed that the French constituted the largest single group (1,082,940 people), followed by the Irish (846,000 people), the English (706,000 people), the Scots (549,946 people), and the Germans (202,000 people). The aboriginal population was estimated to be 23,000. The 1871 census figures probably underestimated the aboriginal population and excluded the Chinese who were in Canada before Confederation (Kelley & Trebilcock, 1998). Other cultural groups represented in Canada at the time of Confederation included the Dutch (29,000 people), Africans (21,000 people), and people of Welsh, Swiss, Italian, Spanish, and Portuguese origin (Agnew, 1967). Early settlers on the "Beautiful Land" included Chinese, Icelanders, Jews, Danes, Swedes, Norwegians, Mennonites, Italians, Hungarians, Czechs, Poles, Slovaks, Mormons, Ukrainians, Doukhobors, Japanese, Austrians, Americans, South Asians including Sikhs, Armenians, Bulgarians, Croatians, Greeks, Lebanese, Maltese, Romanians, Serbians, and Syrians.

Also contrary to popular belief, culturally pluralistic states have been states of minority populations rather than states with a single majority ethnic group. Canada has been a nation of minority groups. According to Tepper (1994, p. 101), "the numerical predominance of a single group in Canada ended over half a century ago." In 2001, 23 percent of the population reported Canadian as their only ethnic origin and 39 percent reported Canadian as their ethnic origin, either alone or in combination with other origins (Statistics Canada, 2001). The most frequent ethnic origins after Canadian (11.7 million) were English (6 million), French (4.7 million), Scottish (4.2 million), and Irish (3.8 million).

In Ontario, 73.1 percent of the population reported English as their mother tongue, 4.5 percent reported French, and 24.2 percent reported a non-official language (Statistics Canada, 2001). Similarly, in 2001, 82.7 percent of the population in Ontario reported English as their language spoken at home, 2.7 percent reported French, and 14.5 percent reported a non-official language (Statistics Canada, 2001).

ACCULTURATION ORIENTATIONS OF HOST COMMUNITIES

Bourhis, Moïse, Perreault, and Senécal (1997) assert that host communities adopt four acculturation orientations toward immigrants:

integrationist
supportive of immigrants adopting features of the host culture while maintaining aspects of their heritage culture

exclusionary
intolerant of immigrants' heritage culture and of immigration in general

assimilationist
intolerant of immigrants' heritage culture, demanding that they relinquish that culture and adopt the host culture

- An **integrationist** host community encourages immigrants to adopt important features of the host culture and values and to maintain aspects of their heritage culture;

- An **exclusionary** host community is intolerant of the wish of immigrants or other cultures to maintain their heritage cultures, and does not allow them to adopt features of the host culture. Host community members do not favour interaction with immigrants and consider their citizenry with ambivalence;

- An **assimilationist** host community demands that immigrants relinquish their cultural identity and adapt totally to the host culture. Assimilation refers to the social process whereby relations among members of different ethnic communities result in the participation of these individuals in ethnocultural institutions other than those of the ethnic community to which they belong (Kallen, 2003). Over time, members of the host community consider those who have been culturally absorbed to be full-fledged citizens; and

segregationist
opposed to immigrants and other cultures, preferring that immigrants return to their countries of origin

- A **segregationist** host community distances itself from immigrants or other cultures but allows them to maintain their heritage culture. Members of the host community believe that immigrants can never be incorporated culturally or socially as rightful members of the host society and prefer that they be deported to their countries of origin.

Host communities use features of immigrant communities to justify their acculturation orientations. For example, host communities may exhibit linguistic ethnocentrism. *Linguistic ethnocentrism* is a factor that contributes to social distance and segregation between the host community and immigrant community. An example of linguistic ethnocentrism is attributing positive qualities to some but not other languages—for example, the English accent is aristocratic, the French accent is beautiful, and the German accent is elegant, but the Spanish accent does not have nice tones, and Asian accents are too complex, harsh, and hard to understand (Fernandez, 1991).

ACCULTURATION ORIENTATIONS OF IMMIGRANT GROUPS

Acculturation refers to those "phenomena which result when groups of individuals having different cultures come into continuous first-hand contact, with subsequent changes in the original cultural patterns of either group or both groups" (Berry, 1990, 1998). In this process, each population acquires from the other new cultural attributes that may eventually be absorbed into its own system. Viewed as part of a general learning process, acculturation refers to the process of learning those cultural ___ of an ethnic community to which one does not belong (Kallen, 2003). Immigrants show one of four modes of acculturation:

1. **marginalization** involves the simultaneous rejection of one's culture of origin and the host culture. Those who are marginalized are disenchanted with their own cultural identity and the alternative identity accorded by the host culture;

2. **assimilation** represents rejection of one's culture of origin in favour of absorption into the host culture;

3. **separation** involves rejection of the host culture and maintenance of one's culture of origin; and

4. **integration** involves embracement of the host culture and maintenance of one's culture of origin.

Integration is the mode of acculturation most preferred by immigrants and most desired by the host culture. First, cultural groups tend to be most predisposed to this strategy and least predisposed to the marginalization strategy (Berry et al., 1989). Second, integrationists show good psychological adjustment and personal satisfaction, while marginalizers show relatively higher alienation, ill health, and dissatisfaction with life (Berry, 1998). This is an important consideration not only from an economic perspective (better productivity, lower health care costs) but also from the perspective of law and order because members of immigrant groups who are integrated are less likely to engage in disorderly or criminal activity. Third, and most significant from a national unity perspective, integrationists do not practise separation or isolation from the host culture or self-segregation, nor does retaining of their cultural identity lessen their commitment to the welfare of the host nation (Berry & Sam, 1997).

INTERPLAY OF ACCULTURATION ORIENTATIONS

The **interactive acculturation model** suggests an interplay between the acculturation orientations of the host communities and those of the settlement groups. This interplay results in either concordant relationships or discordant relationships (Bourhis et al., 1997). A concordant, or positive, relationship exists when the acculturation orientation of the host country is the same as those of the immigrant cultures (for example, the host community wants immigrants to integrate and the immigrants want to integrate). A discordant, or negative, relationship exists when the acculturation orientation of the host culture does not match those of the immigrant cultures (for

acculturation
process of acquiring cultural attributes of an ethnic community to which one does not belong

marginalization
simultaneous rejection of the culture of origin and the host culture

assimilation
rejection of one's culture of origin in favour of absorption into the host culture

separation
individual rejection of the host culture and maintenance of the culture of origin

integration
embracement of the host culture of settlement and continued maintenance of the culture of origin

interactive acculturation model
concept that suggests interplay between orientations of host communities and those of settlement groups

example, the host community wants immigrants to assimilate while the immigrants want to integrate). Discordant relationships can create conflict, discontent, and disorder.

DIVERSITY ACCULTURATION ORIENTATIONS

diversity acculturation orientation model
concept that suggests interplay between orientations of host communities and those of people of diversity

The **diversity acculturation orientation model** addresses the acculturation orientations of host cultures and those of people of diversity. For example, applying the model to sexual orientation invokes concordant and discordant relationships between the host community and the gay and lesbian community to make explicit their acculturation orientations. A host community may find it acceptable for gays and lesbians to maintain their sexual orientation and may facilitate their integration into mainstream culture. Another host community may view gays and lesbians as deserving segregation from mainstream society.

CANADIAN IMMIGRATION POLICIES

Culturally pluralistic states are nations of aboriginal people, immigrants, and refugees. Immigrants were received in colonized and colonizing countries for nation building, defence, population replenishment, or economic reasons. Except for indigenous people, the people who now make up Canada, the United States, and Australia were all immigrants at one time or another (Harper & Vienneau, 1994, p. A1). The pioneer nation builders were courageous, driven by what they considered to be the best way to fulfill their dreams, and they made great sacrifices. By modern standards, they may not have been sensitive to diversity, but they were sincere in their beliefs and ideologies.

The evolution of Canadian immigration policies is presented in the sections below in some detail for illustrative purposes. Although Lee-Chin (2000) asserts that people do not learn from the past and are apt to commit the mistakes of history, people still need to know their history. They also need to recognize the achievements and failures of their predecessors and parents regarding nation building. Such knowledge is particularly crucial for police. By understanding the dynamic forces and historic treatment that have influenced the people they serve and protect, police learn that all individuals are worthy of acceptance and respect, no matter what group they belong to.

Pre-Confederation to 1899

A brief sketch of the major historical developments in Canadian immigration policy is provided in table 4.1. The *Act Respecting Aliens* was passed in the first Parliament of Lower Canada in 1794. Its objective was to restrict admission of Americans to Canada in view of their opposition to the British Crown. After Confederation, immigration became the responsibility of the federal government.

The first 30 years after Confederation constituted the "Golden Age" of Canadian immigration (Kelley & Trebilcock, 1998). Employers, trade unions, and British nationalists significantly influenced debates on immigration policy during these

TABLE 4.1   Historical Landmarks in Canadian Immigration Policy

1794	*Act Respecting Aliens* to prohibit immigration of Americans	1956	*Immigration Regulations* to introduce four-fold classification of admissible immigrants
1869	First *Immigration Act* to protect immigrants	1962	*Immigration Regulations* to remove race and nationality as grounds for admissible immigrants
1885	*Chinese Immigration Act* to introduce head tax		
1906	*Immigration Act* to control/deport undesirable immigrants	1967	*Immigration Regulations* to introduce point system for immigrant admissibility
1910	*Immigration Act* to restrict immigrants unsuitable to the climate of Canada and its requirements	1976	*Immigration Act* to strengthen due process for immigrants
1914	*War Measures Act* proclaimed	1993	*Immigration Act* to revise point system and reform refugee policy
1922	*Empire Settlement Agreement* signed with Britain		
1947	*Chinese Immigration Act* repealed	2002	*Immigration and Refugee Protection Act* to maintain safety and respect for Canadian norms of social responsibility
1952	*Immigration Act* to identify nationality, citizenship, and ethnic group for immigrant admissibility		

years, and Canada's 1869 *Immigration Act* protected immigrants from the health hazards of ocean travel and from exploitation by service providers of immigrants (for example, ship captains and innkeepers). The Act allowed newcomers to enjoy a "charmed status" after landing in the country. The government provided travel assistance to selected immigrants and affordable homesteads to those intending to settle. Immigrants were also allowed to naturalize (become citizens) after three years of residence and assume the status of a British subject with all the rights enjoyed by other British subjects. However, the 1869 Act did include some notable entry restrictions: it barred admission to immigrants with physical disabilities or criminal tendencies, or those deemed unable to support themselves, and it required the posting of a $300 bond for every "lunatic, idiot, deaf, dumb, blind or infirm person" without an immigrant family (Serge, 1993, p. 10). Ten years later, a regulation prohibiting the landing of indigents and paupers was also passed.

In the 1870s and 1880s, pauper British child immigrants, female immigrants, and Chinese immigrants became the focus of public attention. In relation to the thousands of British immigrant children who settled in the country, concerns centred on child abuse on the one hand and their "inferior stock" on the other. For example, Canadian law enforcement officials complained that British immigrant children coming from "depraved slums" and "ghettos" were corrupting Canadian youth and increasing the ranks of the criminal class. The medical establishment also claimed that these children suffered from moral depravity and genetic impairment. Despite this negative publicity, policies against children immigrating from Britain did not materialize. Rather, legislation was passed to ensure that the children were protected and provided with the necessities of life.

Regarding immigrant women, there were fears that they were being lured into prostitution and that they needed protection from "seduction from the path of virtue." Initiatives were introduced to protect the morality of immigrant girls and to assist immigrant women with the immigration process. For example, the federal government established the position of superintendent of female immigration to oversee the settlement of single women in the country.

The Chinese labourer immigrants who were brought to work on the western leg of the Canadian Pacific Railway gave rise to racial and economic concerns. Chinese immigrants were considered sojourners and an inferior race. They were also considered lacking in British instincts or aspirations and unassimilable in Canadian society. Finally, these immigrants were seen as an economic liability in that they were driving wages down and putting local people out of work. As a result, in July 1885 the federal government passed the *Chinese Immigration Act*, which regulated and restricted Chinese immigration into Canada by imposing a $50 head tax.

1900 to 1945

At the start of the 20th century, there was a willingness "to allow the West to remain unpopulated rather than settle it with people 'who stand in no hereditary relation with the rest of Canada'" (Tepper, 1994, p. 100). Law enforcement officials expressed the view that increased immigration contributed to the rise in crime rates, and blamed foreigners for the prevailing "violence and apparent lawlessness in [the] city slums" (Kelley & Trebilcock, 1998, p. 135). In the Western cities, the North-West Mounted Police attributed the alarmingly higher rates of physical assault, sexual assault, and incest to the "low class" of the Eastern European settlers (Kelley & Trebilcock, 1998). They also complained of ethnic mistrust of the police and reluctance on the part of witnesses from ethnic communities to testify in court. The federal government passed the 1906 *Immigration Act* for the explicit purpose of enabling the government to deal with "undesirable" immigrants. The list of excludable immigrants was expanded to include the blind, the deaf and dumb, carriers of contagious disease, convicts of crimes of "moral turpitude" (for example, prostitutes and pimps), the destitute, epileptics, the infirm and insane, and paupers. The new Act also empowered the government to deport immigrants found undesirable (for example, an inmate of a jail) during the first two years of settlement.

The 1910 *Immigration Act* amplified the 1906 *Immigration Act*. The federal government prohibited the entry of any immigrant of any race who was deemed unsuitable to the climate and requirements of the country; immigrants of any specified class, occupation, or character; and any immigrant who came to the country other than by continuous journey. These and other measures enabled the government to selectively restrict immigration of Chinese, East Indian, Japanese, and African-American settlers. An added consequence was that the measures reinforced racial stereotypes among resident Canadians. For example, Asians were seen not only as dishonest, unclean, immoral, and unassimilable but also as a menace to the aspirations of local workers. The $50 head tax imposed on all Chinese people entering Canada in 1885 was boosted to $100 in 1900 and further raised to $300 with the passage of the *Chinese Immigration Act* of 1923, an Act that restricted admission of Chinese immigrants to female domestic servants and farm workers, and restricted other people of colour or "visible minorities."

World War I intensified prewar hostility toward immigrants, particularly those now considered "enemy aliens" (Germans, immigrants from the Austro-Hungarian and Ottoman empires, and Bulgarians). The federal government proclaimed the 1914 *War Measures Act*, which authorized the government to do whatever was necessary (arrest, detain, exclude, or deport) for the security, defence, peace, order, and welfare of the nation. Canada interned thousands of "enemy aliens" in camps across the country and summarily deported them.

In the United States, government policies and propaganda also led to the persecution of "enemy aliens." In the United States, the government created the Committee
on Public Information to use propaganda techniques for the purposes of uniting "a
multiethnic, pluralistic society behind the war effort," recruiting men to the armed
services, coaxing civilians to support the war effort by purchasing war bonds, and influencing civilians to put pressure on other civilians to refrain from antiwar acts that
could hurt the war effort (Wheeler & Becker, 1994, pp. 134–35). The government-
sponsored propaganda was so effective that it led to vigilante-style persecution of
Americans of German heritage and the German language and culture. As an example, a German American of draft age was lynched for not being in uniform even
though the man was physically ineligible by virtue of having only one eye. American
children of German heritage were badgered, and many German words were prohibited. For example, people started calling hamburgers "liberty steaks," and frankfurters
"hot dogs" (Wheeler & Becker, 1994).

Canada's hostility toward "enemy aliens" and other "undesirable" or "non-
preferred" immigrants lingered in the years following World War I. The government
prohibited the immigration of "enemy aliens" even though the war was over. It also
extended this prohibition to Mennonites, Hutterites, and Doukhobors because of
their "undesirable" customs and unassimilability. Finally, it applied its exclusionary
policy to Jewish orphans languishing in Ukraine and to Armenians starving in refugee camps. Fewer than 1,300 Armenian genocide survivors were accepted into
Canada, compared with the 80,000 taken by France and 23,000 by the United States
(Kelley & Trebilcock, 1998).

On the other hand, Canada took a generous approach to the settlement of British immigrants after World War I. The 1922 *Empire Settlement Agreement* between
Canada and England provided special immigration schemes (for example, trans-
portation assistance, agricultural training, and supervision) for bringing British
agriculturalists and their families, farm labourers, domestic workers, and young
immigrants to the new land. The government also created the Women's Division of
the Department of Immigration and Colonization primarily to attend to the special
needs of unaccompanied female immigrants from the British Isles. These immigrants were interviewed in Britain by female immigration officers, provided with
ship conductresses to supervise their travel, and met on arrival by female immigration officers to guide them through their medical examinations and place them on
trains to various parts of the country (Kelley & Trebilcock, 1998).

Canada's preference for immigrants who were assimilable was no secret. It was
noted annually in the *Canada Year Book* (Kelley & Trebilcock, 1998). The preferential
treatment of certain classes of immigrants had public and professional support. As
far back as the 1920s, the Canadian National Committee for Mental Hygiene (the
forerunner of the Canadian Mental Health Association) urged the federal government to be more vigilant in its examination of newcomers to Canada "to prevent
[Canada] from being a dumping ground for defectives and degenerates from other
countries" (Griffin, 1989, p. 30). The most preferred immigrants were those who
spoke English and were from the United Kingdom and the United States. Scandi-
navians and Dutch were also considered assimilable and enjoyed preferred status,
but not those from the Orient (for example, Chinese).

Deportation was used as a means of dealing with the host community's aversion to the "defective, degenerate, inferior, and undesirable." On the average, 1,700

or more people were deported every year between 1920 and 1930. Many of these people had entered the country as immigrants on permit to work in railway construction. They were assessed as undesirable if they came down with an illness or had a disabling work accident, and they were "granted" deportation. Similarly, more than 5,700 people were deported from Canada between 1930 and 1935 for the sin of being recipients of public support or welfare. One of those deported had been a resident of Canada for 18 years. She was deported because she was an epileptic at the time of her entry into Canada (Kelley & Trebilcock, 1998).

Canada's involvement in World War II prompted internal security measures that culminated in the excessive and arbitrary internment of immigrants from countries with which Canada was at war. In addition to suspending the civil liberties of thousands of Italians and Germans, the government removed more than 22,000 Japanese immigrants and Japanese Canadians from their homes and relocated them to internment camps. The property of those interned was subsequently confiscated and sold at bargain prices. The Canadian government has since apologized to and compensated Japanese who suffered internment.

1946 to 1961

The period from 1946 to 1961 saw an economic boom and selective reopening of the doors of Canadian immigration (Kelley & Trebilcock, 1998). The *Canadian Citizenship Act* of 1946 allowed Canada to create its own class of citizenship separate from that of the United Kingdom for the first time. The *Chinese Immigration Act* was repealed in 1947, a separate Department of Citizenship and Immigration was created in 1950, and a new *Immigration Act* was passed in 1952 and proclaimed into law in 1953.

The 1952 *Immigration Act* empowered Canada to limit admission of people (Kelley and Trebilcock, 1998) on the following grounds:

- nationality, citizenship, ethnic group, occupation, class, or geographical area of origin;

- "peculiar" customs, habits, modes of life, or methods of holding property;

- unsuitability with regard to the climatic, economic, social, industrial, labour, health or conditions or requirements existing in the country; or

- probable inability to become readily assimilated or to assume the duties and responsibilities of Canadian citizenship.

The prohibited classes in the Act were as follows: idiots; morons; epileptics; beggars; insane people; diseased people; physical defectives who were likely to pose a public burden or a threat to public health; and those convicted of moral turpitude, including prostitutes, political subversives, homosexuals, drug addicts, and drug traffickers.

The 1956 *Immigration Regulations* listed four categories of admissible immigrants:

- British subjects born or naturalized, and citizens from select countries (for example, Ireland, the United States, and France) capable of finding employment for themselves;

- refugees from Europe or citizens from select European and Scandinavian countries willing either to find employment under the auspices of the Canadian government or to establish themselves in agriculture or a business, trade, or profession;

- citizens of any country of Europe or the Americas, or of the Middle East who had relatives in Canada willing to act as sponsors; and

- citizens of any countries other than those already listed who were family members of a Canadian citizen residing in Canada who had applied for their entry and was in a position to sponsor them.

1962 to 1992

The 1962 *Immigration Regulations* were historic because, for the first time in Canadian immigration policy, race and nationality were no longer grounds for consideration for independent immigration. In 1967, immigration regulations removed lingering traces of racial discrimination in Canada's immigration policy, and a new point system was adopted. This point system considered short-term and long-term factors for immigrant selection, such as a job in Canada, a knowledge of French or English, a relative in Canada, and job skills. It was from this point on that many developing countries started to suffer from brain drain as many of their most qualified workers came to work and live in Canada, depriving their home countries of their skills and talents.

In 1976, a new *Immigration Act* was passed following extensive consultation at the national level. This Act offered increased due-process protection for immigrants, and a more humanitarian refugee policy. The Act also removed the prohibited classes of immigrants and replaced them with broad categories that pertained to public health and security protection. The Act barred entry to persons convicted of crimes prohibited by Canadian criminal law.

1993 to 2001

Immigrants from 1967 and onward were chosen on the basis of either who they knew or what they knew. The 1993 *Immigration Act* and the amended 1995 Act and Regulations incorporated provisions to better control and select those who are allowed to enter Canada with a view to ensuring that national development and economic prosperity are sustained. The Act fulfilled several functions:

- linking the immigration movement to Canada's population needs and labour market needs;

- allowing Canadian citizens and permanent residents residing in Canada to sponsor close relatives;

- providing settlement assistance to eligible immigrants (including refugees) through a variety of programs and services designed to help newcomers become participating members of Canadian society as quickly as possible;

- confirming Canada's commitment and responsibilities to refugees under the United Nations Convention;

- introducing security measures to protect Canada from organized crime and international terrorism; and

- protecting the Canadian public by providing for the removal from the country those identified as inadmissible (for example, participants in organized crime, terrorists, hijackers, and war criminals).

The 1993 Act resulted in many changes to Canadian immigration policy that are still in effect today. Section 3 of the 1993 Act prohibits discrimination against immigrants on the grounds of race, national or ethnic origin, colour, religion, or sex. Section 6 of the Act identifies three classes of immigrants: the family class, Convention refugees (discussed below under the heading "Refugee Policies Pre-9/11"), and independent immigrants.

Family class immigration allows sponsorship of relatives, including parents and children.

Independent immigrants include assisted relatives, skilled workers, entrepreneurs, self-employed persons, and investors who apply on their own initiative. The three categories of entrepreneurs, self-employed persons, and investors make up Canada's Business Immigration Program. To immigrate as entrepreneurs, individuals must be able to demonstrate that they intend and have the ability to establish, purchase, or make a substantial investment in a business in Canada that will make a significant contribution to the country's economy. Specifically, they must demonstrate that they intend and have the ability to create or maintain at least one job for a Canadian citizen or permanent resident other than the entrepreneur and dependants, and provide active and ongoing participation in the management of the business. Self-employed persons are similarly defined. Self-employed persons are immigrants who intend and have the ability to establish or purchase a business in Canada that will create employment for themselves and make a significant contribution to the economy or the cultural or artistic life of the country. Finally, investors are defined as individuals with a proven track record in business, an accumulated personal net worth of Cdn $800,000 or more, and an investment of Cdn $400,000 in Canada before the issuance of their visa.

Independent immigrants are selected on the basis of a point system to maximize their success in Canada. (Table 4.2 shows the point system under which independent immigrants were evaluated from 1993 to 2001.) The indicators emphasize what applicants know rather than who they know.

CANADIAN REFUGEE POLICIES PRE-9/11

Several countries accept refugees for humanitarian reasons. Canada has been home to refugees since before Confederation. The United Empire Loyalists, for example, flocked to Canada (along with many non-British subjects) during the American Revolution in 1776. Similarly, the Puritans found refuge in Canada in the 1600s after suffering religious persecution in England. Many Scots settled in Canada after being forced from their homes during the Highland clearances of the 1600s, and the Irish sought refuge in Canada during the devastating potato famine of the 1800s.

In the early 20th century, Canada became a haven for people persecuted for political reasons. Extensive refugee movements occurred in Europe and Asia after

TABLE 4.2   Canadian Immigration Point System, 1993–2001

Indicator	Maximum points allocated
Education	16
Education and training	18
Work experience	8
Occupation	10
Arranged employment or designated occupation	10
Demographic factor (this number is set by the government)	10
Age	10
Knowledge of English or French	15
Personal suitability	10
Bonus for relative in Canada	5
Bonus for self-employed immigrants	30

Source: Office of the Auditor General of Canada (2000).

World War I (Holborn, 1975). In the years 1918–22, as a result of the Bolshevik Revolution, the international community absorbed about 1.5 million Russian refugees. By 1923, an estimated 320,000 Armenian refugees were scattered throughout the Near and Middle East and Europe after fleeing the first premeditated genocide of the 20th century carried out by the Young Turks of Turkey (Holborn, 1975). The first official Armenian refugees to make Canada their home were the Georgetown boys—100 Armenian orphan boys who settled on farms near Georgetown, Ontario (Kaprielian, 1982; Kazarian, 1997).

Like many other countries, Canada has continued its humanitarian tradition with respect to refugees. The past four decades, however, have witnessed a shift from a predominantly east–west refugee pattern to a south–north pattern (Nef & da Silva, 1991). Thus, refugees after World War II were primarily from Eastern Europe, while currently they mainly originate from such countries as Somalia, Cambodia, Vietnam, and Guatemala.

Welcoming refugees should be seen not as an immigration issue but as a human rights issue. The preamble to the 1951 *United Nations Convention and Protocol Relating to the Status of Refugees* (United Nations, 1983, p. 150) notes that the UN has "affirmed the principle that human beings shall enjoy fundamental rights and freedoms without discrimination" and has "on various occasions, manifested its profound concern for refugees and endeavoured to assure refugees the widest possible exercise of these fundamental rights and freedoms." Article 1 of the Convention defines a refugee as any person who

> owing to a well-founded fear of being persecuted for reasons of race, religion, nationality, membership of a particular social group or political opinion, is outside the country of nationality and is unable, or owing to fear, is unwilling to avail himself of the protection of that country; or who, not having a nationality and being outside the country of his former habitual residence as a result of such event, is unable, or owing to such fear, is unwilling to return to it.

The 1976 Canadian *Immigration Act* formalized the prevailing ad hoc approach to refugee determination and selection to form a refugee policy. The Act identified three options to granting qualified refugees permission to resettle in Canada: overseas selection, special programs, and inland refugee-status determination. Currently, Canada is moving away from government-based assistance to refugees and allowing non-government agencies to assume increased involvement in the provision of supports and services.

IMMIGRATION AND REFUGEE POLICY EVALUATION

Immigration and refugee policies need periodic makeovers (see, for example, De-Voretz, 1996; Gwyn, 1993; Kelley & Trebilcock, 1998; Stoffman, 1993; Watson, 1992; Will, 1993). Critics of refugee policy have used overhauls of the refugee system as an opportunity to demonize immigrants and refugees as criminals, system bilkers, a drain on the economy, and the like. However, such failures are national issues rather than newcomer issues. Condemning or victimizing immigrants and refugees is unhealthy, and, more important, the very survival of many countries depends on immigrants to supplant shrinking populations and sustain their cultural, social, and economic viability. This is a primary reason that many countries actively attempt to draw the "cream of the crop" immigrants for permanent settlement. Canada accepts 0.7 percent of its total population in migrants each year (8.8 per 1,000 Canadians); Australia accepts 1.4 percent of its population (7.6 per 1,000), the United States 0.4 percent (2.5 per 1,000), and New Zealand 0.3 percent.

Nevertheless, viable solutions for dealing with security concerns and difficulties associated with executing orders of deportation of criminals are needed. Those with criminal records should be prohibited from entering the host country, and those criminals who are subject to a deportation order should be deported. An important factor that mitigates against the execution of deportation orders is the provision of eligibility for appeal under Canada's immigration policies. Failing to act quickly can have tragic consequences. For example, in April 1994, a young woman was slain at a popular Toronto café during a robbery. One of the men charged in the fatal shooting was an immigrant with a lengthy record of assault and weapons convictions. He had been ordered deported in 1993 but the order had not been carried out. In June 1994, a Toronto police officer was shot by an immigrant who had been ordered deported in March 1991 for drug and weapons convictions, but the order had not been carried out. Amendments to the *Immigration Act* passed in 1995 have made it easier to remove a permanent resident with a serious criminal background from the country.

In 1996, a review of Canada's immigration and refugee policy was initiated with a view to making fundamental policy reforms and introducing new legislation. Consultations with the provinces, territories, and all major stakeholders were also initiated between 1996 and 1998, culminating in the release of the white paper *Building on a Strong Foundation for the 21st Century: New Directions for Immigration and Refugee Policy and Legislation,* the tabling of the *Immigration and Refugee Protection Act* (Bill C-31) in April 2000, and the reintroduction of the *Immigration and Refugee Protection Act* as Bill C-11 in February 2001.

IMMIGRATION AND REFUGEE POLICIES POST-9/11

The new *Immigration and Refugee Protection Act* and its accompanying Regulations were purported to represent a simpler, more modern, and more coherent law and legislation. The primary objectives of the Act were to better respond to Canada's global challenges of the 21st century, to ensure that Canada can preserve immigration as a source of diversity, richness, and openness to the world, to enhance Canada's advantage in the global competition for skilled workers, to maintain and enhance its strong humanitarian tradition, to deter migrant trafficking and punish those who engage in this form of slavery, and to maintain confidence in the integrity of the immigration and refugee protection program. The Act received royal assent in November 2001, and came into force on June 28, 2002. The Act introduced new terminology and distinguished between a foreign national and a permanent resident. A "permanent resident" is defined as "a person who has acquired permanent resident status and has not subsequently lost that status under section 46," and a "foreign national" is defined as "a person who is not a Canadian citizen or a permanent resident, and includes a stateless person."

The objectives of the Act invoked several key principles and values that defined Canadian society:

- principles inherent in the *Canadian Charter of Rights and Freedoms*;
- respect for the multicultural character of Canada;
- the need to support the development of minority official languages communities;
- commitments to human rights in accordance with international human rights instruments to which Canada is signatory; and
- integration of immigrants into Canadian society.

The Act articulated objectives relating to refugee protection separate from those relating to immigration on the ground that immigration and refugee programs served different purposes. The objectives for the refugee program focused on the fundamental expression of Canada's humanitarian ideals—namely, saving lives, providing fair consideration to those who come to the country claiming persecution, and offering a safe haven to those with a well-founded fear of persecution and to those at risk for torture or cruel and unusual treatment or punishment in their country of origin.

Family Reunification

The Act formally recognized the existence of the family class, thus giving it a greater measure of permanency and introduced changes to the family class to expand the family class and to expedite the process of family reunification. Membership in the family class was defined to include a foreign national who is the spouse, common-law partner, child, or parent of a Canadian citizen or permanent resident and any other prescribed family member (Citizenship and Immigration Canada, 2002). An important legislative change related to the joint application for sponsorship of spouses, common-law and conjugal partners, and dependent children. "Common-law partner" was defined to include same-sex common-law partners.

Skilled Workers, Business Immigrants, and Temporary Foreign Workers

The Act introduced changes to the selection system for skilled workers with a view to opening up the category to a broader range of applicants with the skills and education needed to drive economic growth and innovation in the country (see table 4.3). Changes to the business immigrant categories were introduced to enhance the integrity of the business immigration program through a more objective assessment of business experience. Finally, the Act created a new in-Canada class for certain temporary workers, including graduates from Canadian schools who have Canadian work experience and meet the selection criteria as skilled workers. The creation of the in-Canada class is expected to produce positive benefits for the country and better meet the needs of people who make the transition from filling a specific temporary shortage to filling a permanent need.

Safety and Norms of Social Responsibility

The Act differentiated between permanent residents and foreign nationals to provide more transparency with respect to residency criteria. For example, permanent residents must be physically present in the country for at least 730 days in every five-year period after becoming a permanent resident or they risk losing their status. The Act also enhances the rights of permanent residents by requiring that they be issued permanent resident documents that are fraud resistant and include a tamper-proof photo.

The Act also strengthens enforcement measures to ensure national and border safety by targeting those who abuse the system. The Act identifies security, human or international rights violations, criminality, health, financial reasons, misrepresentation, and non-compliance as generic grounds for inadmissibility. This approach supports the notion that the best way to stop undesirable foreign nationals from entering Canada is to stop them before they enter it and to increase surveillance on those already in the country. The process of preventing the importation of threats to national security includes the establishment of overseas screening offices to intercept threats, reliance on an advance passenger information system to predetermine those who may be cause for concern, use of new technologies such as ultra-violet

TABLE 4.3   Skilled Worker Selection Grid

Indicator	Maximum points allocated
Education	25
Language	24
Experience	21
Age	10
Arranged employment	10
Adaptability	10
Total	100

Source: Citizenship and Immigration Canada (2002).

light testing and digital fingerprinting for security clearance, and temporary closure of border areas, air cargo, ports, and railways in the event of a high-level security threat.

The Act also stipulates penalties for and the inadmissibility of persons engaged in transnational crimes such as trafficking in persons or money laundering and of foreign nationals who violate Canadian law at entry to the country and those "described in travel sanctions imposed in concert with an international organization of states, of which Canada is a member." Furthermore, the Act prohibits the possession and use of fraudulent immigration-related documents and the improper use of otherwise legitimate immigration documents and, excepting refugees, stipulates penalties for document-related offences.

The Act introduces the security certificate process as a strategy to remove from the country those who pose a security risk, including terrorists. To deal more effectively with cases involving security and organized crime and to provide for a more expeditious removal of dangerous security threats, the security certificate process allows the use of confidential information at admissibility hearings, detention reviews, and immigration appeals. There is a prohibition on the release of confidential information that can cause potential injury to national security or the safety of persons.

Although the Act stipulates arrest of permanent residents and refugees under security certificates by warrant only, there is no such requirement for foreign nationals. The Act provides for the detention of foreign nationals on the grounds of danger to the public, flight risk, and refusal to provide information concerning identity, and considers specific factors prior to detention orders or during detention. Factors considered include the foreign national's involvement with or being under the influence of criminally organized smuggling or trafficking operations, being a fugitive from justice in another jurisdiction, having a conviction in Canada or abroad or outstanding charges for serious offences, and being affiliated with organized crime.

HOST COMMUNITY ORIENTATIONS: POLICE ABILITIES, KNOWLEDGE, AND SKILLS

Canada is one of the most ethnically diverse nations in the world, representing more than 200 different ethnic ancestries. Canada's multicultural society has been shaped over time by the aboriginal people of the country, by the different waves of immigrants and their descendants, and by the recruitment of immigrants from different countries of the world. According to the 2001 census, Canada welcomed more than 13.4 million immigrants during the past century, the largest number having arrived during the 1990s. In fact, 18.4 percent of its population was deemed to have been born outside Canada, the highest proportion in 70 years, representing emerging new ethnic groups from eastern Europe, central Asia, the Middle East, Africa, and Central and South America (Statistics Canada, 2001). In Toronto, 44 percent of the residents are foreign born, and 43 percent of the student population speaks a language other than English at home.

A nation's most precious resource is its people. Canadian citizens, permanent residents, foreign nationals, temporary workers, and refugees are assets to the host community rather than liabilities. For example, only about 3.5 percent of newcomers to Canada of working age receive social assistance, in comparison with 5.5 percent of those born in the host country (Gibbens & Lacoursière, 1993). Immigrants and refugees enrich the cultural, economic, and demographic mosaics of the country rather than impoverish it. Both Canadian citizens and would-be Canadians contribute to nation building, provide a source of capital, and facilitate international trade. As the United Nations High Commissioner for Refugees (1991) has noted, "A bundle of belongings isn't the only thing a refugee brings to his new country." People of diversity who are allowed to integrate provide the least threat to the host community and the most positive outcome from the perspective of law and order.

Yet the September 11, 2001 terrorist attacks on the United States influenced not only the two neighbouring countries' immigration attitudes and practices but those of the whole world. Two fundamental changes involving Canada and the United States occurred. First, a view of immigration as a threat to national security developed, and, second, the powers of law enforcement were expanded to curb the national security threat and wage a war against terrorism (Axelrod, 2000; Kruger, Mulder & Korenic, n.d.).

Law enforcement agencies and their officers have been given a dual mandate of closing the back door to criminals and others who would abuse Canada's openness and generosity or threaten its security while opening the front door to genuine refugees and to immigrants. In particular, the new phenomenon of homegrown threats to national security poses a challenge for law enforcement. For example, the July 7, 2005 subway bombing in London, England that killed 56 people and injured over 700 others was carried out by four British nationals. Such terrorist attacks seem to suggest that urban and suburban youth of successful immigrant parents are "having their fuses lit by orators, religious or secular, who spew their hatred of democratic institutions and the lifestyles that goes with them" (*The Montreal Gazette*, 2006). These events raise important issues regarding the limits of freedom of expression, the meaning of citizenship for disaffected youth, the family as the bedrock for social responsibility, and the need to implement laws that enhance national security without washing away democratic values and human right principles.

civil order policing model
law enforcement model that places national security at the forefront of police services

civil liberty policing model
law enforcement model that places civil liberties at the forefront of police services

Thus, the dilemma for law enforcement agencies is the tension between a **civil order policing model** and **civil liberty policing model**. The civil order model of policing places public order and national security at the forefront of police services. It views all foreign nationals with suspicion and applies liberally a host of practices for the purpose of protecting Canada and Canadians at home and abroad, ensuring that Canada is not a base for attacks on its allies, and maintaining international security. On the other hand, a civil liberty model of policing places human rights at the forefront of police services and promotes the mandate of protection of civil order within the limits of the law.

Law enforcement officers need to be cognizant of the serious negative consequences of equating immigration with terrorism and "causing the foreign national and the terrorist to be understood as one and the same in governmental [and law enforcement] discourse." (Kruger, Mulder, & Korenic, 2004, p. 78). Officers need to remember that very few immigrants pose threats to national security, very few asylum seekers are involved in terrorism, and Canada's immigration policy is not the root cause of international terrorism.

Policing also needs to be careful not to construe multiculturalism negatively, and not to view immigrants as less than Canadian, or paper citizens, or citizens of convenience. Initiatives such as the Police–Community Roundtable on Security (similar to the federal government's Cross-Cultural Roundtable on Security), which was introduced in February 2005 and held its inaugural meeting in March 2005 (Heritage Canada, 2006), are important because they engage Canadians and the government and its agencies including law agents in a long-term dialogue on issues relating to national security and their effects on the diverse and pluralistic Canadian society, and allows the establishment or the strengthening of partnerships at the national and international levels. Securing Canada by reducing the threat of terrorist activity and preventing terrorists and extremists from operating in Canada and abroad is an imperative that requires an integrated approach to policing. An integrated policing approach to security aims at strengthening and building partnerships with a variety of partners at the national level including the Public Safety and Emergency Preparedness Canada, Department of Justice, Minister of State for Multiculturalism, Canadian Security Intelligence Service, and Canada Border Services Agency. The integrated policing approach also aims at demystifying the prevailing negative perceptions of the diverse communities regarding security measures and practices.

The safety of Canadian society and respect for Canadian norms of social responsibility are paramount. Law enforcement efforts to balance respect for the letter of the law and a police relationship with people of diversity that is integrationist, respectful, and just, and that involves the community for the protection of civil order is advantageous to policing. Hostile, rejecting, overly suspicious, and disrespectful police conduct serves only to create bitter feelings, cynicism toward police, and lawlessness. A list of dos and don'ts of policing immigrants and refugees is provided in table 4.4.

TABLE 4.4 Dos and Don'ts of Policing Immigrants and Refugees

Dos

- Support an accepting host culture.

- Support an integrationist host culture orientation.

- Help immigrants and refugees become contributing members of society.

- Educate immigrants and refugees about policing in the host culture.

- Recognize that law-abiding citizens are citizens with a sense of acceptance, belonging, and fairness.

- Promote an immigration and refugee policy that is tough on organized crime, international terrorism, and war criminals.

- Support an immigration and refugee policy that allows the expeditious removal of persons involved in organized crime, war criminals, hijackers, and terrorists.

Don'ts

- Don't expect people of diversity to assimilate.

- Don't marginalize people of diversity.

- Don't bash immigrants and refugees.

- Don't disregard people's civil liberties.

CHAPTER SUMMARY

Police symbolize host community beliefs and practices. Host communities display attitudes of willingness or reluctance toward people of diversity. Host communities also influence immigration and refugee policies, and approaches to settlement and adaptation. People of diversity who wish and are allowed to integrate contribute the most to the country's demographic, social, legal, and economic livelihood and to civic order. A social climate that is hostile to and rejects social diversity and a policing approach that discriminates against certain types of diversity are likely to compromise respect for police and police safety. Law enforcement practices need to be guided by a balance between national security and civil liberty.

KEY TERMS

host community

settlement patterns

integrationist

exclusionary

assimilationist

segregationist

acculturation

marginalization

assimilation

separation

integration

interactive acculturation model

diversity acculturation orientation model

civil order policing model

civil liberty policing model

REFERENCES

Agnew, W.H. (1967). The Canadian mosaic. In Canada, Dominion Bureau of Statistics, *Canada one hundred, 1867–1967* (pp. 82–98). Ottawa: Queen's Printer.

Associated Press (2006, June 7). Suspects charged in Canada: Terrorists' plot is said to include beheadings. *International Herald Tribune*, p. 6.

Auditor General of Canada, Office of. (2000, April). Citizenship and Immigration Canada: The economic component of the Canadian immigration program. www.oag-bvg.gc.ca/domino/reports.nsf.

Axelrod, A. (2000). *American history*. Indianapolis, IN: Alpha Book.

Berry, J.W. (1990). Psychology of acculturation: Understanding individuals moving between cultures. In R.W. Brislin (Ed.), *Applied cross-cultural psychology* (pp. 232–52). Newbury Park, CA: Sage.

Berry, J.W. (1998). Acculturation and health: Theory and research. In S.S. Kazarian and D.R. Evans (Eds.), *Cultural clinical psychology: Theory, research and practice* (pp. 39–60). New York: Oxford University Press.

Berry, J.W., & D. Sam. (1997). Acculturation and adaptation. In J.W. Berry, M.H. Segal, and C. Kagitcibasi (Eds.), *Handbook of cross-cultural psychology: Social behavior and applications.* Vol. 3 (pp. 291–326). Needham Heights, MA: Allyn and Bacon.

Berry, J.W., U. Kim, S. Power, M. Young, & M. Bujaki. (1989). Acculturation attitudes in plural societies. *Applied Psychology: An International Review* 38: 185–206.

Bourhis, R.Y., L.C. Moïse, S. Perreault, & S. Senécal. (1997). Towards an interactive acculturation model: A social psychological perspective. *International Journal of Psychology* 32: 369–86.

Canadian Heritage. (2006). Annual Report on the operation of the Canadian Multiculturalism Act: 2004–2005. http://www.pch.gc.ca/index_e.cfm.

Citizenship and Immigration Canada. (2002). Bill C-11: *Immigration and Refugee Protection Act.*

DeVoretz, D. (1996). *Diminishing returns.* Vancouver: Simon Fraser University.

DePalma, A. (2006, June 5). Mosque is target as Canadians arrest 17 in terror sweep. *International Herald Tribune*, p. 4.

Dickason, O.P. (1992). *Canada's First Nations: A history of founding peoples from earliest times.* Toronto: McClelland & Stewart.

Fernandez, J.P. (1991). *Making a diverse workforce: Regaining the competitive edge.* Lexington, MA: Lexington Books.

Gibbens, R., & A. Lacoursière. (1993, November 20). Stream of newcomers imperative. *The London Free Press*, p. E5.

Griffin, J.D. (1989). *In search of sanity: A chronicle of the Canadian Mental Health Association, 1918–1988.* London, ON: Third Eye Publications.

Gwyn, R. (1993, July 4). Immigration, though undebated, in our best interest. *The Toronto Star*, p. B3.

Hall, J. (1992, November 22). Guide for immigrants demeaning, lawyer says. *The Toronto Star.*

Harper, T., & D. Vienneau. (1994, October 29). Clampdown on immigration. *The Toronto Star*, pp. A1, A3.

Holborn, L.W. (1975). *Refugees: A problem of our time: The work of the United Nations High Commissioner for Refugees 1951–1972.* Metuchen, NJ: The Scarecrow Press.

Immigration Act, RSC 1985, c. I-2, as amended.

Immigration and Refugee Protection Act, SC 2001, c. 27.

Kallen, E. (2003). *Ethnicity and human rights in Canada: A human rights perspective on race, ethnicity, racism and systemic inequality.* NY: Oxford University Press.

Kaprielian, E. (1982). Armenians in Ontario. *Polyphony* 4: 5–11.

Kazarian, S.S. (1997). The Armenian psyche: Genocide and acculturation. *Mentalities* 12: 74–87.

Kelley, N., & M. Trebilcock. (1998). *The making of the mosaic: A history of Canadian immigration policy.* Toronto: University of Toronto Press.

Kruger, E., M. Mulder, & B. Korenic. (2004). Canada after 11 September: Security measures and "preferred" immigrants. *Mediterranean Quarterly* 15:72–87.

Lagasse, J.H. (1967). The two founding peoples. In Canada, Dominion Bureau of Statistics, *Canada one hundred 1867–1967* (pp. 74–81). Ottawa: Queen's Printer.

Lee-Chin, M. (2000, June). Chairman's message. *AIC Group of Funds semi-annual report.* Burlington, ON: AIC Group of Funds.

The Montreal Gazette (2006, August 12). Editorials: Muslim leaders must make themselves heard, p. B6.

Nef, J., and R. da Silva. (1991). The politics of refugee generation in Latin America. In H. Adelman (Ed.), *Refugee policy: Canada and the United States.* (pp. 52-80). North York, ON: York Lanes Press.

Serge, J. (1993). *Canadian citizenship made simple: A practical guide to immigration and citizenship in Canada.* Toronto: Doubleday.

Statistics Canada. (2001). Profile of languages in Canada: English, French and many others. 2001 Census: Analysis series.

Statistics Canada. (2002). Fact sheet 16: Skilled workers. http://www.cic.gc.ca/english/pub/fs-skilled.html.

Stoffman, D. (1993). *Toward a more realistic immigration policy for Canada.* Toronto: C.D. Howe Institute.

Tepper, E.L. (1994). Immigration policy and multiculturalism. In J.W. Berry and J.A. Laponce (Eds.), *Ethnicity and culture in Canada* (pp. 95–123). Toronto: University of Toronto Press.

United Nations. (1983). *Convention and Protocol Relating to the Status of Refugees Final Act of the United Nations Conference of Plenipotentiaries on the Status of Refugees and Stateless Persons and the Text of the 1951 Convention Relating to Refugees. Resolution 2198 Adopted by the General Assembly and the Text of the 1967 Protocol Relating to the Status of Refugees.* New York: United Nations.

United Nations High Commissioner for Refugees. (1991). Poster no. B/0100/1/91.

Watson, P. (1992, March 22). Snoozing adjudicator a problem for refugees. *The Toronto Star,* pp. A1, A14.

Wheeler, W.B., & S.D. Becker. (1994). *Discovering the American past: A look at the evidence. Volume I: To 1877.* Boston: Houghton Mifflin.

Will, G.F. (1993, July 30). America's debate on immigration. *International Herald Tribune,* p. 7.

EXERCISES AND REVIEW
Personal Reflections
Read each statement below and circle whether you agree or disagree with it.

1. Almost all refugee claimants come from countries that commit serious human rights violations.

   AGREE   DISAGREE

2. Immigrants make police work harder because they commit more crimes than the average citizen.

   AGREE   DISAGREE

3. Policing is becoming more difficult because this country seems to be giving refuge to all the criminals of other countries.

   AGREE   DISAGREE

4. Immigrants are more likely to abuse the social programs of a country than the average citizen.

   AGREE   DISAGREE

5. Immigrants take jobs away from "real" citizens.

   AGREE   DISAGREE

6. Everyone has the right to flee persecution in their own country and seek and enjoy asylum in other countries.

   AGREE   DISAGREE

7. Immigrants and refugees may have a negative view of law enforcement because of their experience in their countries of origin.

   AGREE   DISAGREE

8. The majority of newcomers develop no nationalistic feelings for their new country.

   AGREE   DISAGREE

9. Immigrants are a burden on the economy.

   AGREE   DISAGREE

10. Most refugee claims tend to be bogus.

   AGREE   DISAGREE

11. Except for aboriginal peoples, we can all trace our ancestry to immigrants.

    AGREE   DISAGREE

12. Most newcomers are poor and uneducated and do not speak or want to speak English or French.

    AGREE   DISAGREE

13. When every other safeguard fails, asylum in a foreign country becomes the ultimate human right.

    AGREE   DISAGREE

14. Immigrants and refugees are the main sources of problems that arise between police and the community.

    AGREE   DISAGREE

15. Most foreign nationals come to Canada from conflicted societies to create vibrant international terrorist networks.

    AGREE   DISAGREE

SCORING: Give yourself one point for agreeing with the following statements: 1, 6, 11, and 13. Give yourself one point for disagreeing with each of the remaining statements. The higher the score, the more positive your attitude toward newcomers. Compare your score with a classmate's and try to reconcile any differences in opinion.

Diversity IQ: Multiple Choice

Circle the best answer.

1. Which of the following is a historical reality?

    a. colonized countries were discovered by the colonizers

    b. colonized countries were "discovered" by their aboriginal peoples

    c. cultural pluralism in modern Western nations is a very recent phenomenon

    d all culturally pluralistic nations are countries with a majority culture

2. Host countries accept immigrants for what reason(s)?

    a. demographic

    b. economic

    c. humanitarian

    d. all of the above

3. Race ceased to be one of the grounds for admissibility under Canada's immigration policy in

    a. 1906

    b. 1952

    c. 1962

    d. 1993

4. Which of the following statements are myths about immigrants and refugees?

    a. they take jobs away from "real" citizens

    b. they are a drain on the economy of the host society

    c. they love to milk the system

    d. a and c

    e. all of the above

5. Refugees are people fleeing

    a. political, racial, religious, or other persecution

    b. war or natural disasters

    c. a and b

    d. none of the above

6. Which of the following factors are related to successful human adaptation?

    a. host culture acculturation orientation

    b. personal acculturation orientation

    c. a and b

    d. none of the above

7. The integration of newcomers depends on

    a. their willingness to integrate

    b. the willingness of the larger society to help them integrate

    c. their willingness to integrate and on the willingness of the larger society to foster their integration

    d. the efforts of the larger society to assimilate them

8. The acculturation strategy that is most conducive to healthy law-enforcement–community relations is

   a. assimilation

   b. integration

   c. segregation or separation

   d. marginalization

9. The majority of newcomers prefer to

   a. marginalize

   b. live in ghettos

   c. integrate into the host society

   d. engage in terrorist activities

10. According to the proposed diversity acculturation orientation model,

    a. the acculturation orientation of police is not important

    b. diversity should be restricted to ethnicity

    c. a more inclusive approach to diversity needs to be considered

    d. all of the above

Diversity IQ: True or False?

____ 1. Having a heritage culture or dual identity does not diminish one's sense of attachment or commitment to a host society.

____ 2. Refugee policies are developed to keep people out of a country.

____ 3. Economics is not a factor in the immigration policies of host countries.

____ 4. Welcoming refugees is more of a human rights issue than an immigration issue.

____ 5. Open debate on immigration and refugee issues is conducive to national growth and development.

____ 6. An assimilationist host community assumes the equality of immigrants.

____ 7. Marginalized people feel alienated and have a lower quality of life.

____ 8. The most precious resource of any country is its people.

____ 9. Disadvantaged individuals are less likely to be law-abiding.

____ 10. Integration involves embracing the host culture and abandoning the culture of origin.

Application Now

1. List principles, strategies, and practices that police services and police officers should consider to provide a social, economic, political, and policing climate that is conducive to integrating the members of the communities they serve and maximizing national security.

   Principles

   Strategies of Police Services

   Practices

2. List the benefits to a host society and to police of having integrated communities.

   Benefits to the host society

Benefits to the police

Food for Thought

1. A prevailing practice is to identify people of diversity as members of *minority* or *majority* groups.

    a. Pretend that you are a police officer. Write down your reactions to being labelled a member of a majority or dominant group.

    Now, write down your reactions to being labelled a member of a minority group.

    Do the labels evoke different reactions? If so, how and why?

    b. What do you think are the psychological and social consequences of being labelled a member of a majority or minority group?

    Majority person or group

Minority person or group

c. What are some consequences of being labelled a minority, in terms of the criminal justice system in general and policing in particular?

Criminal justice system

Policing

2. Divide the class into groups of three to five. Read the story below, and then compare your analyses as a group. Appoint a representative to report your group's findings to the class for general discussion.

Police Deliver Baby

I am a recent immigrant and a 27-year-old mother of a toddler. I flagged down a cab in front of my apartment around 5 a.m. when I realized that I was going into labour. The cab driver called 911. Two female police officers arrived moments before the ambulance and firefighters. One of the officers thought she still had time to get me to hospital, but I knew that it was too late. One officer supported me from behind while the other delivered a healthy baby girl. Both officers were encouraging—they were really great. The ambulance and firefighters arrived a minute later and whisked me off to hospital. The cab driver was so happy—he was like a proud grandfather. The officers were also beaming. It was an experience we'll all remember.

Source: Adapted from Hemingway (1997), p. A5.

a. What are the implications of this experience for the mother's adjustment to the host culture?

b. What are the likely implications of this experience for the mother's attitude toward police officers?

c. What are the likely implications of this experience for neighbourhood attitudes toward police officers?

From Thought to Action

1. Critique the list of dos and don'ts in table 4.4 (on p. 121). What should be deleted from the list and what should be added?

Lessons from History

1. In 1991, an 85-page guidebook was published by the government of a culturally pluralistic country and distributed to its foreign visa offices. The *Newcomer's Guidebook* contained the following instructions to prospective immigrants:

    a. Spitting, urinating or defecating anywhere except in a private or public toilet is against the law.

    b. Genital exposure is called "indecent exposure" and is against the law.

    c. Extended public displays of affection (passionate kissing, fondling) are considered impolite and offensive in public.

    d. You should always arrive on time at school, on the job or for any business appointment.

    e. Breastfeeding babies in public is offensive.

    f. You can wear whatever style of clothes you wish in the host country; however, you will probably want to modify what you are used to wearing.

    Source: Hall (1992).

    a. What impression of newcomers do these instructions create? What do you think of the instructions?

    b. What image of the host country does the *Newcomer's Guidebook* create?

    c. As a police officer, if you were to develop a guidebook for newcomers in the aftermath of 9/11 to help them integrate in your country, what would you include?

2. The media play a major role in shaping police perceptions of the communities they serve and in shaping public perceptions of police. There is widespread concern that the media portray people of diversity (for example, racial and cultural groups) negatively. There is also concern that the media show bias in reporting incidents that involve police and people of diversity. Such distorted media coverage perpetuates negative stereotypes of police and people of diversity.

    a. How can the community learn from the past and improve the fairness of media coverage of police, people of diversity, and police–community relations?

    Police

    People of diversity

    Police–community relations

The Great Debate

Host cultures can force homogenization on newcomers or they can foster a climate that is conducive to integrating people into host cultures without losing their heritage cultures. Divide the class into two groups to debate this topic. Have one group take the homogenization position from the perspective of law enforcement and the second group take the integration position. Have a general discussion after the debate.

Debate the merits of the civil order policing model versus the civil liberty policing model.

CHAPTER 5

Cultural Diversity Values, Beliefs, and Practices

CHAPTER OBJECTIVES

After completing this chapter, you should be able to:

- Explain the concepts of culture, ethnicity, race, and minority.
- Understand core cultural values, beliefs, and practices.
- Refine your understanding of specific cultures in the context of the post-9/11 environment.

PREVIEW SCENARIO

In November 2000, a 73-year-old cop killer, considered armed and dangerous, escaped from prison. The man had been serving a life sentence at a minimum security penitentiary for murdering two police officers about 25 years earlier. Evidently, he and an accomplice had jumped the two officers, ordered them to dig their own graves, handcuffed them, and then shot them with their own guns. The two men had been found guilty and sentenced to death, but their sentence was commuted to life in prison when the death penalty was abolished. The escaped killer was described as having a tattoo on his upper left arm with a heart and the names Carol and Janet. He was also described as five-foot-eight, 155 pounds, green-eyed, brown-haired, and balding. His name was James Hutchinson. (Canadian Press, 2000)

INTRODUCTION

Canada's more than 32 million inhabitants reflect a cultural, ethnic, and linguistic mosaic not found anywhere else on earth. Not everyone in Canada is born in Canada, and as the Preview Scenario shows, not all those who are born in the country are law-abiding citizens. Each year, close to 200,000 immigrants from all over the globe choose Canada as their host country and become law-abiding citizens. These immigrants are drawn by Canada's quality of life and "its reputation as an open, peaceful and caring society that welcomes newcomers and values diversity" (Canadian Heritage, 2004).

Canada is a federation of 10 provinces and 3 northern territories. The country is a land mass of 10 million square kilometres on which live a mosaic community of over 32 million people. Thus, the country has a population density of approximately three people per square metre. The majority of its people (roughly 80 percent) congregate in its cities. Canada's geographic and political boundaries pose challenges for Canadian police work. In combatting crime, protecting civil order, and contributing to international strategies against terrorism, police encounter people from all walks of life and all diversities.

General descriptions of Canada's people of diverse backgrounds invariably mask the complexity of their historical development and the important *cultural similarities* and *cultural differences* that exist among them. Equally important, such descriptions ignore the richness of the lives of individuals. Nevertheless, an understanding of and respect for specific diversities can improve social relations and strengthen national identity, and enhance security and lawful conduct in a free and democratic civil society. This chapter focuses on issues of diversity, including ethnicity, race, and culture. More specifically, it discusses the core values, beliefs, and practices associated with different ethnocultural groups and the challenges for policing ethnocultural communities in the aftermath of the terrorist attacks on the United States on September 11, 2001.

CONCEPTS OF CULTURE, ETHNICITY, RACE, AND MINORITY

There is a great deal of confusion over the terms "culture," "ethnicity," "race," and "visible minority." A major problem is that these terms are used interchangeably (Kazarian, 1998). For example, even though the English and the French are called Canada's "two founding races," as Lagasse (1967) points out, both cultural groups belong to the same Caucasian race.

Culture

Culture can be defined narrowly as folk traditions, on the one hand, to achieve a particular purpose or objective. In its anthropological sense, culture is synonymous with ethnoculture (Kallen, 2003). Both terms refer to the distinctive ways of viewing and doing things shared by members of a particular ethnic community and transmitted by them from one generation to the next through the process of enculturation (distinctive ethnic socialization). In a broader sense, **culture** refers to the pattern of behaviour and results of behaviour that are shared and transmitted among the members of a particular society (Linton, 1945). Triandis (1990) refers to culture as "the man-made part of the environment" (p. 36) and describes two aspects: the objective (for example, roads and bridges) and the subjective (beliefs, attitudes, norms, roles, and values). Individuals have unique world views that are shaped by

culture
pattern of behaviour and results of behaviour that are shared and transmitted among members of a particular society

their culture. These world views in turn affect how they think, feel, act, communicate, and interpret their personal and social environments. The most important point about culture, from a social-scientific perspective, is that it is a learned phenomenon; it is acquired, for the most part, through the ordinary process of growing up and participating in the daily life of a particular ethnic community (Kallen, 2003).

Ethnicity

The term "**ethnicity**" (also called "ethnic identity") is used to define an individual's or a group's identification with a cultural origin (for example, British or Armenian) within a culturally pluralistic context (for example, Canada); thus, an individual may define himself or herself as a British-Canadian or Armenian-Canadian. One can exhibit symbolic ethnicity—that is, by expressing an attachment to and pride in one's ethnic origin—or behavioural ethnicity—that is, by participating in ethnic activities and the social and cultural life passed on from generation to generation. Census Canada defines "ethnic origin" as "the ethnic or cultural group(s) to which an individual's ancestors belonged (Statistics Canada, 2001). While ethnicity refers to identifying with a cultural community at the group or individual level, "cultural group" refers to individuals who share a cultural heritage but do not necessarily identify with it. For example, someone may be a member of the Estonian cultural group but consider himself or herself Canadian. Canadian in this context is a legal definition given to an individual when the government of Canada, through its immigration policy, bestows upon the individual legal rights and privileges associated with the label and identity "Canadian." While cultural group is inherited, ethnicity develops through the process of learning and socialization. Globalization and intermarriages among ethnic groups are contributing to the emergence of multiple ethnic ancestries and identities.

ethnicity
individual or group identification with a culture of origin

Race

The word "**race**" first occurs in the English language about 1500 CE. A study of its etymology, or origin, shows that it was adopted from the French word *race*, which is connected to the Italian word *razza* and the Spanish word *raza*. Beyond this, its origin is obscure (Kallen, 2003). It was not until the 18th century, however, that the term was used to indicate major divisions of humankind by stressing certain common physical characteristics such as skin colour (Kallen, 2003). In essence, it is an approach to categorizing humankind or *Homo sapiens* according to common ancestry or origin and on the basis of physical characteristics.

Originally, the term "race" was used to refer to both biological characteristics (as in "white race," "black race," "yellow race," or "red race") and cultural traits and values (as in "peasant race") (Berry and Laponce, 1994). The word is increasingly used to refer to such groupings as language, national origin, ethnicity, culture, and religion. However, social scientists and others stick to the definition of race as physical or biological.

race
classification based on biological or cultural traits

Minority

The term "minority" refers to a group's placement in a subordinate social category where the group's members have subordinate social status relative to the majority, and wield a lesser degree of political, economic, and/or social power (Kallen, 2003: 284). For example, blacks in South Africa constitute the majority of the population numerically, but hold the minority power politically, economically, and socially. The term "minority" is not and should not be reduced to a racial classification of those who are not white. Any racial group can hold the majority power in any given society and have bestowed upon them the label of majority group.

The term "minority" refers to groups that are seen as having less social, political, and economic power than the host group. Minority group status may be based on race, religion, political affiliation, nationality, or some other characteristics that are different from those of the majority group. In Canada, a **visible minority** is defined as an individual, other than an aboriginal person, who is non-Caucasian in race or non-white in colour (Employment and Immigration Canada, 1987, p. B-3). This definition is used by the Canadian government solely for the purpose of hiring members of groups that are underemployed, under-represented, or not represented in the government and private sector.

visible minority
an individual, other than an aboriginal person, who is non-Caucasian in race or non-white in colour

CRITIQUE OF THESE CONCEPTS

Some critics have called for the abolition of the term "race" from everyday language and academic discourse. They argue that it carries a negative connotation and has the potential to be misused. Others have called for the abolition of the term "culture," arguing that it is seen as a euphemism for race or ethnicity. Similarly, Winterdyk and King (1999) have suggested that the designation of "minority" evokes negative associations, including lack of prestige, privilege, and power.

Discussion of terms such as "culture," "ethnicity," "race," and "minority" is not just an academic exercise. These concepts are being tested in the same way that the idea of a woman being a legal person was tested some years ago. Bonnett (2000) describes a 1998 quibble over terminology in Britain's *Race Relations Act*. A supervisor argued that his alleged racial remarks about a Danish employee were not racist because the employee was the same race as the supervisor—both were white. The supervisor equated race or skin colour with national origin or ethnicity. The court rejected this argument, asserting that whiteness did not preclude allegations of racism. The court ruled that the supervisor had contravened the *Race Relations Act*, and awarded compensation to the employee for *ethnic* abuse from the supervisor.

In another British case, a white supremacist group campaigned against the construction of a mosque. A London municipal council brought the issue to court under the *Race Relations Act*. The High Court, however, rejected the council's application on the grounds that "Muslims were a religious rather than an ethnic group," and so they fell outside the provisions of the Act (Bonnett, 2000). As noted by Bonnett (2000), the High Court demonstrated the practice of confusing race with national, cultural, or religious identity.

CULTURAL BELIEFS AND PRACTICES: CORE DIMENSIONS

There are 10,000 cultures and 6,170 distinct languages in the world (Moynihan, 1993; Triandis, 1995). It is impossible to study all of these cultures and languages in detail, but we can become familiar with key characteristics, or what psychologists call *dimensions*, of cultures. Several such "personalities" of cultures or core cultural beliefs and practices have been identified, and are described below.

Note that dimensions are continuums, not categories. That is, cultures or cultural beliefs and practices are seen as partaking more of one characteristic than of another, rather than as being entirely either one or the other. A dimensional approach to cultures and cultural beliefs and practices allows us to see them in relation to each other, and avoids the tendency to stereotype people, cultures, or cultural beliefs and practices in simplistic, value-laden categories.

Achievement Versus Relationship Culture

In **achievement cultures** people primarily live to work, whereas in **relationship cultures** they work to live (Hall, 1976; Hofstede, 1980). Individuals from achievement cultures tend to focus on work and getting the job done. Individuals from relationship cultures emphasize leisure and fun, the separation of work life from private life, close family ties, and nurturing social relations. In relationships between a person from an achievement culture and a person from a relationship culture, conflicts can develop when the achievement-oriented person is preoccupied and self-absorbed, while the relationship-oriented person is trying to prolong the social interaction in an effort to nurture the relationship. Individuals from relationship cultures work as hard as those from achievement cultures, but tend to be better at separating their work lives from their private lives.

achievement culture culture that focuses on work

relationship culture culture that focuses on social relations

Tight Versus Loose Culture

Tight cultures impose clear-cut societal norms. Such cultures have only minimal tolerance for people who deviate from established norms and expectations. Predictability, certainty, and security are dominant values in tight cultures. Unlike individuals from **loose cultures**, which are less concerned about rules and conformity, individuals from tight cultures tend to be more anxious, insecure, and fearful of reprisal for violating norms.

tight culture culture that values predictability, certainty, and security

loose culture culture that tolerates deviation from established norms and expectations

Low-Context Versus High-Context Culture

Cultures can be described in terms of communication style. In **low-context cultures**, words are extremely important because they convey most of the message being sent. Low-context cultures include Canada, Britain, France, Germany, the United States, and most Scandinavian countries. In these countries, police officers use direct and logical language, usually without emotion, and they expect each and every word they use to convey the message they want to communicate. Low-context cultures are also time-oriented—that is, schedules are an important part of completing tasks.

low-context culture culture that relies on words to convey most of the message being sent

In contrast, words in the absence of emotion and a context have very little meaning in **high-context cultures**. In these cultures, words convey only part of the message being sent. Instead, the spoken message needs to be understood in the context of the communication or social interaction. Goodman (1994) points out that there can be many different meanings to the word "maybe" in Japanese culture, ranging from "perhaps" to "no." The context in which "maybe" is used will determine its exact meaning.

People from high-context cultures prefer to get to know strangers before developing a work relationship with them. Long personal conversations before reaching agreements or responding to instructions are often a feature of these cultures, to the annoyance of individuals from low-context cultures. Individuals from high-context cultures are also task-oriented—completing a task is more important than the schedule. Thus, not showing up for an appointment or being late may be non-issues for these people. High-context cultures include aboriginal cultures and African, Caribbean, Asian, and Latin-American cultures.

Collectivism Versus Individualism

Cultures can be understood as **collectivist** ("we"-oriented cultures) and **individualist** ("me"-oriented). Collectivist cultures are characterized by hierarchical structures and by identification with, loyalty to, and dependence on in-groups. The self-concepts of individuals from these cultures tend to depend on their in-groups rather than on distinct identities. Individual and group interdependence is a critical feature. People from collectivist cultures value immediate and extended family (sometimes including ancestors), family honour, security, hierarchical relationships, obedience, conformity, group decisions, group "face," and group harmony. They are likely to downplay their own goals and remain loyal to group goals. They believe that parents are obligated to care for their children, and children are obligated to care for their parents. In collectivist cultures, elderly parents are expected to live with their children and to command their respect. Because people from collectivist cultures emphasize long-term relationships, they are hesitant to commit themselves to personal or business relationships unless trust has been established.

People from individualist cultures are likely to pursue personal goals, and, when faced with a conflict between their own goals and those of the group, are likely to obey their own desires. They tend to value independence, self-reliance, and competition over cooperation. They may also mistrust authority. Table 5.1 summarizes the differences between individualist and collectivist cultures.

Relative to European peoples, aboriginal, African, Asian, and Latin-American peoples are collectivist given their relative de-emphasis on the welfare of the individual in favour of the welfare of the community. Canada has been a collectivist country in the sense that it has "recognized collectivities as fundamental units and emphasized group rights over those of individual citizens" (Lock, 1990, p. 239). As Lock describes, "Whereas in America 'life, liberty, and the pursuit of happiness' were enshrined as fundamental ideals, in Canada 'peace, order, and good government' were laid down as overarching goals" (1990, p. 239).

Collectivist individuals may be found in individualist cultures, and individualist individuals may be found in collectivist cultures. Individuals may also embrace individualism and collectivism at the same time. There are three variations to the ex-

high-context culture
culture that relies on context to convey the meaning of a message

collectivist culture
"we"-oriented culture that values family, group harmony, and conformity

individualist culture
"me"-oriented culture that values the pursuit of personal goals, self-reliance, non-conformity, and competition

TABLE 5.1   Differences Between Individualist and Collectivist Cultures

Individualism	Collectivism
Pursuit of one's own goals	Loyalty to one's group
Nuclear family structure	Extended family structure
Self-reliant	Group-reliant
Time and energy invested for personal gain	Time and energy invested for group gain
Receptive to career changes	Relatively unreceptive to career changes
Relatively little sharing of material/ non-material resources	Sharing of material/non-material resources
Emphasis on competition	Emphasis on cooperation
Relatively non-conformist	Conformist
Mistrust of authority	Respectful of status and authority

pression of collectivist values in which the welfare of the individual is de-emphasized: familism, spiritualism, and romanticism (Gaines, 1997).

Familism is a cultural value orientation that expresses collectivism by emphasizing the welfare of the immediate and extended family. Latino culture may be considered familistic because of the family orientation of its members. *Spiritualism* is a cultural value orientation that emphasizes the welfare of all living entities, both natural and supernatural. Spiritualism is embraced particularly by Eastern religions and people of Asian descent. *Romanticism* is a cultural value orientation that emphasizes the welfare of personal relationships. As Gaines (1997) points out, romanticism is particularly operative in interethnic or interracial relationships in which couples defy the odds against their long-term success.

Finally, a vital difference between collectivist and individualist cultures is construal of the self (Markus & Kitayama, 1991). People in individualist cultures exhibit **independent self-construal**. They construe the self as independent and reliant on the self for its well-being whereas people in collectivist cultures exhibit **interdependent self-construal**. They construe the self as interdependent and its well-being reliant on family, kin, or the in-group. Individuals who construe the self as interdependent view their self as an extension of family, kin, and in-group such that the identity of the self is intertwined with that of family, kin, and the in-group. Thus, a person with an interdependent self construal is likely to sacrifice his happiness, or even life, if called on by family, kin, and/or the in-group. Similarly, the family, kin, and/or the in-group will react with anger or even violence if the interdependent self is threatened physically or psychologically. Insulting the person with the interdependent self is by extension also insulting the in-group of the individual. For example, insulting the religious leader of a collectivist community is the same as insulting the community. The insult may not evoke a response from the leader but it may evoke a community response, in some cases a violent response.

independent self-construal
view of the self as independent and self-reliant for its well-being

interdependent self-construal
view of the self as interdependent and reliant on family, kin, or the in-group for its well-being

CULTURAL BELIEFS AND PRACTICES: SPECIFIC CULTURAL GROUPS

Canada is a multicultural and multiethnic society in that it is represented by more than 200 ethnic groups. The mosaic nation's cultural groups can be classified into three major categories: aboriginal people, non-visible ethnic minority groups, and visible ethnic minority groups. A list of the top 10 ethnic groups representing the three major categories is provided in table 5.2. In the present section, the three major cultural groups and select subgroups within them are described briefly for the purpose of discussion. Other groups have not been dealt with because of space limitations; a single chapter simply cannot begin to cover the entire international world within Canada.

First Nations People

The First Nations population makes up 3.4 percent of the population in Canada. It is a community that is growing almost twice as fast as the rest of the population in Canada and a group in which half of its members make their homes in the cities across the country. The majority of aboriginal people report being North American Indian (62 percent), followed by Metis (30 percent), and Inuit (5 percent). Ontario is home to 188,315 aboriginal people.

Native cultures have evolved despite the harm done to them from European colonization. At the time of European settlement, more than 56 aboriginal nations existed, speaking more than 36 languages (Canadian Heritage, 2004). Aboriginal people in Canada continue to confront unique socio-cultural and economic challenges including loss of their aboriginal languages, high rates of poverty, and discrimination.

Native ethics, values, and rules of behaviour have contributed to the development of cooperation and harmonious interpersonal relationships among aboriginal people and in the past ensured their individual and collective survival in natural

TABLE 5.2   Top 10 Ethnic Groups in Canada, 2001

Group	(%)*
Canadian	39.4
English	20.2
French	15.8
Scottish	14.0
Irish	12.9
German	9.3
Italian	4.3
Chinese	3.7
Ukrainian	3.6
North American Indian	3.4

* The numbers add up to more than 100 percent because some respondents reported more than one ethnic origin.

Source: Statistics Canada (2001).

TABLE 5.3   Native Ethics of Behaviour

Non-interference	Physical, verbal, and psychological coercion are avoided, as is exertion of pressure by means of advising, instructing, coercing, or persuading.
Non-competitiveness	Rivalry is averted and social embarrassment of individuals is prevented.
Emotional restraint	Both positive (joy and enthusiasm) and negative (anger and hostility) emotions are suppressed.
Sharing	Generosity is encouraged while hoarding material goods is discouraged.
Concept of time	There is a belief in "doing things when the time is right."
Attitude toward gratitude and approval	Gratitude and approval are rarely shown, verbalized, or expected.
Principle of teaching by modelling	To learn, one is *shown* how rather than *told* how. Actions convey useful and practical information.

Source: Brant (1990).

and harsh environments. To sustain a cooperative and friendly social climate for survival, aboriginal peoples assumed a social pattern of behaviour that dictated the suppression of conflict (Brant, 1990). According to Brant (1990), conflict suppression among the members of an extended family, clan, band, or tribe was established through ethics, or the application of harmony-promoting principles of behaviour. Native ethics or principles of behaviour are listed in table 5.3. These have evolved over time to become social norms in North American Native culture.

Non-interference helps to promote positive relations between people. It takes the form of permissiveness in the context of adult–child relationships, as described by Brant (1990, p. 535) in the following passage:

> A Native child may be allowed at the age of six, for example, to make the decision on whether or not he goes to school even though he is required to do so by law. The child may be allowed to decide whether or not he will do his homework, have his assignment done on time, and even visit the dentist. Native parents will be reluctant to force the child into doing anything he does not choose to do.

Non-competitiveness is a way of avoiding conflict between groups and between individuals. Aboriginal cultures are collectivist cultures that emphasize group harmony over individual success.

Emotional restraint is considered desirable because it promotes self-control and discourages the expression of strong and violent feelings. However, suppressing emotions may contribute to alcohol abuse as an outlet for some individuals. Domestic violence and violence within the community that result from intoxication are serious issues for aboriginal people living on reserves.

Sharing is consistent with aboriginal collectivist cultures. In addition to its historical survival value, sharing helps to suppress conflict by minimizing the likelihood of greed, envy, arrogance, and pride within the community. It also contributes to equality and democracy. Personal striving for prosperity and success and acquiring education and other assets require individuals to give up the ethic of sharing. Native society is therefore likely to discourage or disapprove of individual ambition. In addition, individual ambition has resulted in the "skimming of Native society" (Brant, 1990), where young, attractive, and talented Native people or those with a postsecondary education have essentially left the reserve to live in non-Native society and marry non-Natives.

The *concept of time* in contemporary Native life is another manifestation of the need for harmonious relationships (Brant, 1990). Aboriginal people are unlikely to be inconvenienced or annoyed by delays in starting scheduled meetings or social functions.

Gratitude and approval are rarely expressed. Both are considered superfluous because doing something for someone else carries its own intrinsic reward.

Teaching in aboriginal culture is done by modelling.

Another feature of aboriginal cultures is that *excellence is expected at all times.* A negative consequence of this core value is performance anxiety. Native people may avoid taking risks for fear of making mistakes or subjecting themselves to public scrutiny and possible ridicule. In Native cultures, praise and rewards for being good are not expected because being good is what one expects from oneself. Praise is likely to be seen as deceitful, or as embarrassing in group contexts when the praise is not given to the whole group. Praise that is not shared with peers is seen as disharmonious to peer relationships.

Non-Visible Ethnic Minority Peoples

Non-visible ethnic minority groups represent those that are not listed by Employment and Immigration Canada (1987). They include the two founding peoples of Canada, the English and the French, and a host of other cultural groups from Europe including Germans, Italians, and the Dutch. As indicated in table 5.2, English, French, Scottish, and Irish are the most frequently reported non-visible ethnic minority groups in Canada. In this section we focus mainly on the French and the English.

Generally, people of French heritage value their language and its preservation, their French culture and its distinctiveness, their religion and the Catholic church, and their families.

While there are differences among the English, Scottish, Irish, and Welsh cultures, they also share potential common values (see table 5.4). People of British and Irish cultures are individualistic, as manifested in their emphasis on the work ethic, self-reliance, emotional reserve, the nuclear family structure, privacy, democracy, and mistrust of authority. The *work ethic* is a particularly powerful value.

Self-reliance is tied to the British work ethic. British self-reliance is shown in a reluctance to express affection (one exception being the public outpouring of emotion at the death of Princess Diana in 1997), respect for personal privacy, and reluctance to disclose personal issues—for example, marital discord—to others (including one's own children). The reluctance to self-disclose is based on the perception that personal issues reflect personal failures and that disclosing them overburdens others. In the face of personal issues—for example, divorce—British people are likely to believe that the best remedy is to work or try harder.

TABLE 5.4   Comparison of Cultural Values and Practices

British	Black	Latino	Asian
Individualism	Collectivism	Collectivism	Collectivism
Nuclear family structure	Extended family system	Familism (*la familia*)	Extended family system
Individual initiative and risk taking	Family strength	Family honour	Group decision making
Achievement orientation	Education	Importance of process over outcome	Obligation to group
Competition	Cooperation	Cooperation	Cooperation
Work ethic, task-and-outcome orientation	Black language, soul, and oral tradition	*Dignidad*—Spanish pride, personal reputation, opinions of others, and saving face	Harmonious interpersonal relationships
Materialism	Religion	Religion	Spiritualism
Rationalism	Emotional expressiveness	Emotional expressiveness	Indirect expression of emotions
Direct communication	Direct communication	Indirect communication	Indirect communication
Assertiveness	Openness, directness	Courtesy, tact, and diplomacy	Fatalism, patience, and formality

Visible Ethnic Minority Peoples

People of visible minorities constitute 13.4 percent of the Canadian population (Statistics Canada, 2001). The rate of increase of visible minorities between 1996 and 2001 was six times that of the general population of the country. In 1981, 1 in 20 Canadians was a visible minority; in 2001, it was 1 in 7. Thus, almost 4 million individuals who identify themselves as visible minorities have made Canada their home. In addition, 3 out of 10 visible minority people are born in Canada, and Chinese, South Asians, and blacks constitute the three largest visible minority groups, accounting for two-thirds of the visible minority population. In terms of urban settlement, 36.9 percent of the population of Vancouver, 36.8 percent of the population of the Toronto Census Metropolitan Area (GTA), and 13.6 percent of the population of Montreal are visible minority people. In the GTA, 25 percent of Chinese and 25 percent of South Asians are foreign born, as are 20 percent of blacks, 8 percent of Filipinos, 6 percent of Arabs and West Asians, 5 percent of Latin Americans, 3 percent of South East Asians, 3 percent of Koreans, and 1 percent of Japanese.

BLACK PEOPLES

According to the 2001 Canada census, a total of 662,215 people identified themselves as black (Statistics Canada, 2001). Black peoples have a long and tragic history of colonization and slavery. The beginnings of their slavery in the United States are traced to 1619. A trickle of Africans brought from England to work as farm labourers swelled to a slave population in the millions. Similarly, a fairly loose labour system evolved into a "system of chattel slavery that tried to control nearly every aspect of the slaves' lives" (Wheeler and Becker, 1994, p. 170).

The French brought African slaves to Canada in the early 1600s. In 1689, the settlers of New France were given explicit permission to import more slaves from Africa. Thousands of people of colour settled in the Maritimes beginning in 1776. Many of those individuals came with their white masters fleeing the American Revolution, but many also came as free people. Slavery was legalized in 1709 and outlawed in 1834, at a time when Canada was under British rule. Although black people were invited to settle on Vancouver Island in 1859, segregated schools continued to exist in many parts of Canada until 1964. More historical details on people of African heritage in North America is provided in the *Handbook of Cultural Health Psychology* (Kazarian, 2001).

Black heterogeneity, difference, and ethnic classifications for people of African descent are often vaguely defined, and the concepts underlying them are poorly understood. Combining heterogeneous African populations under a single label such as "black" creates practical problems of comparability between places and times, and reinforces the simplistic notion that there is one fixed black identity, culture, politics, and social class. There is considerable diversity within and between populations of African descent, and this fact must be understood for research purposes, nourished, respected, and celebrated.

LATIN-AMERICAN PEOPLES

People of Latin-American heritage come from a variety of Latin countries and constitute many races and cultures. As an umbrella term, "Latino" identifies people who claim Spanish-speaking ancestry. Another term that is used is Hispanic. A list of core values and practices of Latino culture is provided in table 5.4.

The majority of people of Latin-American heritage are Roman Catholic. According to Gaines (1997), the "cult of masculinity" in Spanish culture and the Don Juan image of the Spanish man are based on mythology rather than reality. Gaines asserts that *la familia*, not machismo, is central to Latino culture. Familism has such a strong influence on interpersonal behaviours in Latino culture that "when the two sets of value [machismo and familism] come into conflict, familism tends to prevail" (p. 51). A more appropriate portrayal of the Latino male is that of *dignidad*—Spanish pride.

ASIAN PEOPLES

People of Asian heritage come from different countries—for example, China, Southeast Asia, Japan, Korea, the Pacific Islands, and the Philippines. Even though Asian people constitute a heterogeneous group, they share some core cultural values and practices, summarized in table 5.4. Confucianism, Buddhism, Hinduism, Taoism, and Islam have influenced these values and practices. Family and group loyalties are fundamental to Asians. The Asian self is seen as an extension of the family and the in-group. Family loyalty is practised through filial piety—children honouring their parents. The characterization of the Asian man as passive and the Asian woman as exotic is a stereotype.

ARAB PEOPLES

The fastest-growing visible minority groups in Canada are Arabs and Western Asians. The majority of people of Arab heritage living in Canada are Lebanese, Syrian, Egyptian, Chaldean/Iraqi, and Palestinian/Jordanian. Even though there are Christian Arabs, the majority are Muslim. The various Arab groups share the Arabic language, although there are some differences in vocabulary and accent.

Arab culture is a culture of honour and shame, and a self-construal that is interdependent. This influences and guides the individual behaviour of nuclear and extended family members. Female premarital sex and loss of virginity before marriage bring shame and dishonour to the family. Medical conditions may also be a source of shame for the family. As in many other cultures, mental illness may be concealed because of the shame its knowledge in the community may bring to the family and the potential limits it may place on the marriage opportunities of other family members. Arab culture also values the virtues of hospitality and generosity, in addition to feeling pride in their ethnic heritage and the historical contribution Arabs have made to civilization.

CULTURAL DIVERSITY BELIEFS AND PRACTICES: POLICE ABILITIES, KNOWLEDGE, AND SKILLS

Culture, race, and ethnicity affect individual values, practices, and codes of conduct. Diverse values and customs enrich the quality of life of a country, but also have the potential to be the source of conflict, misunderstanding, and violence.

In Canada, ethnocultural groups and their community leaders have the responsibility to respect others' rights and freedoms, live peacefully with members of other groups, recognize that there is one secular law for all, obey the law of the land, and protect the civil order of the nation. Conflict and misunderstanding are more likely in contexts where a "we are superior and they are inferior" ideology exists or where a system of different laws for different groups prevails. Ethnocultural groups in Canada and police services and agencies in the country need to recognize and sustain a core value that respects diversity—namely, **diversity equity**. Diversity equity means that, although different groups exist, there are no superior or inferior ones.

Police need to be vigilant in opposing distorted portrayals of ethnocultural groups and individuals. The demonization of Arabs generally and Arab communities in Western countries by some Canadians in the aftermath of 9/11 is illustrative. To such people, "Arab" and "Muslim Arab" have become synonymous with "terrorist," and the Arab–terrorist connection has been perpetuated on the grounds that some Arab communities and their leaders failed to express unequivocal condemnation of terrorism or were slow in making their declaration, or that some Muslims even reacted with jubilance to the 9/11 tragedy. Police need to remember that very few Arabs are fundamentalists, extremists, radicals, fascists, or terrorists and that terrorists are likely to defy demographic, racial, or ethnic profiles. They may spring out of all demographics—male and female, young and old, immigrants and citizens; and all colours and nationalities—African, Asian, European, Hispanic, and Middle Eastern. Colour-blind and democratic law enforcement is required to protect civil order and curb terrorist threats. All those who pose a legitimate terrorist threat or threat

diversity equity
equity based on belief that there are no superior or inferior cultural groups

TABLE 5.5   Dos and Don'ts of Policing Cultural Diversity

Dos

- Learn about the culture of people of diversity.

- Recognize that people of diversity are neither all saints nor all villains.

- Learn some helpful words and phrases in other languages.

- Focus on similarities among people as much as on differences.

- Be willing to work on the concerns of people of diversity.

- Recognize that you can learn a lot from people of diversity.

- Be empathic, respectful, honest, and patient with people from other cultures.

- Prevent conflict by establishing trust and good communication.

- Remember that one bad apple does not mean that all are rotten.

Don'ts

- Don't be judgmental and defensive.

- Don't blame all the problems of the world on people of diversity.

- Don't be afraid of making honest mistakes in communicating with people of diversity—no one is perfect, and they will understand.

to national security, regardless of their race, ethnicity, and religion, must be fair game for democratic policing measures, including screening, scrutiny, surveillance, and criminal prosecution. Symptomatic approaches to terrorist threats, however, may be limited in that they fail to eradicate the underlying causes of the problem. Sound police–community relations and mutually respectful and trusting attitudes and open communication are good ingredients for counter-terrorism.

Police should be neither complacent nor overzealous. Protection of civil order is an imperative. But communicating to ethnocultural groups and their leaders that police are committed to using security measures and practices that respect civil liberties is also an imperative. By disconnecting the association between terrorism and particular ethnic groups and by incorporating and maintaining a diversity equity core value, police can promote a world view that recognizes the humanity of people, nourishes the humanity of policing, and nurtures a climate of mutual trust that promotes a safe and a secure Canada. A list of dos and don'ts of policing ethnocultural groups is provided in table 5.5.

CHAPTER SUMMARY

This chapter has described some cultural groups in an attempt to promote awareness of diverse values, practices, and viewpoints. It is important to keep in mind that these groups actually represent a variety of cultures and ethnic origins, as well as individuals with personal beliefs and attitudes. Stereotyping people is a simplistic and lazy substitute for getting to know and understand them. Focusing on people's similarities instead of their differences can help in reducing conflict and misunderstanding. Establishing a mutually respectful and trusting relationship between law enforcement and cultural groups contributes to protection of civil order.

KEY TERMS

culture	low-context culture
ethnicity	high-context culture
race	collectivist culture
visible minority	individualist culture
achievement culture	independent self-construal
relationship culture	interdependent self-construal
tight culture	diversity equity
loose culture	

REFERENCES

Berry, J.W., & J.A. Laponce. (1994). Evaluating research on Canada's multiethnic and multicultural society. In J.W. Berry and J.A. Laponce (Eds.), *Ethnicity and culture in Canada* (pp. 3–16). Toronto: University of Toronto Press.

Blank, R., & S. Slipp. (1994). *Voices of diversity: Real people talk about problems and solutions in a workplace where everyone is not alike.* New York: American Management Association.

Bonnett, A. (2000). *Antiracism.* London: Routledge.

Brant, C.C. (1990). Native ethics and rules of behaviour. *Canadian Journal of Psychiatry* 35: 534–39.

Canadian Heritage. (2004). Canadian diversity: Respecting our differences. http://www.pch.gc.ca/progs/multi/respect_e.cfm.

Canadian Press. (2000, November 10). Escapee, 73, "armed and dangerous." *The London Free Press*, p. A8.

Employment and Immigration Canada. (1987). *Profiles of Canadian immigration.* Ottawa: Supply and Services Canada.

Gaines, S.O.J. (1997). *Culture, ethnicity, and personal relationship processes.* New York: Routledge.

Goodman, N.R. (1994). Cross-cultural training for the global executive. In R.W. Brislin and J. Yoshida (Eds.), *Improving intercultural interactions: Modules for cross-cultural training programs* (pp. 34–54). Thousand Oaks, CA: Sage.

Hall, E.T. (1976). *Beyond culture.* New York: Doubleday.

Hofstede, G. (1980). *Culture consequences: International differences in work related values.* Beverley Hills, CA: Sage.

Kallen, E. (2003). *Ethnicity and human rights in Canada: A human rights perspective on race, ethnicity, racism and systemic inequality.* New York: Oxford University Press.

Kazarian, S.S. (2001). Health issues in North American people of African heritage. In S.S. Kazarian & D.R. Evans (Eds.), *Handbook of cultural health psychology.* San Diego: Academic Press.

Kazarian, S.S., & Evans, D.R. (1998). Cultural clinical psychology. In S.S. Kazarian & D.R. Evans (Eds.), *Cultural clinical psychology: Theory, research and practice.* New York: Oxford University Press.

Lagasse, J.H. (1967). The two founding peoples. In Canada, Dominion Bureau of Statistics, *Canada one hundred, 1867–1967.* (pp. 74–81). Ottawa: Queen's Printer.

Lett, A.H. (1968). A look at others: Minority groups and police–community relations. In A.F. Brandstaller & L.A. Radelee (Eds.), *Police and community relations: A source book* (pp. 121–28). Beverley Hills, CA: Glencoe Press.

Linton, R. (1945). *The cultural background of psychology.* New York: Appleton-Century.

Lock, M. (1990). On being ethnic: The politics of identity breaking and making in Canada, or, *nevra* on Sunday. *Culture, Medicine, and Psychiatry* 14: 237–54.

Markus, H.R., & Kitayama, S. (1991). Culture and the self: Implications for cognition, emotion, and motivation. *Psychological Review* 98: 224–53.

Moynihan, D.P. (1993). *Pandaemonium: Ethnicity in international politics.* Oxford: Oxford University Press.

Race Relations Act 1976 (UK), c. 74.

Ripley, B. (2006, August 19). Terrorism defies comprehension, cure. *The London Free Press*, p. F5.

Statistics Canada. (2001). Canada's ethnocultural portrait: The changing mosaic, 2001 census. http://www.statcan.ca/menu-en.htm.

Triandis, H.C. (1990). Theoretical concepts that are applicable to the analysis of ethnocentrism. In R.W. Brislin (Ed.), *Applied cross-cultural psychology* (pp. 24–55). Newbury Park, CA: Sage.

Triandis, H.C. (1995). A theoretical framework for the study of diversity. In M.M. Chemers, S. Oskamp, & M.A. Costanza (Eds.), *Diversity in organizations: New perspectives for a changing workplace* (pp. 11–36). Thousand Oaks, CA: Sage.

Wheeler, W.B., & S.D. Becker. (1994). *Discovering the American past: A look at the evidence. Volume I to 1877.* Boston: Houghton Mifflin.

Winterdyk, J.A., & D.E. King (Eds.). (1999). *Diversity and criminal justice in Canada.* Toronto: Canadian Scholars' Press.

EXERCISES AND REVIEW
Personal Analysis

Read each statement and circle whether you agree or disagree with it.

1. Law enforcement agencies need to understand differences among cultures but not similarities.

   AGREE   DISAGREE

2. Teaching police about cultural similarities and differences is a waste of time.

   AGREE   DISAGREE

3. Cops have better things to do than listen to whining cultural groups.

   AGREE   DISAGREE

4. Police already know everything that needs to be known about cultures.

   AGREE   DISAGREE

5. Police have developed an aversion to some cultures that is difficult to change.

   AGREE   DISAGREE

6. Police will never get respect from some cultural groups no matter what they do.

   AGREE   DISAGREE

7. If police wait long enough, they will eventually see a cultureless society.

   AGREE   DISAGREE

8. Cultural groups need to learn as much about police culture as police need to learn about them.

   AGREE   DISAGREE

9. After everything is said and done, some cultures are far better than others.

   AGREE   DISAGREE

10. Ignorance of cultures is likely to breed contempt.

    AGREE   DISAGREE

SCORING: Give yourself one point each for agreeing with statements 8 and 10. Give yourself one point each for disagreeing with the remaining statements. Higher scores are likely to reflect more positive perceptions of the benefit of learning about other cultures. Compare your score with a classmate's and try to reconcile any differences in opinion.

Diversity IQ: Multiple Choice

Circle the best answer.

1. Which of the following is true about culture?

    a. it refers to a person's world view

    b. it refers to the transmission of biological characteristics

    c. it refers to just the concrete and tangible aspects of life

    d. all of the above

2. A police officer who refers to her Ukrainian heritage is identifying her

    a. race

    b. ethnic identity

    c. minority status

    d. none of the above

3. A police recruit from a collectivist culture is likely to value

    a. cooperation

    b. group decision-making

    c. strong identification with the police agency

    d. all of the above

4. A police recruit from an individualist culture is likely to value

    a. self-reliance

    b. competitiveness

    c. a direct approach to communication

    d. all of the above

5. A police officer from an achievement culture is likely to focus on

    a. family life

    b. work

    c. competition

    d. all of the above

6. In a low-context culture,

    a. time and schedules are unimportant

    b. verbal communication is direct and logical

    c. emotion conveys much of a spoken message

    d. words are not as important as the context of a message

7. In the aftermath of 9/11, Arabs

    a. have been demonized

    b. have been glorified

    c. have forfeited their citizenship

    d. all of the above

8. Treating certain groups of people as terrorists

    a. boosts their fragile ego

    b. does not help the cause of counterterrorism

    c. helps fight terrorism

    d. none of the above

9. Diversity equity

    a. is a belief that all people are the same

    b. promotes the differences among people

    c. rejects the idea that some groups of people are inferior or superior

    d. all of the above

10. When a police officer is shot and wounded, fellow officers feel a sense of concern and a need to stick together. This is a good example of the value of the

    a. extended family

    b. nuclear family

    c. polygamous family

    d. collectivist family

Diversity IQ: True or False?

_____ 1. The best way for a police officer to learn about cultures is to study each of them in detail for years.

_____ 2. People from one culture may feel superior to those from another culture.

_____ 3. A police recruit from an individualist culture who is paired with an officer from a collectivist culture is likely to face differences in world views.

_____ 4. Police culture is a low-context culture because of the way it uses language and its emphasis on the work schedule.

_____ 5. Individuals from collectivist cultures are likely to pursue individual goals and downplay group goals.

_____ 6. Collectivist cultures are community-minded.

_____ 7. Ethnicity is a person's identification with a national origin.

_____ 8. All people of any specific ethnic heritage are the same.

_____ 9. Poverty is the root cause of terrorism.

_____ 10. It is possible to be individualist in a collectivist culture, and vice versa.

Application Now

1. What implications does focusing on cultural differences rather than on similarities have for policing?

2. How would you go about involving police and the community to develop and implement policing approaches that are responsive to ethnic and racial groups?

Food for Thought

1. Police have a duty to serve and protect their communities. An important aspect of their duties in the aftermath of 9/11 is using individuals' personal details to pinpoint terror suspects. However, this practice may raise the ire of religious leaders who may question the legitimacy of law enforcement agents' singling out ordinary citizens or travellers who fit profiles similar to those who have carried out acts of terrorism or who have posed a threat to national security. In fact, religious leaders may warn that the targeting of those who look like terrorists could alienate these individuals and the communities to which they belong and make matters worse by creating a backlash. As a result, these individuals and their communities might respond by refusing to cooperate with police. How should police resolve this dilemma?

2. Police officers want to be respected not for their culture but for their abilities and professionalism. What moral dilemmas could police officers from, say, a European, Asian, or black culture encounter in dealing with co-workers or suspects from the same culture and those from other cultures?

    Own culture

    Other cultures

From Thought to Action

1. As a police officer, you will encounter people from many different cultural and racial groups. What reactions (thoughts, feelings, and actions) are you likely to have about the following individuals if you stop them for speeding?

    a. An Arab man

    b. A French man who speaks minimal English

    c. An Irish woman who looks intoxicated

    d. A Scot

e. A transsexual

f. A single white mother on welfare

g. A young black man in a brand new car

h. A Chinese man

     i. A lesbian holding hands with her lover

2. Identify factors that may contribute to your reactions to the people listed above.

3. Of the factors you identified, which provide a rational basis for your reactions and which provide an irrational basis for your reactions?

    Rational

    Irrational

4. What lesson can be learned from the above exercises?

5. Consider how the following factors may influence your reactions to individuals from various ethnic groups.

Your upbringing

Media portrayal of specific cultural or religious groups

Police culture

Past personal experience with individuals from specific religions

A person's appearance

A person's skin colour

The situation you and the other person may be in—for example, a traffic violation versus a domestic violence call

Your ability to "see" a person as a human being independent of his or her diversity

A person's core cultural values

6. a.   Identify the advantages and disadvantages of individualist and collectivist cultures.

Individualist culture

Advantages

Disadvantages

Collectivist culture

Advantages

Disadvantages

b. Which of the two cultural dimensions do you prefer, and why?

7. Newcomers tend to be vulnerable to victimization and may fear police because of experiences they have had with police corruption and brutality in their countries of origin. What would you do to encourage newcomer adherence to the law and cooperation with police when serious crimes occur in a neighbourhood or when police suspect terrorist plans?

8. Explain the behaviour of the police officer in the following scenario. Form groups and role-play the situation, then share your thoughts and feelings with the group.

    A police officer arrested two Muslim women who were wearing *hijabs* (veils) as they walked from a local mosque to a convenience store. The officer frisked the women, handcuffed them, and took them to the police station on the grounds that wearing a mask in public is against the law. The women were later released without charge.

9. Critique the list of dos and don'ts in table 5.5 (on p. 148). What do you think should be deleted from the list and what should be added?

Lessons from History

Lett (1968) identified Americans' prevailing views of cultural and religious groups in the 1950s. Match each culture with the stereotype that goes with it. (Answers are found on page 164.)

Cultural group		*Cultural stereotype*	
_____	1. Orientals	A.	shiftless and sex crazy
_____	2. Mexicans	B.	sly
_____	3. Puerto Ricans	C.	drunkards
_____	4. "Negroes"	D.	villains
_____	5. Jews	E.	pig-headed and belligerent
_____	6. Irish	F.	dirty and uncontrollable
_____	7. Germans	G.	grafters and racketeers
_____	8. Italians	H.	dishonest

a. How prevalent are these stereotypes today?

b. What effects do you think such negative views have on these groups' quality of life and on society generally?

c. What effects do you think such negative views of these groups have on policing?

The Great Debate

Several countries are following the lead of US President George W. Bush in fighting a war on terror. The war on terror is based on the premise that "terror is an enemy that requires fighting militarily." There is also a counternotion that "terror is not an enemy you can fight militarily," the implication being that a person full of enough hatred will use his suicide to end the lives of as many others as possible, no matter what (Ripley, 2006).

In groups, debate the notion that terror is an enemy one fights militarily. Have one group take one position and a second group take the opposite position. Follow the debate with a class discussion.

LESSONS FROM HISTORY KEY: 1. B   2. D   3. F   4. A   5. H   6. C   7. E   8. G

CHAPTER 6

Religious Diversity

CHAPTER OBJECTIVES

After completing this chapter, you should be able to:

- Explain the concept of religion.
- Recognize the multiple religious beliefs and practices in pluralistic societies.
- Discuss specific religious groups and their beliefs and practices.
- Analyze personal perspectives on religion.
- Use concepts of religious diversity to analyze and facilitate police–community interactions.

PREVIEW SCENARIO

"Young Muslims Worried, Frustrated in GTA," read the headline of the article written by Toronto Star staff reporter Surya Bhattacharya (2006) in the aftermath of "news of yet another series of arrests [in England] involving young Muslims" and a terrorist plot to explode at least 10 planes bound for the United States using sports drink containers and liquid explosives. The British arrests came two months after 17 men were also arrested on terrorism-related charges in Canada. US President George W. Bush commented that the arrests of the 24 Britons (22 men and two women between the ages of 17 and 35) and the dismantling of an attack that could have been more devastating than 9/11 served as a "stark reminder that this nation is at war with Islamic fascists who will use any means to destroy those of us who love freedom, to hurt our nation." On the other hand, Ziyaad Al-Khateeb, a University of Toronto (U of T) life sciences student, told Bhattacharya that he felt "sad, especially on a Friday, going to prayers," adding: "These people (extremists) never represent religion properly. Secondly, they're giving a bad image to the religion and, thirdly, that's how non-Muslims will view us now." Arsheen Devjee, a U of T student specializing in religion, indicated to Bhattacharya that the news evoked frustration and the feeling that "it's going to happen here." Ms. Devjee wondered what sort of frustration drives young Muslims to extremism, while Al-Khateeb believed that "if extremists went back and learned their religion from scratch,

165

such incidents would not occur." Others Bhattacharya (2006) interviewed expressed a "them-versus-us" mentality, in that they considered themselves mainstream or moderate Muslims and could not identify with the mindset of extremist or fundamentalist Muslims. Although the young Muslim interviewees described the personal worries of Muslims over showing their religious identity in the form of a *hijab* or *kufi* (Muslim skullcap) and fear of being told off in public or attacked verbally, they commented that Muslim parents were the most worried: "They tend to freak out when such news breaks out … . [T]hey worry, what if we're detained, harassed or arrested?" (Bhattacharya, 2006; Shephard, 2006)

INTRODUCTION

This chapter discusses the concept of religion, the beliefs and practices of a number of religious groups, and the experiences of Muslims, post-9/11, and the implications for enabling police to work better and smarter in protecting themselves and their fellow citizens. Canada is a multi-ethnic, multilingual, and multi-faith country. New immigrants to Canada have brought not only new cultures, ethnicities, and languages but also new faiths. In 2001, 43 percent of the population in Canada identified themselves as Roman Catholic, 29 percent as Protestant, 2 percent as Muslim, and 1 percent each as Buddhist, Hindu, or Sikh. The changing sources of immigrants have also contributed to shifts in the country's religious make-up such that there have been decreases in the last decade in the number of Canadians reporting Protestant and Catholic religious affiliations and substantial increases in the number of Canadians reporting the religions of Islam, Sikhism, and Buddhism (Statistics Canada, 2001).

WHAT IS RELIGION?

religion
a spiritual belief system

All humans have basic needs. **Religion** and spirituality identify ways of satisfying those needs. The spiritual needs identified by various religions and how they are satisfied vary. For example, Christianity identifies *sin* as a fundamental human issue and advocates salvation from sin. Buddhism, on the other hand, regards *ignorance* as the fundamental issue and prescribes enlightenment. Religions use sacred speech and narrative (myth, prayer, song), sacred acts and rituals, and sacred places for religious expression (Forman, 1993).

RELIGIOUS BELIEFS AND PRACTICES

religious beliefs
tenets of particular faiths

religious practices
concrete expressions of
religious beliefs

Religion plays a significant role in the lives of many people. Each religion has its own world view and concept of a higher power. Religions give individuals within a family of faith a common link to the past and the future (White, 1997). However, **religious beliefs** and **religious practices** in pluralistic societies have the potential to create divisiveness, animosity, and intolerance when ignorance, misunderstanding of religious doctrines, or differences in world views exist. For example, some

Americans interviewed by CNN after the terrorist attacks on the United States on September 11, 2001 believed that America needed to go into Iraq and turn all Muslims living in Iraq into good Christians in order for them to be saved. The same was often said of Canada's First Nations people by the colonizers, of blacks who were taken as slaves, and of most conquered or colonized people around the world. History is replete with examples of hegemonic Christianizing of a colonized and dominated people through the use of religion. Thus, the history of one's religious struggles against forms of domination will assist in a better understanding of the group's resistance, trust, and level of integration into mainstream society. To that end, gaining an understanding of the many religions and the beliefs and practices associated with them is an important step in appreciating religions and developing an attitude of acceptance and respect.

Needless to say, not everyone has a religion or believes in religion. For example, atheists profess no particular religion and do not believe in a higher power. Similarly, agnostics believe in the impossibility of knowing God or determining how the universe began. Atheists and agnostics have their own values and codes of ethical conduct. They deserve as much recognition, respect, and protection as those with firm religious beliefs and practices.

The religions that are discussed in this chapter are listed in table 6.1. Of course, all of the religions in the world cannot be discussed in a single chapter. Those that have been included here should not be seen as more significant or superior to those religions not discussed in the chapter, and those that are excluded should not be seen as insignificant or inferior.

Bahá'í Faith: Embracing All Peoples

Bahá'u'lláh is the founder of the Bahá'í Faith, which is associated with the trinity of oneness of God, oneness of religion, and oneness of humanity. A Bahá'í is a follower of Bahá'u'lláh. This religion teaches that there is only one God; that there is only one religion, which is revealed progressively by God; and that all people are equal

TABLE 6.1   Some Religions of the World

Religion	Number of believers in the world
Bahá'í Faith	5 to 6 million
Buddhism	376 million
Christian Science	500,000
Christianity	2.1 billion
Hinduism	1 billion
Islam	1.3 billion
Jehovah's Witnesses	> 12 million
Judaism	14 million
Shintoism	> 100 million
Sikhism	23 million
Taoism	not available
Wicca	> 100,000

in the sight of God. The Bahá'í Faith endorses several other basic principles and practices (Bahá'í Faith, 2007):

- unity (oneness) of humankind;

- unity in the foundation of all religions, the great religions expressing a single divine plan;

- religion as the source of unity;

- religion as a progressive and evolutionary process;

- compatibility of science and religion;

- independent investigation of truth;

- equality of men and women;

- elimination of all forms of prejudice;

- universal peace;

- universal education;

- a universal auxiliary language—an international language everyone learns in addition to his or her mother tongue;

- spiritual solutions to economic problems; and

- an international tribunal.

The Bahá'í do not have a clergy. They consider the family the foundation of human society, marriage a means for the spiritual development of both partners, and morality as a direct influence on spiritual development and happiness. In addition to the Ten Commandments (see table 6.3), the moral code of the Bahá'í Faith dictates the following practices:

- avoiding backbiting and gossip, promiscuity, gambling, and alcohol and drug use;

- daily prayer and reading of holy writings;

- fasting;

- observing Bahá'í holidays;

- maintaining chastity before marriage;

- teaching the cause of God;

- contributing to the Bahá'í Fund, which supports the work of the Faith;

- considering work a form of worship; and

- respecting and obeying the government of the land.

Buddhism: Seeking Enlightenment

In 2001, 300,300 Canadians identified themselves as Buddhists. Buddhism was founded in northern India by the ascetic Siddhartha Gautama (566–480 BCE), who became Buddha, "the enlightened one." Gautama was from an aristocratic family but discovered suffering and left home to search for redemption from it. He saw the truth of salvation as he sat under a tree in deep meditation.

Buddhism is not a religion in the Western sense. Buddhists do not worship a creator God. Instead, they follow a path of practice and spiritual development that aims at the full development and freedom of body, speech, and mind and that leads to the personal qualities of awareness, kindness, and wisdom; to insight into the true nature of life; and ultimately to Enlightenment or Buddhahood. The three basic tenets of Buddhist teaching are *impermanence* (nothing is fixed or permanent), *actions have consequences*, and *change is possible*. There are different types or levels of Buddhism, but all invoke non-violence, lack of dogma, tolerance of differences, and the practice of meditation.

Four Noble Truths are associated with Buddhism (Boeree, 2000):

1. Suffering is inherent in life.

2. Attachment to things and craving sensual pleasures are cause for suffering.

3. Release from suffering (Nirvana) is achieved by eliminating selfish, sensual, and material desires.

4. There is an Eightfold Path to achieve Nirvana:

    a. right view—understanding the Four Noble Truths;

    b. right aspiration—sincerely wanting to overcome attachment;

    c. right speech—avoiding slander and gossip;

    d. right action—conducting oneself morally;

    e. right livelihood—doing work that harms no one;

    f. right effort—focusing on good thoughts and nurturing good qualities;

    g. right mindfulness—integrating thoughts, body, and feelings to overcome desire; and

    h. right concentration—disciplining the mind through meditation.

The Four Noble Truths and the Eightfold Path translate into five rules of Buddhist living:

1. Avoid harm and be kind.

2. Avoid taking what is not given and be generous.

3. Avoid sexual misconduct and excess and be content.

4. Avoid false speech and be truthful.

5. Abstain from intoxicants and be aware.

The Buddhist moral code forbids killing, stealing, lying, and sexual promiscuity. In marital relationships, husbands are expected to be respectful, faithful, and supportive of their wives. Wives are expected to show diligence, hospitality to relatives, and faithfulness to their husbands.

Christian Science: Healing Through Divine Laws

Christian Science aims to save the universe from evil and to heal disease by spiritual means alone. It is based on the words and works of Jesus Christ, draws its authority from the Bible, and follows the teachings of its founder, Mary Baker Eddy. Eddy's personal experience with spiritual healing through divine laws led to her discovery of the Science of Christianity that Jesus lived and taught. In 1875, she wrote and published *Science and Health with Key to the Scriptures*, which is used as a textbook and to prepare Christian Science practitioners for ministering Christian healing.

Christian Scientists subscribe to the belief that moral, spiritual, and physical healing can occur through *divine laws*—that is, through scientific prayer, or spiritual communion with God. Scientific prayer recognizes an ill person's direct access to God's love. Scientific prayer knows God, or divine Mind, as the only healer. It brings the transforming action of the Christ, the idea of divine Love, to the ill person's consciousness. The ill person's transformed or spiritualized thought changes his or her condition.

Christian Science healing is a specific treatment that is distinct from faith healing, psychotherapy, Scientology, and positive thinking. Hypnotism, spiritualism, and suggestion are not part of Christian Science healing, nor are blind faith or control of one human mind over another. No formulas, chants, rituals, esoteric practices, or secret writings are associated with Christian Science healing (First Church of Christ, Scientist, 2001).

While some authoritative sources have pointed out that some Christian Scientists reject medical treatment from physicians and hospitals (for example, White, 1997), the Christian Science community refers to the freedom of choice of its members in caring for themselves and their families, "just as anyone who normally resorts to medical care could choose to use spiritual means" (Church of Christ, Scientist, 2001). More specifically, Christian Science takes the position that those who "depart from the use of Christian Science by choosing some other kind of treatment" are "neither condemned by the Church nor dropped from membership."

Christian Science teaches strict adherence to the moral code of the Ten Commandments (see table 6.3) and Christ's Sermon on the Mount. The sermon speaks to seeking spirituality; being mild-tempered, peaceable, merciful, and a lover of righteousness; loving those who are disliked; giving to the needy; being non-judgmental; and treating others as one would like to be treated. The sermon also condemns murder, being wrathful with others, adultery, lustful thoughts, and irresponsible divorce actions that break up homes and victimize children.

Christianity: Love Your Neighbour

Christianity is the most popular religion in the world. About 33 percent of the world's population is Christian. Christianity became a moral force in the first century CE.

Jesus of Nazareth is the central figure in Christianity. The basic Christian beliefs are stated in the Nicene Creed. Christians believe in one God; in one Lord, Jesus Christ, the son of God and saviour whose birth, death, and resurrection provide hope for eternal life with God; and in the Holy Spirit. The principle of love ("love your neighbour as yourself") represents the fundamental ethical instruction for

Christians. Christians hold children in high regard and are obligated to support their church and to give to the poor.

A number of branches of Christianity date back to Christ's disciples (for example, Catholic and Orthodox). The Roman Catholic Church is the largest and most universal. In 2001, 43 percent of Canadians identified themselves with the Roman Catholic Church. The head of the Catholic Church is the Pope (Latin for "father") whose pronouncements are considered infallible. The Catholic Church opposes birth control, abortion, and the ordination of women.

In 2001, Protestant denominations made up 29 percent of the Canadian population. Martin Luther (1483–1546), a German monk and reformer, sparked a major schism in the Catholic Church called the Protestant Reformation. He advanced the ideas that the Bible is the only rule of faith and practice and that ordinary Christians are competent to profess their faith without adhering to the proclamations of popes. Luther's reformist movement resulted in the establishment of non-Catholic sects. Today, there are over 1,000 Christian denominations, which are often categorized into conservative, mainline, and liberal groups.

Hinduism: Museum of Religions

In 2001, 297,200 Canadians identified themselves as Hindu. *Hindu* is the Persian word for India. India and the Ganges River make up the sacred geography of Hinduism. Hindus believe that God lives on the Ganges (Lawrence, 2000). Hinduism is called a "museum of religions" because of the immense diversity of its beliefs and practices. There is no specific founder or holy book that is Hinduism's basic scriptural guide.

Hinduism has four primary denominations: Saivism, Vaishnavism, Shaktism, and Smartism. Even though all of the denominations rely on the Vedas—the most sacred books of Hinduism—as scriptural authority, they hold divergent beliefs and are considered independent religions. Nevertheless, all four denominations share beliefs in dharma, all-pervasive divinity, one supreme being that is manifested in many deities (gods and goddesses), reincarnation, sacraments, the guru tradition, and yoga.

Dharma is a central concept in Hinduism. It refers to a way of life, the ritualization of daily life, or self-actualization.

No one particular deity is central to Hinduism. Hindus may worship a particular god (for example, Krishna) or goddess; a spirit, trees, and animals; or a Supreme Spirit. Of all the deities, Brahma, Vishnu, and Shiva are the most significant. Brahma is the creator of the universe and life; Vishnu the preserver of life, the guide of the cycle of birth and rebirth, and saviour of the world from evil; and Shiva the destroyer of all evil.

Reincarnation is a process of many births to attain knowledge and gain freedom from the cycle of reincarnation. In this process, *kharma* is resolved through successive lives. Kharma is the law of cause and effect, and Hindus believe that each person creates a personal destiny through his or her thoughts, words, and actions.

Gurus are teachers with superior spiritual knowledge, and they are considered essential guides for attaining that knowledge.

The word "yoga" means union, and it is a philosophy and discipline whose purpose is to unite the person's consciousness with divine consciousness. There are several levels, or types, of yoga (Himalayan Academy, 2000).

The following are other basic principles of Hinduism (Himalayan Academy, 2000):

- Spiritual transformation comes from personal discipline, good conduct, and meditation.

- All life is sacred, so individuals must practise non-injury.

- No particular religion is above all others.

Islam: There Is No God but God

Islam is one of the fastest-growing faiths in North America, Europe, and the Caribbean. In Canada, the Muslim population more than doubled in the decade between 1991 and 2001 such that 579,200 people identified themselves as Muslims in 2001 (Statistics Canada, 2001).

Like Judaism and Christianity, Islam is also a one God religion and the second most popular religion in the world. It may become the dominant religion of the world during the 21st century. Islam is a global faith that spans diverse races, nationalities, and cultures (Abu-Harb, 2001). One out of five people in the world is a Muslim.

In Arabic, *Islam* means achieving peace personally and spiritually through submission (surrender, obedience) to Allah (God) and commitment to His guidance. A *Muslim* is a person who has surrendered to the will of God. A person becomes a Muslim by believing and proclaiming that "There is none worthy of worship except God," and that "Muhammad is the Messenger of God." Muslims do not worship the Prophet Muhammad, but follow his teachings.

The *Qur'an* ("recitation") is the holy text of Islam. Muslims believe that the Qur'an contains the words of God communicated to Muhammad through the archangel Gabriel. They also believe that the Qur'an completes the Jewish and Christian scriptures rather than contradicts either.

Belief in fate is seen in the Islamic doctrine of predestination ("Nothing will befall us but what God has written down for us"). However, the Islamic doctrine of the hereafter, with its stress on reward and punishment, also requires that people assume responsibility for their deeds.

The two main Islamic schools of thought are Sunni and Shiite, but there are other schools as well, including Sufi, Ismaili, and Druze. The five basic religious practices of Islam are listed in table 6.2.

Islam is not just a religion; it is a way of life. There is no division between the secular and the sacred for Muslims; law is not separate from religion. Religious law, *fiqh*, relies on the following sources: the Qur'an, Muhammad's way of life, oral traditions, reasoning, and community consensus. Proper food is known as *halal*. Muslims are prohibited from eating pork and consuming blood, alcohol, and animals that have not been slaughtered properly or those that have died naturally. Parents are highly respected, and caring for them in old age is seen as an honour and a blessing. Consequently, institutional homes for the elderly are virtually unknown in the Muslim world.

The Muslim community identifies the following myths associated with Islam:

TABLE 6.2 The Five Pillars: Basic Religious Practices in Islam

Iman (faith)	*Iman* signifies the belief that the sole purpose of life is to serve and obey God through the teachings and practices of Muhammad. Muslims are required to declare their faith by bearing witness that there is no God but Allah and that Muhammad is his final messenger.
Salat (prayer)	Muslims are required to pray five times a day, at dawn, noon, afternoon, evening, and night.
Zakat (alms giving)	A certain percentage of earnings is expected to go to the poor or needy. This obligation is based on the belief that everything belongs to Allah.
Siyam (fasting)	Fasting is beneficial for health, self-purification, and self-restraint; it reminds Muslims of their purpose in life and promotes empathy for poor and hungry people. All adult Muslims are expected to fast (abstain from food, drink, and sexual relations) from sunrise to sunset during the holy month of Ramadan.
Hajj (pilgrimage)	Adult Muslims with the physical and financial means are required to make at least one pilgrimage to Mecca (in Saudi Arabia), the birthplace of Islam, during the 12th month of the Islamic calendar.

- *Muslims are a threat to the "new world order." The Western media's use of such terms as jihad (Holy War), Islamic fundamentalism, Islamic terrorism, fascist, and Islamic militia reflect stereotypes.* By all accounts, fundamentalist or extremist Muslims constitute a very small percentage of Muslims around the world.

- *The "sword of Islam" means forcing people to accept Islam.* Islam implores people to be peaceful and submit to the will of Allah even though the religion has been misconstrued by extremists to advance holy wars, suicide bombings, and acts of terror.

- *Muhammad is God's only messenger.* In fact, Jesus is held in high esteem by Muslims.

- *The God worshipped by Muslims is separate from the God of the Jews and Christians.* Muslims call God "Allah," which is the literal translation of the word God into Arabic, the universal language of Islam. It is noted that Christian Arabs also call God Allah.

- *All Arabs are Muslims.* Not all Arabs are Muslim as there are also Christian Arabs. Although Arabs make up about 20 percent of the Muslim world, they are considered the keepers of Islam, because the Qur'an is written in Arabic and prayers are performed in the Arabic language.

- *Islam oppresses women.* Even though, according to the *Qur'an*, men and women are equal before God and their roles are complementary, the West associates Islam with the subordination of women. According to Muslim theologians, governments oppress women, not Islam.

Jehovah's Witnesses: Spreading the Word

Jehovah's Witnesses are recognized by their religious activity of going from house to house or standing on the streets with Bibles, Bible literature, and *Watchtower* and *Awake!* magazines. This religion originated in the United States, as did its founder, Charles Taze Russell (1852–1916). Jehovah's Witnesses have published and use their own version of the Bible known as the *New World Translation of the Holy Scriptures*. They have elders but no clergy. The following are basic beliefs and practices of Jehovah's Witnesses (Watch Tower Bible and Tract Society of Pennsylvania, 2001):

- There is only one God, Jehovah. Jesus is Jehovah's son and inferior to Him.

- The Bible is Jehovah's word and is the truth.

- The end of the world is imminent. God's Kingdom will be ushered in when the wicked are destroyed in the battle of Armageddon, God's war to end wickedness. Armageddon will restore paradise, purify the world, establish God's Kingdom on earth for 1,000 years, and destroy Satan, his demon forces, and all rebels against God.

- Accepting blood orally or intravenously violates God's divine law to "abstain from blood." So, devout Jehovah's Witnesses refuse to accept blood transfusions.

- The Memorial of Christ's Death is recognized at Passover as the only holiday that requires celebration. Other holidays are worldly or pagan.

- Christians must keep separate from the world. Jehovah's Witnesses dissociate themselves from politics because they regard the world as being under Satan's control, refusing formal allegiance to political systems and interpreting all pledges of allegiance to national emblems as idolatry. Jehovah's Witnesses do not run for public office, join the military, or vote in elections.

- Humanity was created, it did not evolve.

- Spiritual cleanliness, moral cleanliness, mental cleanliness, physical cleanliness, and clean speech must be maintained. The Bible teaches people to respect marriage, to raise children with the right principles, and to emphasize the importance of the family.

- Christians must publicly testify to spiritual truth. Jehovah's Witnesses assert that the more individuals and families they influence to live by Christian principles, the less crime, delinquency, and immorality will exist in society.

Judaism: First Monotheistic Religion

Judaism is about God, the *Torah*, and Israel. As a way of life, Judaism describes the relationship between God and the Jewish nation and their mutual obligations. The Hebrew Bible is called the *Tanach*. It consists of the *Torah* ("teaching"), the *Neviim* (prophets), and the *Ketuvim* (writings, or wisdom literature). As the central symbol of Judaism, the *Torah* contains within it the 613 *mitzvot* (plural of *mitzvah*, commandments or divine rules of conduct) that God gave to the Jewish people. Ten of those *mitzvot*, the Ten Commandments, are listed in table 6.3.

TABLE 6.3 The Ten Commandments

1. I the Lord am your God. … You shall have no other gods beside Me.
2. You shall not make for yourself a sculptured image. … You shall not bow down to them or serve them.
3. You shall not take in vain the name of the Lord your God.
4. Remember the Sabbath day and keep it holy.
5. Honour your father and your mother.
6. You shall not murder.
7. You shall not commit adultery.
8. You shall not steal.
9. You shall not bear false witness against your neighbour.
10. You shall not covet.

Several principles of faith are associated with this religion:

- God exists.
- God is one and unique, incorporeal, eternal, knower of the thoughts and deeds of persons, and rewarder of the good and punisher of the wicked.
- Prayer is directed to God alone and to no other. Even in prayer, Jews do not address God by name because naming God is an act of idolatry, which the Torah prohibits (Lawrence, 2000).
- Moses's prophecies and the words of the prophets are true.
- The written *Torah* and the oral *Torah* (teachings contained in the *Talmud* and other writings) were given to Moses (the greatest of the prophets), and there will be no other *Torah*. The *Talmud* ("study") contains commentaries on and interpretations of Jewish law, in addition to proverbs and parables.
- The Messiah will come, and the dead will be resurrected.

Judaism is described as a set of rules and practices known as *halakhah*, which means law, or "the path that one walks." Observing *halakhah* is believed to support spirituality in life. *Halakhah* consists of the 613 *mitzvot*, laws instituted by the rabbis (teachers) and long-standing customs. Needless to say, *halakhah* touches on every aspect of life, including relations to God, the *Torah*, other people, and animals; clothing; prayers and blessings; dietary law (*kashrut*); marriage, divorce, family, and sexual relations; and criminal law. Nevertheless, observing Jewish law is subordinate to preserving life. Jews live by the commandments, they don't die by them (Krauthammer, 2000). Food must be *kosher*. Pork is prohibited, as are all animals that do not chew their cud, wild birds, insects, and shellfish. Bestiality, cross-dressing, incest, and sodomy are prohibited. Women are highly regarded, but certain restrictions on women apply in strict Jewish communities. The equal status of women to men in Judaism is supported by the view that God has no body and gender, and has both masculine and feminine qualities.

Four major movements or groups in Judaism follow:

- *Orthodox Judaism* views the *halakhah* as binding on Jews. Because God gave the *Torah* to Moses, its 613 *mitzvot* are divine and binding on all Jews. Of the four major movements, Orthodox Judaism is the most traditional. Men and women sit separately to worship and women are not ordained as rabbis.

- *Conservative Judaism* views *halakhah* as binding on Jews, but believes in the evolutionary nature of the Torah. Consequently, conservative Jews change religious rules and practices over time. Conservative Judaism allows its members to ride in a car to attend service on Shabbat (the day of rest, Saturday), permits the ordination of women as rabbis, and allows men and women to sit together during worship in Conservative synagogues. On the other hand, Conservative rabbis are unlikely to perform or attend a marriage between a Jew and an unconverted non-Jew.

- *Reform Judaism* is a liberal religious movement that views Jewish Law as non-binding. It allows individual autonomy and choice on the personal meaningfulness of religious laws.

- *Reconstructionist Judaism* views Judaism as a civilization. It does not view Jews as the chosen people and does not consider Jewish law to be binding.

Shintoism: The Way of the Gods

Shintoism is an ancient religion of Japan. Historically, it was the state religion of Japan. Today it has 13 denominations.

Shinto means "way of the *kami*." *Kami* are "the sacred spirits that exist both in the celestial realm and in nature and human beings" (White, 1997, p. 98). *Kami* is also translated as "God" or "divinity." Shintoism is an animistic religion that sees the sacred in all things, including animals and plants, trees and mountains, and so on. Human ancestors are also held in high regard. Basically, all forms of life are celebrated in Shinto, as is the connection among gods, people, and the world.

Shintoism has no written scriptures, formal teachings or dogma, or group worship. Instead, small shrines believed to be the homes of the *kami* are places for individual worship. Shinto festivals and rituals replace the sermons and study of scripture that characterize other religions. There are three elements of Shinto worship:

- purification, usually with water;

- offerings to the *kami*, usually money or food; and

- prayer or petition (a request for something).

Shintoism supports attitudes of respect for life, appreciation of beauty, and love of purity and simplicity (Watt, 1982).

Sikhism: Religion of Disciples

In 2001, 278,400 Canadians identified themselves as Sikhs. Sikhism is the religion of the state of Punjab in northern India. In Punjabi, *Sikh* means disciple or learner. Sikhs believe in human unity and equality of the sexes. They are anti-class and strive to eliminate all prejudices based on race, colour, and religion.

Sikhism was founded by Guru Nanak in 1469, who was succeeded by nine more gurus (teachers or authorities). The last one, Guru Gobind Singh, appointed as his successor the Sikh holy book the *Guru Granth Sahib*, which contains the writings of all 10 gurus. These scriptures are unique in being the head of the Sikh religion (Brar, 1998a). There is no clergy in Sikhism. Table 6.4 lists the five principles of faith, five stages of spiritual development, five virtues, and five vices associated with Sikhism.

Khalsas are Sikhs who have gone through a special ceremony to dedicate themselves to the principles of Sikhism. The word "Khalsa" means pure. Sikhs are expected to be Khalsas or working toward becoming Khalsas. Khalsas must wear five articles of faith (Brar, 1998b):

- *Kesh:* Uncut hair, symbol of spirituality and dedication. Sikh men must wear a turban, a symbol of royalty and dignity; it is optional for Sikh women. The turban cannot be covered by anything else and cannot be replaced with a hat.

- *Kangha:* Comb, symbol of cleanliness and discipline.

- *Kara:* Steel bracelet, to remind its wearer to show restraint.

- *Kachha:* Drawers, symbol of self-control and chastity.

- *Kirpan:* Ceremonial sword, symbol of dignity and the Sikh struggle against injustice. The sword is a religious symbol only and is never used as a weapon.

TABLE 6.4   Doctrines of Sikhism

Principles of faith	Stages of spiritual development
Human equality	Duty
Worship of God	Knowledge
Charity for the poor	Effort
Dignity of work	Grace
Service to others	Truth

Virtues	Vices
Faith	Lust
Truth	Greed
Compassion	Materialism
Patience	Conceit
Self-control	Anger

Taoism: Universal Energy in Balance

Taoism is China's oldest religion, dating back to 206 BCE. It is believed that Lao Tzu, who wrote the *Tao Te Ching*, founded this religion. The word "Tao" comes from a Chinese word for "the way." Taoism is a philosophy of life with great emphasis on non-aggression, non-competition, balance, the pursuit of health, and physical immortality. Its influence can be seen in such practices as acupuncture, Chinese herbal medicine, meditation, and the martial arts.

Until the 20th century, Taoism was the state religion of China. But from 1911 on, because of political upheaval and the growth of Confucianism and Buddhism in China, Taoism began to wane. During the Chinese communist years that began in 1949, when religion was banned, many Taoist monks were imprisoned or killed and Taoist temples were destroyed. This religion almost died out entirely, but it has been enjoying a resurgence since the 1980s (Centre of Traditional Taoist Society, 1999).

Taoists believe that Tao is an energy force that flows through all life. The goal of life is harmony between the individual and this universal energy.

The ancient yin and yang symbol represents Tao. Yin is the dark side and yang is the light side. The two sides symbolize pairs of opposites: good and evil, feminine and masculine, and so on. Taoists believe that yin and yang must be in balance in people. This balance is achieved through mental, physical, and spiritual health. Illness is believed to be caused by a lack of balance in the body's energy (chi). Practices such as meditation and Tai Chi help to restore the balance (Ontario Consultants on Religious Tolerance, 2000).

Wicca: Harm None

The Wicca religion's belief system and way of life date back to Druidic nature worship practices in Ireland, Scotland, and Wales and tribal peoples in other parts of the world. The repeal of the anti-witchcraft laws in Britain in 1951 helped to revive interest in the old religion. Gerald B. Gardner, considered the grandfather of Wicca, declared himself a witch in England after the repeal. Two of his students, Raymond and Rosemary Buckland, emigrated to the United States in 1962 and began teaching Gardnerian witchcraft. Wiccan worship groups, known as covens, sprang up gradually in various states and Canada.

The ethical and moral code of Wicca is based on three main tenets: Wiccan Rede (pronounced "reed"), the Law of Three, and the Golden Rule. The Wiccan Rede dictates that a Wiccan can do whatever he or she wants as long as it harms nothing, no one, or oneself. The Law of Three states, "Whatever you do will return to you three-fold." For example, a Wiccan who casts a bad spell will receive three spells as powerful as the cast spell. Similarly, a Wiccan who does a good deed will receive three good deeds in return.

The Golden Rule states, "Do unto others as you would have them do unto you." It ensures that Wiccans take responsibility for their actions and the consequences rather than blaming them on others.

RELIGIOUS BELIEFS AND PRACTICES POST-9/11

The 9/11 terrorist attacks on the United States, the suicide bombings and the killing of innocent people in several cities, including London in 2005 and Madrid in 2004, the riots by unemployed mostly Muslim youth in France in 2005, the rage ignited by the Danish cartoons of the Prophet Muhammad in 2005, and a host of other international events (for example, the war in Iraq) have invoked two mutually antagonistic worldviews—Westerners perceiving Muslims as medieval and their religion as fascist, and Muslims depicting Westerners as modern Crusaders, and America and the fundamentalist Christian Church as the devil. These disparate worldviews have also evoked in the West a revival of interest in the Muslim religion itself—whether it is a violent or a peaceful religion—and intensive soul-searching over a host of related issues including the process of nation building, the meaning of citizenship, the impossibility of integration of certain ethnocultural and religious groups to host cultures, immigration policies regarding preferred and non-preferred immigrants, and national security. More specifically, the West has been preoccupied with the possibility that growing Islamic identity is a barrier to Muslim integration in host counties; that Islam is a threat to Western democracies, that the Islamic faith is antagonistic to a peaceful culture and is increasingly being offered as a licence to kill by Islamic leaders in *madrassahs* (religious schools), and that the war on terror and the ideal of the democratization of non-democratic countries will lead to world peace.

The Pew Research Center, as part of its Global Attitude Project for 2006, has published editorials and commentaries, and conducted extensive international surveys on these issues. The Pew survey involved 14,000 people in 13 nations, focusing on Muslim and Western perceptions, the tensions between religious identity and national identity, and the ideals of a peace culture, as opposed to a war culture (Bortin, 2006; Rampe, 2006). The international surveys found that "Westerners and Muslims around the world have radically different views of world events, and each group tends to view the other as violent, intolerant and lacking respect for women" (Bortin, 2006, p. 2). The less-than-ideal relationship between Muslims and the West was attributed to a host of factors including 9/11; Al-Qaida being seen as representative of Islam; America's war on terror being seen as a war on Islam; the labelling of Muslims as fundamentalists and terrorists and the use of these labels as an excuse to persecute Muslims; the West connecting Islam to terrorism; the Israeli–Palestinian conflict; perceived Western bias toward Israel (a friend of the Jew is an enemy in the eyes of most fundamentalist Muslims); the perception that the West uses a double standard on terrorism; and the US-led war in Iraq. Muslims tend to blame the poor relationship between Muslims and the West on the foreign policies of the West, particularly in the Middle East, and the participation of Western nations in the fight against the Taliban in Afghanistan and the war in Iraq, and corruption among Arab governments, whereas Western people attribute the less-than-ideal relationship to Islamic fundamentalism and Islamist militants, inadequate education, and lack of democracy.

In relation to the tension between confessional identity and citizenry, the Pew survey showed that 81 percent of Muslims in Britain, 69 percent in Spain, 66 percent in Germany and 46 percent in France see themselves as Muslims first and as citizens of their country second.

In relation to the ideal of a peace culture, the Pew survey reported varying but sizable support for suicide bombings by Muslims in the countries surveyed. Rates of support for suicide bombings ranged from 17 percent in Turkey to 31 percent in Pakistan.

RELIGIOUS BELIEFS AND PRACTICES: POLICE ABILITIES, KNOWLEDGE, AND SKILLS

Police need to recognize the role that religious beliefs and practices play in their lives and those of others. Police may be involved in conflicts that have religious overtones, and that have the potential to become or be seen as racist because of the manner in which they are handled. Religious literacy can assist them in dealing with the issues that underlie these conflicts, engaging in effective community policing, fostering positive police–community relations, communicating effectively, and resolving conflicts successfully.

The religious group that is perceived to present the greatest challenge to policing in the post-9/11 environment are Muslims and by association the Arab and Muslim community. Law enforcement agencies need to know the dynamics of the relationship between Muslims and the host cultures that police services represent. They also need to de-homogenize the Muslim people and religion in relation to terrorism and divorce the concept of Islam from terrorism and suicide bombing. To this end, the racial profiling of all Arabs and Muslims as terrorists or a threat to national security is equally important to cease, in order to build positive and meaningful community relations. There are Muslim terrorists but very few Muslims and Arabs are terrorists. Muslims themselves see a struggle within Islam between moderates and radicals. Law enforcement agencies also need to recognize that the mistreatment of Muslims fuels anti-police sentiment in the Muslim community and undermines the efforts of law enforcement to fight terrorism and promote the idea of a peaceful culture. The case of Maher Arar is instructive in this regard. Arar, a Muslim Canadian, was en route to Canada from a family visit abroad when he was arrested in the United States on the basis of faulty intelligence information from Canada. He was subsequently returned to Syria, his country of origin, and tortured on suspicion of terrorist ties. This case invokes human rights issues, provokes anger in the community, and erodes trust between state and citizen. A state that is against its citizens fails to inspire attachment and commitment, resulting in alienation and lack of trust. A state that is against its citizens is not worth defending or dying for.

Reaching Muslims in the post-9/11 climate and dialoguing with Muslim communities is both a challenging task and a duty. Religious beliefs and practices contribute to the cultural values and the moral code and social conduct of individuals, as do the perceptions of religious groups of host cultures and the institutions that represent them. Police may find the beliefs and practices of various religions puzzling or even abhorrent. Such reactions are normal, but labelling religious beliefs and practices as primitive or savage is unproductive. Similarly, officers who cling to religious prejudices and allow them to cloud their judgment fail to uphold their responsibility to treat all groups fairly. Finally, national and international strategies for intelligence gathering are important, as are cutting-edge technologies applied to border security and counterterrorism. Equally important, however, are efforts to establish, re-establish, and enhance trust between law enforcement and cultural and religious

TABLE 6.5   Dos and Don'ts of Policing Religious Diversity

Dos	Don'ts
■ Value the religions of your country.	■ Don't be a religious illiterate.
■ Learn about religious beliefs, practices, rituals, laws, and holidays.	■ Don't believe all media portrayals of religions.
■ Recognize that the roles of men and women may be different in different religions.	■ Don't judge other religions as primitive, ungodly, or evil.
■ Recognize that in some households it is expected that you remove your shoes when you enter a home (for example, Hindus, Japanese) in all seasons.	■ Don't greet everyone by shaking hands with them; wait to see if a hand is offered.
■ Recognize that shaking hands, kissing, or touching may be considered inappropriate in some religions or in certain situations (for example, aboriginal religions, Buddhism, Anabaptism, Islam, Orthodox Judaism).	■ Don't offend or be offended by diverse religious beliefs and practices.
■ Endorse a civil society that is based on principles of citizenship and equality rather than confessionalism.	■ Don't use religion as the only filter through which you view others.
■ Raise youth awareness on the rule of law, pluralism, human rights, democracy, and a culture of peace.	■ Don't treat the symptoms of terrorism; consider its root causes
■ Dispel the myth that all Muslims are terrorists.	

communities, particularly the Muslim community, as a strategic approach to democratic community policing and protection of civil order (Ewatski, 2006). Police who are dedicated to their profession transcend cultural and religious differences and serve and protect members of all religions and cultures indiscriminately without compromising their mandate to serve and protect. A list of dos and don'ts of policing religious diversity is provided in table 6.5.

CHAPTER SUMMARY

Pluralistic societies include many religious beliefs and practices. These beliefs and practices may be at odds with those of individual police officers, different religious groups not from the dominant culture, or the host culture. An understanding of and respect for different religions, a willingness to respond to religious conflict with a view to effective conflict resolution, and a consideration of proactive approaches to prevent religious conflict and minimize, if not eliminate, the threatening forces of terrorism are important for police credibility and safety, and the ideal of a peaceful culture. Involving religious leaders and those who understand the religious group in question as experts in solving and addressing conflicts that have religious overtones will assist in reducing conflict and in building or restoring the trust of religious groups. Furthermore, employing alternative dispute resolution, a practice adopted by many religious groups to solve conflicts among their members, can also be an effective tool in addressing and understanding some of the differences that divide rather than unite.

KEY TERMS

religion

religious beliefs

religious practices

REFERENCES

Abu-Harb, I.A. (2001). Some basic Islamic beliefs. In *A brief illustrated guide to understanding Islam* (ch. 3). Houston, TX: Darussalam. http://www.islam-guide.com/frm-ch3-2.htm.

Bahá'í Faith. (2007). *Welcome to the Bahá'í faith.* http://www.bahai.us.

Bhattacharya, S. (2006, August 12). Young Muslims worried, frustrated in GTA. *Toronto Star*, p. A13.

Boeree, C.G. (2000). The basics of Buddhist wisdom. In *An introduction to Buddhism.* http://www.ship.edu/~cgboeree/buddhaintro.html.

Bortin, M. (2006, June 22). For Muslims and the West, Antipathy and Mistrust. *International Herald Tribune*, pp. 2, 7.

Brar, S.S. (1998a). Introduction to Sikhism. http://www.sikhs.org/summary.htm.

Brar, S.S. (1998b). The Khalsa. http://www.sikhs.org/khalsa.htm.

Center of Traditional Taoist Studies. (2007). Enlightenment. www.tao.org.

Eddy, M.B. (1994). *Science and health with key to the scriptures.* Boston: The First Church of Christ, Scientist.

Ewatski, J. (2006, April 20). Trust as counterterrorism. Paper presented at the 5th International Counterterrorism Conference, Washington, DC.

First Church of Christ, Scientist. (2007). About Christian Science. http://www.tfccs.com.

Forman, R.K.C. (Ed.). (1993). Religions of the world (3rd ed.). New York: St. Martin's Press.

Himalayan Academy. (2000). Hinduism: The basics. http://www.himalayanacademy.com/basics.

Krauthammer, C. (2000). CNN Editorial, August 14.

Lawrence, B.B. (2000). *The complete idiot's guide to religions online.* Indianapolis, IN: Alpha Books.

Ontario Consultants on Religious Tolerance. (2000). Taoism. http://www.religioustolerance.org/taoism.htm.

Rampe, D. (2006, July 7). Muslims and Europe: Surprisingly positive. *International Herald Tribune*, p. 4.

Shephard, M. (2006, August 12). A friend or foe in the war on terror? *Toronto Star*, p. A13.

Statistics Canada (2001). Overview: Canada still predominantly Roman Catholic and Protestant. http://www12.statcan.ca/english/census01/home/index.cfm.

Watch Tower Bible and Tract Society of Pennsylvania. (2001). Jehovah's Witnesses—Who are they? What do they believe? http://www.watchtower .org/library/br78/index.htm.

Watt, P. (1982). Shinto and Buddhism: Wellsprings of Japanese spirituality. Asia Society's *Focus on Asian Studies, Asian Religions* 2 (1): 21–23.

White, G.C. (1997). *Beliefs and believers.* New York: Berkley Books.

EXERCISES AND REVIEW

Personal Analysis

Read each statement and circle whether you agree or disagree with it.

1. Law enforcement officers need to understand the religious diversity of the communities they are sworn to serve.

   AGREE   DISAGREE

2. Religious groups have to adjust to the way police do things rather than police having to adjust to the way the religious groups do things.

   AGREE   DISAGREE

3. Police officers treat everyone equally because that is the way they were trained.

   AGREE   DISAGREE

4. Police have to reject their own religion if they are to understand the religions of others.

   AGREE   DISAGREE

5. Police benefit little from learning about the religions of the communities they serve and protect.

   AGREE   DISAGREE

6. Police safety and respect are maintained only by police adopting an "us against them" mentality.

   AGREE   DISAGREE

7. The changing religious demographics of a society dictate rethinking policing to make it more responsive to religious diversity.

   AGREE   DISAGREE

8. In dealing with religious diversity, the police way is the only way.

   AGREE   DISAGREE

9. Police benefit little from listening to the concerns of religious groups in the communities they serve and protect.

   AGREE   DISAGREE

10. It is important ethically and morally for police to learn to deal with the religious differences in the communities they serve.

    AGREE   DISAGREE

SCORING: Give yourself one point for agreeing with each of statements 1, 7, and 10. Give yourself one point each for disagreeing with the remaining statements. Higher scores are likely to reflect a more positive attitude toward religious literacy. Compare your score with a classmate's, and try to reconcile any differences of opinion.

Diversity IQ: Multiple Choice

Circle the best answer.

1. Which of the following is true about religion?

   a. all religions are the same

   b. religions define basic human needs and prescribe ways of meeting them

   c. religions are corrupt and scandalous

   d. all of the above

2. Which of the following is *not* a basic teaching of the Bahá'í Faith?

   a. there is one God

   b. all people are equal

   c. diversity should be promoted

   d. men and women are equal

3. Which of the following police officers is likely to require a prayer room at the workplace?

   a. Bahá'í

   b. Muslim

   c. Christian

   d. Christian Scientist

4. Hinduism can be described as

    a. a museum of religions

    b. a belief in one God

    c. a belief that only people are important and of divine nature

    d. all of the above

5. Which of the following is least likely to join the police services?

    a. Jehovah's Witness

    b. Muslim

    c. Christian Scientist

    d. Christian

6. Which of the following is most associated with extremist Muslims?

    a. peacemakers

    b. terrorists

    c. rainmakers

    d. camel riders

7. Which of the following is a Buddhist Noble Truth?

    a. Nirvana is achieved by eliminating desire

    b. suffering is not normal

    c. it is impossible to eliminate suffering

    d. all of the above

8. Which of the following represents an important tension between Westerners and Muslims post-9/11?

    a. globalization versus nationalism

    b. religious identity versus national identity

    c. world war versus world peace

    d. none of the above

9. Which of the following is true about Muslims?

    a. Most of them are terrorists

    b. Most of them are fundamentalists

    c. Most of them are moderates

    d. Most of them believe in the cause of suicide bombers

10. Which of the following is one of the Ten Commandments?

    a. You shall murder.

    b. You shall not bear false witness against your neighbour.

    c. You shall not disobey your police chief.

    d. Honour your mother-in-law.

Diversity IQ: True or False?

____ 1. Some religions are really primitive.

____ 2. It is best to shake hands with all religious people.

____ 3. All Muslims are Arabs.

____ 4. Members of some religious groups may be targets for persecution by members of a host community.

____ 5. There are no religious villains in the world.

____ 6. Some religions do not have clergy.

____ 7. Religions play no part in police work.

____ 8. Most religions endorse backbiting and gossip.

____ 9. Suicide bombers love to live and let others live.

____ 10. Police should follow acceptable protocol in relating to people from various religious groups.

Application Now

1. What implications does religious diversity have for individual police and police services?

2. On the basis of statistical data on police calls and other reliable sources, you suspect that youth violence in a particular neighbourhood may have religious undertones. Which of the following options would you consider first in addressing the violence issue, and why?

   Option 1: Invite young people from different religious groups for a meeting to discuss issues of youth violence in the neighbourhood.

Option 2: Invite different religious leaders for a meeting to discuss issues of youth violence in the neighbourhood.

Option 3: Invite parents and religious leaders for a meeting to discuss issues of youth violence in the neighbourhood.

Option 4: Consult with various religious leaders on viable approaches to addressing issues of youth violence in the neighbourhood.

Food for Thought

1. What images did you have of the following individuals before and after reading about them in the text? Share your reactions with your classmates.

   a. A Muslim woman wearing a veil (*hijab*)

   b. A Chinese Buddhist

   c. A Christian Scientist

   d. A Jehovah's Witness

   e. A Wiccan

f. A Sikh wearing a turban

g. A Hindu woman wearing a *sari* (garment consisting of cloth that is worn so that one end forms a skirt and the other end forms a head or shoulder covering)

h. A Muslim man with a beard

i. A white Protestant woman

2. Identify factors that may have contributed to your reactions to the people from the various religious groups.

3. Of the factors you identified, which of them provide a rational basis for
    your reactions and which provide an irrational basis for your reactions?

    Rational

    Irrational

4. What lessons can be learned from the above exercises?

5. Consider how the following factors may influence your reactions to
    individuals from various religions.

    Your upbringing

Media portrayal of specific religions

Police culture

Past personal experience with individuals from specific religions

Your ability to "see" a person as a human being independent of his or her religion

A person's core religious values

6. Do you believe there is any benefit to police collaborating with clergy or even forming police–clergy teams to respond to crisis situations? Why or why not? Tips: Police may refer troubled families to their local clergy for help and guidance; police may use clergy to defuse highly charged emotional situations.

From Thought to Action

One important and worthwhile approach to education and police–community relations is to learn firsthand about the religions of the communities that police serve. Develop a profile of the religions in your neighbourhood. Invite religious leaders to come and speak about their beliefs and practices, and to discuss best practices to resolve conflict. For example, ask a Jehovah's Witness religious leader how police should handle complaints about Jehovah's Witnesses knocking on people's doors and asking to be invited in. Also consider doing more reading on the religions covered in this chapter, or conduct your own research on religions not covered in the chapter (for example, Falun Gong, Hare Krishna, Satanism, and witchcraft; you may be interested in researching the controversy that erupted around the Harry Potter book series, which critics said promoted Satanism). Use the knowledge you gain to add to table 6.5.

Lessons from History

Some religious groups have survived persecution from states and state police. What core values and beliefs contribute to the persecution of religious groups? What are the consequences of religious persecution to the religious groups, to the country, to policing generally, and to counterterrorism in particular?

Core values and beliefs of religious groups

Consequences

The Great Debate

An important issue for policing in a diverse society is whether people of different faiths need to adjust their ways to the host culture or whether the host culture and police need to adjust their ways to the diversity of the people they serve and protect. For example, it could be argued that individuals from a religious group have to abide by the laws of the country (for example, by enlisting in the army in a time of war or following secular laws) even though these laws may contradict their religious beliefs and practices.

Debate this topic by dividing the class into two groups. Have one group take the position that the religious groups need to adjust their ways to the host culture. Have the second group take the position that the police should adjust their ways to the religious beliefs and practices of the people. Follow the presentations with a general class discussion.

PART III

Process and Outcome Considerations

CHAPTER 7

Policing Diversity-Motivated Beliefs and Practices

CHAPTER OBJECTIVES

After completing this chapter, you should be able to:

- Explain the concept of diversity-motivated beliefs and practices.

- Define such terms as stereotype, prejudice, racism, and racial profiling.

- Identify strategies to prevent hate crimes.

PREVIEW SCENARIO

On November 1, 1999, at 12:55 a.m. on the Don Valley Parkway, Constable O pulled over DeCovan "Dee" Brown, a black Toronto Raptors basketball player, on his way home from a Halloween party. He was wearing a baseball cap and a jogging suit and driving a brand new Ford Expedition. When stopped by Constable O, he was travelling "in excess" of the 90 kilometre per hour speed limit. Constable O detected the smell of alcohol on Brown's breath, and requested that Brown submit to a breathalyzer test on the spot. According to Constable O, Brown failed the test, and he was arrested for "driving over eighty milligrams of alcohol in one hundred millilitres of blood," a criminal offence under s. 253 of the *Criminal Code* of Canada. Eighty milligrams of alcohol in 100 millilitres of blood is the legal limit prescribed by law, under ss. 253-255 of the *Criminal Code*. Brown was then taken to a nearby police station, given a second breathalyzer test, which showed a blood alcohol concentration of 140 milligrams of alcohol in 100 millilitres of blood, and then released. In the ensuing trial, the only issue that was raised by Brown's defence lawyer was the reason for Constable O stopping Brown. In Brown's defence, his lawyer raised the following questions: did the police officer stop Brown because Brown was speeding and had twice crossed out of and back into the lane he was travelling, or did he stop Brown because he was a young black male wearing a baseball cap and a jogging suit and driving an expensive new car? Brown's defence counsel contended that Constable O's stopping Brown was an arbitrary detention under s. 9 of the *Canadian Charter of Rights and Freedoms* and that the decision to stop Brown was based on racial profiling rather than the fact that he was speeding. Section 9 of the Charter, which deals with detention or imprisonment, states: "Everyone has the right not to be arbitrarily detained or imprisoned." The evidence used by Brown's lawyer in his defence against Constable O to support his claim for a racial profiling writ is as follows: Constable O pulled alongside and looked into Brown's car before following and stopping him, prepared a second set of notes after becoming aware that Brown was a well-known professional athlete to justify his reasons for stopping him, and conducted a licence check to determine whether Brown's car was stolen before pulling Brown over. There were also discrepancies between the times recorded in the officer's notebook and those that he gave to the breathalyzer technician. Justice Fairgrieve, who presided over Brown's trial, dismissed Brown's contention that he was stopped because he was a black male driving an expensive car, and convicted and fined Brown $2,000, and at one point suggested that Brown should apologize to Constable O for making "serious and quite nasty, malicious accusations." On appeal, however, Justice Trafford of the Ontario Superior Court of Justice overturned Justice Fairgrieve's decision on grounds that remarks and interventions made during the trial (presentation of evidence, cross-examination, defence submissions, and sentencing) gave rise to a "reasonable apprehension of bias." In a subsequent appeal in 2003, the Ontario Court of Appeal ruled that the Superior Court justice had properly applied the principle of "reasonable apprehension of bias" in determining that the trial judge "showed such an antipathy and resistance to the application that he was unable to hear and determine it with an open and dispassionate mind." In April 2003, the *Toronto Star* declared that "Ontario's highest court has recognized the existence of racial profiling," and the *Globe and Mail* observed, "Racial profiling by police exists, the Ontario Court of Appeal concluded yesterday." Similarly, the Canadian Race Relations Foundation (CRRF) applauded the Ontario Court of Appeal on "a historic judgment validating the existence of racial profiling by police." The CRRF emphasized that "the groundbreaking ruling paves the way to more serious discussions on how to end racial profiling and racial discrimination altogether" and praised the Ontario Court of Appeal for "being a leader in judicially recognizing that some police officers subconsciously target Black people as being more likely involved in criminal activity." (Mordin, Laskin, & Feldman, 2003; Canadian Statistical Assessment Service (CANSTATS), 2003a; Canadian Race Relations Foundation, 2003)

INTRODUCTION

The terrorist attacks on the United States on September 11, 2001, the initiatives of the West to democratize non-Western, non-democratic regimes, and the US-led war on terror have highlighted significant clashes between Western and Middle

Eastern values, beliefs, and practices, strained relations between Middle Eastern and Western people internationally and nationally, heightened Western concerns about national security, and challenged the ever-changing profession of policing. The resulting climate of increased antipathy, mistrust, and violence has led law enforcement in Canada to rethink its race-motivated beliefs and practices in the communities it serves and protects. This chapter discusses diversity-motivated beliefs and practices as a social issue and as a law enforcement issue.

CONCEPT OF DIVERSITY-MOTIVATED BELIEFS AND PRACTICES

Diversity-motivated beliefs and practices is an umbrella term that refers to negative views and activities that members of a society assume toward people of diverse populations—for example, a racially motivated verbal attack directed at an individual or a group, or a physical attack on a gay person without provocation. Diversity-motivated beliefs and practices are intimately tied to three concepts: prejudice, racism, and hate crimes.

diversity-motivated beliefs and practices
negative views of and activities against people of diversity

Prejudice

Simpson and Yinger (1972) define **prejudice** as an emotional, rigid attitude, rooted in prejudgment, toward a particular group or category of people. Prejudice includes prejudging people or individuals who share certain physical attributes such as a particular skin or hair colour. A prejudiced person jumps to conclusions, usually with unsubstantiated evidence or facts. Prejudice has three components: cognitive (thoughts), affective (feelings), and behavioural (actions). Thus, a person who is prejudiced against police *thinks* ill of police ("Police don't serve and protect; they oppress and harass"), *dislikes* the police, and *behaves* in a discriminatory way toward police.

prejudice
bias against a person or group, without justification, because of presumed objectionable qualities ascribed to the person or group

Although prejudice is hidden in the mind of the prejudiced individual, it reveals itself through stereotyping, bullying, and discrimination. Stereotyping is a rigid, cognitive map or "picture in one's head" based on often unsubstantiated and inaccurate beliefs about members of a given social category (Glaser & Possony, 1979). **Stereotyping** involves making generalizations about individuals or groups that may or may not be accurate. Stereotypes simplify the world by using names and labels—for example, "women are overemotional" or "the Irish are all drunks." People use stereotypes to establish social inequality and dominance—the person who stereotypes feels superior to the person targeted for stereotyping.

stereotyping
making generalizations that are usually derogatory about individuals or groups

Bullying involves open or subtle acts or remarks that tease, frighten, threaten, hurt, or disempower. Examples of bullying include singling a person out; picking on a person; criticizing, demeaning, or devaluing a person in front of others; blaming a person for one's misfortune or the ills of the world; and shouting at a person to get one's way.

bullying
open or subtle acts or remarks that tease, frighten, threaten, hurt, or disempower people

Racism

Article 1 of the *International Convention on the Elimination of All Forms of Racial Discrimination* defines "racial discrimination" as

> any distinction, exclusion, restriction or preference based on race, colour, descent, or national or ethnic origin which has the purpose or effect of nullifying or impairing the recognition, enjoyment or exercise, on an equal footing, of human rights and fundamental freedoms in the political, economic, social, cultural or any other field of public life. (Office of the High Commissioner for Human Rights, 1969)

The more general term **discrimination** refers to negative behaviour toward a group or its members. As an overt act, discrimination deprives people of their civil and human rights and is against the law. Discrimination is often a byproduct of **racism**, the belief that some races are superior or inferior to others. The source of racism is the false belief that physical features make some people better than others. Racism, and in particular anti-black racism, is part of the psyche of some pluralistic communities such that some members hold overtly racist views whereas for others racism operates subconsciously on the basis of negative racial stereotypes. Furthermore, a country's institutions, including the criminal justice system, can reflect and perpetuate those negative stereotypes.

Systemic racism may be found in both societies and organizations, as well as in the criminal justice system, in the form of institutional cultures that reflect and perpetuate negative racial stereotypes and policies and procedures that discriminate against some racial groups and prevent them from full participation and equal opportunity in society. Systemic discrimination is a related concept. According to Kallen (2003), systemic discrimination is based on the principle that bias can be built into the institutional system through the uneven and unequal application of rules and procedures that may affect vulnerable minorities in different ways. It can be defined as any action that has the discriminatory effect of denying or excluding persons regardless of intent or awareness.

Racism is not in people's imagination. It is a pervasive and chronic problem in Canada that adversely affects individuals and groups by impeding their maximum growth, functioning, and success in society. The Ethnic Diversity Survey conducted in 2002 by the Multiculturalism Program in partnership with Statistics Canada revealed that 36 percent of Canadian visible minorities reported ethnoculture-based discrimination or unfair treatment in the last five years (Canadian Heritage, 2006). Discrimination or unfair treatment was reported by nearly 50 percent of blacks, 34 percent of South Asians, and 34 percent of Chinese who were surveyed.

Hate Crimes

A **hate crime** is a criminal offence against a person or an entire group of people that is motivated in whole or in part by hatred of or bias or prejudice against the victim's race, national or ethnic origin, language, colour, religion, sex, age, mental or physical ability, sexual orientation, or any other similar factor. Hate crimes involve intimidation, harassment, and physical force or threat of physical force against a person, a family, or a property. In Canada, hate crimes fall under the hate propaganda offences. The *Criminal Code* defines **hate propaganda** as any writing,

discrimination
illegal and negative behaviour that deprives a group or its members of their civil rights

racism
predictions, decisions, and actions based on the belief that some races are superior or inferior to others

systemic racism
racism at the social or organizational level that is supported by policies and procedures that discriminate

hate crime
criminal offence against a person or an entire group of people that is motivated in whole or in part by hatred of or bias or prejudice against the victim's race, national or ethnic origin, language, colour, religion, sex, age, mental or physical ability, sexual orientation, or any other similar factor

hate propaganda
any writing, sign, or visible representation that advocates or promotes genocide

sign, or visible representation that advocates or promotes genocide. Communicating hate propaganda is an offence under section 319 of the Code. "Communicating" includes "communicating by telephone, broadcasting or other audible or visible means" (section 319(7)). The Code identifies three specific criminal offences related to hate propaganda: advocating genocide, publicly inciting hatred, and willfully promoting hatred. "Genocide" is defined as "any of the following acts committed with the intent to destroy in whole or in part any identifiable group, namely, (a) killing members of the group; or (b) deliberately inflicting on the group conditions of life calculated to bring about its physical destruction" (section 318(2)). The Code defines "identifiable group" as "any section of the public distinguished by *colour, race, religion or ethnic origin*" (italics added) (section 318(4)), and, as of April 29, 2004, sexual orientation. This definition clarifies that a hate crime involves racial hatred but is not restricted to it. Hate crimes must be willful—that is, committed with the intention of promoting hatred—and do not include recklessness.

Hate propaganda and hate messages can take a variety of forms, including the erection of flaming crosses, heckling at memorial services, and the desecration of synagogues, mosques, and temples. Hate messages and hate literature, and revisionism of historical realities (for example, denying that the Holocaust ever occurred) are also communicated through email, fax machines, telephone hotlines, and the Internet (Gillis, 1993; Swainson & Small, 1993; Kazarian, 1997; Bailey, 1998; Sun Media Newspapers, 1998). Section 320.1 of the *Criminal Code* stipulates the seizure and forfeiture of physical material that constitutes hate propaganda kept on any premises for distribution or sale. Similarly, section 320.1 provides for the courts to order the deletion of hate propaganda available publicly on computer systems, such as a website.

On the other hand, the Code (section 319(3)) stipulates that no one will be convicted of a hate crime

    (a) if he establishes that the statements communicated were true;

    (b) if, in good faith, he expressed or attempted to establish by argument an opinion on a religious subject;

    (c) if the statements were relevant to any subject of public interest, the discussion of which was for the public benefit, and if on reasonable grounds he believed them to be true; or

    (d) if, in good faith, he intended to point out, for the purpose of removal, matters producing or tending to produce feelings of hatred toward an identifiable group in Canada.

Hate crimes and the communication of hate propaganda occur in Canada and other pluralistic countries. A survey conducted jointly by the Canadian Centre for Justice Statistics and 12 major Canadian police forces, including Halton Regional, Toronto, Waterloo, and Windsor, reported a total of 928 hate crime incidents during 2001 and 2002 (Statistics Canada, 2004). (See table 7.1.) Of the 928 reported incidents, 57 percent were motivated by race or ethnicity, 43 percent were motivated by religion, and 9 percent were motivated by sexual orientation. (Note that in some incidents, more than one motivation was reported.) Those most frequently targeted in hate crime incidents motivated by race or ethnicity were blacks (17 percent) and South Asians (10 percent), while those most frequently targeted in hate crime incidents motivated by religion were Jews (25 percent) and Muslims (11 percent).

TABLE 7.1　Hate Crimes in 12 Major Police Forces, 2001–2

	Number	%
Total hate crimes	928	100.0
Jewish	229	25.0
Black	156	17.0
Muslim/Islam	102	11.0
South Asian	96	10.0
Arab/West Asian	72	8.0
East/Southeast Asian	47	5.0

Source: Statistics Canada (2004).

The most common types of hate crime violations were mischief or vandalism (29 percent), assault (25 percent), uttering threats (20 percent), and hate propaganda (13 percent). Hate crime motivations were correlated with offence types to reveal that a little over one half of ethnicity-based hate crimes involved such acts as assault, uttering threats, and criminal harassment against the person, and about two-thirds of anti-religion hate crimes involved such acts as vandalism, arson, other property offences, and hate propaganda. In the case of sexual-orientation-based hate crimes, targeted individuals were more likely than other groups to suffer violent crimes, including assault.

Victims were identified in over 80 percent of the 928 hate crime incidents. Two-thirds of the 794 identified victims were male and their average age was 36 years. Almost all incidents involved a single victim. In cases where the relationship of the accused to the victim was identified, about 83 percent of victims said that they did not know the perpetrator and 15 percent of victims stated that the accused was a casual acquaintance or had a business relationship with them. Roughly one-half (49 percent) of the 447 violent hate crimes involved the threat of force. In 34 percent of these incidents, physical force was actually used. A weapon, usually a knife or other piercing or cutting object, was present in about 17 percent of violent crime incidents, and firearm-like weapons, such as pellet guns, were present in less than 1 percent of hate crime incidents.

Overall, 25 percent of victims of a violent crime suffered an injury as a result of the hate crime incident; the rate of injury of gay and lesbian victims was almost twice (46 percent) the rate among hate crime victims in general. In 45 percent of the cases, the victims suffered minor injuries, and in 7 percent of the cases, they suffered major injuries, two of which resulted in death. In 48 percent of the cases, the level of injury was unknown.

The nature of certain types of hate crime violations—graffiti, vandalism, or anonymous hate messages—is such that it may be difficult to identify a suspect. The majority of the 520 accused on whom detailed characteristics were available were male (84 percent), 10 percent were female, and in 5 percent of the cases the sex of the accused was not recorded. The average age of the accused was 29.

In the majority of cases (86 percent), hate crime incidents involved a single accused, and 10 percent of the accused had a history of involvement in criminal activity. Of those charged with a hate crime, the majority were involved in isolated incidents, 4 percent were involved in previous hate crimes, and 3 percent were connected to a gang or an extremist group.

The incidence of hate crimes and hate propaganda changes in response to national and international events. Hate crimes increased for a short period after the 9/11 terrorist attacks on the United States. In Canada, police reported 232 hate crime incidents for the two months following 9/11, a figure more than three times higher than the 67 hate crime incidents reported for the same two-month period in 2000 (Statistics Canada, 2004). The majority of the hate crime incidents (68 percent) that police associated with the 9/11 attacks were violent in nature, including assault, criminal harassment, and uttering threats. Another 23 percent involved violations against property and 92 percent of these involved vandalism. The remaining 9 percent consisted of other hate crime incidents, including hate propaganda. In terms of motivation, 30 percent of those targeted in hate crime incidents were Muslims, 15 percent were Jews, 15 percent were Americans, and 13 percent were Arabs/West Asians.

Hate crimes and propaganda are taken seriously by the international community and police services, and are addressed in federal statutes and human rights codes. Many nations have ratified the 1948 *Universal Declaration of Human Rights*, the 1970 *International Convention on the Elimination of All Forms of Racial Discrimination*, and the 1976 *International Covenant on Civil and Political Rights*. The *Universal Declaration of Human Rights* requires ratified countries to pass anti-racism legislation, including legislative protection against racist attacks on identifiable groups. Article 4 of the *International Convention on the Elimination of All Forms of Racial Discrimination* requires nations to criminalize hate propaganda and other activities that promote racism. Article 20(2) of the *International Covenant on Civil and Political Rights* calls for hate propaganda to be prohibited by law.

In Canada, federal legal remedies against hate activities are stipulated in the *Canadian Charter of Rights and Freedoms* (under the equality rights and multicultural heritage sections), the *Criminal Code*, and the *Canadian Human Rights Act* (section 13(1)). The provinces have similar legislation—for example, the Ontario *Human Rights Code* (section 13(1)). The fight against diversity-motivated hate activity is supported by the solicitor general, the attorney general, and police services by means of directives, a National Anti-Hate Strategy developed by Canadian Heritage, Multiculturalism, hate crime unit intelligence services, and public education campaigns to identify, report, and reduce hate crime.

DIFFICULTIES WITH FIGHTING HATE CRIMES

Several issues complicate national and international initiatives to curb hate crime. The first is the use of the Internet for hate messages and other controversial and illegal content. Australia, Canada, France, Germany, New Zealand, the Netherlands, the United Kingdom, and the United States are all exploring ways to balance individual rights of free expression and accessibility to information with the collective right of control of hate propaganda. The Council of Europe, the European Union, the Organisation for Economic Co-operation and Development (OECD), and the United Nations, including the United Nations Educational, Scientific, and Cultural Organization (UNESCO), are also addressing Internet-based hate and bias activity.

A second issue relates to the difficulties in tracking and recording hate crimes. A major stumbling block is determining what motivates these crimes. A third issue is the difficulty of gathering statistical data to measure the magnitude of hate and bias activity. Following consultations with police services and the Police Information and Statistics Committee of the Canadian Association of Chiefs of Police, Statistics Canada implemented a national standardized strategy for police-reported, hate-motivated crime data (Canadian Heritage, 2006). A fourth issue relates to publishing hate crime statistics. There is a concern that doing so may spur "some people to commit more violent acts in order to increase the numbers" or allow those involved in hate crimes to "just feed on that statistical data" (Hannan, 1993). A fifth issue has to do with underreporting. Many new immigrants and visible minorities do not report hate crimes because they do not realize that what they have experienced constitutes a hate crime, they fear reprisals from the perpetrator if they report the crime, or they have had bad experiences with police in their country of origin and do not trust the state and the police. Some lack the literacy skills to explain the experience to law enforcers. Hence, underreporting is a major issue for new immigrants and people of colour.

CRIMINALIZATION OF DIVERSITY

Some people espouse an ideology that links people of particular racial and ethnic groups with a disproportionate amount of crime in society. Those who believe in a link between crime and race cite evidence that presumably shows that certain groups have rates of crime that are disproportionate to their representation in the general population. There are two main theories related to the presumed connection between crime and race. The first suggests that race causes criminal activity. It is interesting that this theory is selective in the way it defines race. For example, it makes no reference to criminality and whiteness.

The second theory points to society and the criminal justice system as the real culprits. Those who identify society as the culprit point to the ways in which some racial groups are marginalized and disadvantaged. For example, proponents of this theory have said that the proportionately higher crime rate among blacks and aboriginals in certain areas can be explained by the higher illiteracy, poverty, unemployment, and underemployment rates among blacks and aboriginals than among whites. The marginalization of some black and aboriginal people, coupled with their socially and economically disadvantaged position, tends to expose them to a life of drugs and criminal activity, and increases their likelihood of being involved in violent encounters with police officers and others. Furthermore, the incarceration of members of these groups exposes them to a culture of criminality, so that when they are set free from prison, some maintain these relationships that were formed while in prison. To that end, prison can be seen as a place that contributes to their continued commitment to a life of crime and criminal behaviour.

Those who identify the criminal justice system as the culprit point to the institutionalization of racial bias in the three legs of the system: courts, corrections and parole, and police.

Racial Profiling

racial profiling
police detention or other treatment that singles out any person on the basis of race

Racial profiling is race-based criminal profiling. Racial profiling involves the attribution of certain types of criminal activity to an identified group in society on the basis of race or colour. Racial profiling uses race as a proxy for the criminality or criminal propensity of a racial group and targets individual members of the racial group for differential treatment, including detention that may be arbitrary or abusive. Racial profiling is more likely to occur in areas where members of the identified group look out of place than in areas where they are overrepresented (Harris, 2002). Police practices that may represent racial profiling are listed in table 7.2. Racial profiling is also used by immigration authorities and other government agencies to limit and monitor those whom they perceive to be a threat to national security.

Attitudes underlying racial profiling may be conscious or unconscious. Those engaged in racial profiling may not be overt racists. Their conduct may be based on subconscious racial stereotyping. Police officers who stop young black men driving a brand new car on suspicion of criminal activity may not hold or harbour racist views or be overt racists. Rather, the police officers may be acting on their subconscious beliefs. Then, when they are required to justify their actions, they may invent or fabricate evidence for this purpose.

Racial profiling claims are difficult to prove by direct evidence. Police officers do not come right out and admit to being influenced by prejudice and racial stereotypes in executing their duties—for example, in exercising their discretion to stop a motorist. Racial profiling must be argued by inferences drawn from circumstantial evidence. If a police officer detains an individual and it can be shown in court that the police officer is not being truthful about singling out the accused, it could be argued that the stop was based on racial profiling.

It is worth repeating that the majority of police are devoted to justice and fairness. But, as in any profession, there are always a few individuals who reflect badly on the rest. In some instances, the public has been too quick to scream discrimination without considering the obligations imposed on police officers to perform their duties. For example, the *Criminal Code* stipulates that "[a] peace officer who receives notice that there is a riot within his jurisdiction and, without reasonable excuse, fails to take all reasonable steps to suppress the riot is guilty of an indictable offence" (section 69). This is a classic "damned if you do and damned if you don't" situation for police. Police officers find that some members of the public are quick

TABLE 7.2   Racial Profiling Practices

- Differential use of excessive deadly force
- Differential use of physical force
- Differential verbal abuse of people of diversity
- Differential use of slurs that are racist, sexist, homophobic, and so on
- Discriminatory pattern of arrest
- Differential use of the stop-and-frisk
- Differential use of harsh enforcement of petty offences
- Differential non-enforcement of the law (for example, responding quickly to calls in some neighbourhoods but not to calls in others)
- Differential harassment or surveillance of activists
- Differential police shootings

to accuse police of using excessive force, but are not so concerned when officers are insulted or viciously attacked.

QUALITATIVE EVIDENCE OF RACIAL PROFILING IN POLICING

Qualitative information and evidence of racial profiling in the criminal justice system comes from government inquiries, royal commissions, research studies, and personal anecdotes. Several Canadian and provincial inquiries have supported the view that racial profiling exists in the criminal justice system (McIntyre, 1992; Wortley, 1994; *Report of the Commission on Systemic Racism in the Ontario Criminal Justice System*, 1995; Commission on Systemic Racism in the Ontario Criminal Justice System, 1994). The Commission's (1994) findings suggested that race-based attributes, especially those of black people, in combination with such factors as age, sex, dress, make and condition of car, and perceived lifestyle, provoke police suspicion, at least in Metro Toronto, putting them at high risk of being stopped on foot or in cars.

QUANTITATIVE EVIDENCE OF RACIAL PROFILING AND RACISM IN POLICING

Police are sworn to treat everybody the same—that is, equally and fairly. Three indicators of racial profiling and racism in policing have been used to investigate whether police treat everyone the same: differential treatment, differential use of the stop-and-frisk, and differential use of force.

Wortley (1994) surveyed public opinions of police in a Canadian metropolis and found that "poor people, the young, non-English speakers, and both Black people and Chinese people are treated worse by police than others." The findings also showed that black people were perceived as being treated more unfairly than white people and Chinese people.

There is also evidence of discriminatory use of the stop-and-frisk. Blacks are more likely to be stopped by police than whites and Asians (a rate of 28.1 percent for blacks, 18.2 percent for whites, and 14.6 percent for Chinese) when these citizens are in a car or walking on the street (Wortley, 1994). Men are more likely than women to be stopped by police. Younger people are also stopped more often. In the 18–24 age group, whites have a higher chance (41.3 percent) of being stopped by police than either blacks or Chinese (30.8 percent and 17.9 percent, respectively). For the 25–35 age group, however, the trend is reversed (34.3 percent for blacks, 19.6 percent for whites, and 14.7 percent for Chinese).

The use of force is a legitimate police practice that protects the police and the public. The *Criminal Code*, for example, stipulates that a peace officer who is proceeding lawfully to arrest, with or without warrant, any person for an offence for which the person may be arrested without warrant, is justified, if the person tries to escape arrest, in using as much force as is necessary to prevent escape, unless the escape can be prevented by reasonable means in a less violent manner (section 25(4)). Anyone lawfully assisting the officer has the same authority to use force in making an arrest (section 25(4)). "Every one who is authorized by law to use force is criminally responsible for any excess thereof according to the nature and quality of the act that constitutes the excess" (section 26).

Although police use of force is acceptable, the discriminatory use of force is not. A number of studies support race-based differential use of force by police (Wortley, 1994; CANSTAT, 2002; Wortley & Roswell, 2006 as cited in Gillespie, 2006).

Wortley (1994) found that police were perceived as more likely to use physical force with blacks than with whites (a rate of 54.9 percent for blacks, 42.2 percent for Chinese, and 32.9 percent for whites). The *Toronto Star* scrutinized out-of-sight violations in a police database of all Toronto arrests and charges dating back to 1996 in which race was recorded (CANSTAT, 2002). Out-of-sight violations were those that could only be detected after the vehicle was stopped and the driver questioned—for example, failure to update a driver's licence with a change of address. The *Toronto Star* study reported that although Toronto's black community represented at the time of the study just 8.1 percent of the city's population, about 34 percent of all drivers charged with out-of-sight violations were black. The disproportionate tickets for black drivers were taken as evidence of racial profiling behaviour on the part of the police. In comparison, although 62.7 percent of Toronto's population were white, whites represented 52.1 percent of drivers charged with out-of-sight traffic offences.

The *Toronto Star* also analyzed a database of 10,000 arrests for simple drug possession since 1996, and reported race-based differential treatment. Over 76 percent of the arrested whites were released and sent home with the understanding that they would appear at a police station later but only 61.8 percent of blacks were assigned the same opportunity. Similarly, of those taken to the police station for questioning and jailed instead of being released at the scene, over 15 percent were blacks but only 7.3 percent were whites.

Although the *Toronto Star* studies have been criticized on methodological grounds such as the use of out-of-sight violations as a proxy for racial profiling (CANSTATS, 2002, 2003b), they may be suggestive of random, race-based discretionary stops and leniency, and as such the findings should not be entirely dismissed or ignored. (CANSTATS, 2002).

Finally, Wortley and Roswell (2006, as cited in Gillespie, 2006) examined 784 investigations conducted by Ontario's Special Investigation Unit, concluded that "aboriginal and black residents are more exposed to police use of force than white people," and offered several plausible explanations for race-based police use of force:

- Racial animosity: blatantly racist police officers are more likely to abuse police authority.

- Racial devaluation: mainstream society's devaluation of racial minorities lessens the likelihood of scrutiny of police use of force against them.

- Stereotyping: police stereotypes of black and aboriginal males as being more dangerous than whites increases police apprehension in encounters with the racial groups, which in turn increases their use of force against such racial minorities.

- Crime: racial minority males are more frequently in contact with police officers and therefore are more likely to be involved in use-of-force situations.

- High-crime neighbourhoods: increased wariness of police of people in poor and high-crime neighbourhoods increases their likelihood of using force against them.

- Demeanour: disrespectful and aggressive attitudes toward police, which are more common among racial minorities, are more likely to provoke police use of force against them.

- Integrated fear: a combination of fear-engendering factors—for example, a disturbed racial minority person with a gun—contributes to police use of force.

- Police subculture: police officers who use force are likely to depend on their colleagues to invoke the code of silence.

DIVERSITY-MOTIVATED BELIEFS AND PRACTICES: POLICE ABILITIES, KNOWLEDGE, AND SKILLS

Diversity-motivated hate activities have serious physical, psychological, and social consequences for individual victims and the community. Victims and their families may experience a kaleidoscope of behaviours, emotions, and thoughts: isolation, withdrawal, depression, paranoia, fear, anger, revenge fantasies, and hate. The consequence of hate-motivated activities for the community is a climate that is tense, divided, and disrespectful of the law.

It is instructive for police to reflect on the effects of national and international events, such as acts of terrorism, on hate crimes. Police need to prepare for the potential surge of hate crime incidents that may follow these events and devise strategies for their prevention. The ill-preparedness of police in some Canadian jurisdictions to deal with the increase in violence after the attack on the World Trade Center in New York led to a community backlash for lack of action (Biles & Ibrahim, 2002). On the other hand, proactive strategies were initiated in municipalities such as London, Toronto, and Calgary, in which strong relationships existed between police and the groups targeted for hate crimes. Examples of proactive law enforcement responses included public condemnation of hate crime incidents by chiefs of police across Canada, increases in police patrols to maximize the safety of the groups under attack, and the development of a hate crime unit in London, Ontario (Biles & Ibrahim, 2002b; Pruegger, 2003).

Hate crimes and racial profiling have serious consequences for victims, society, police officers, and police organizations (CANSTATS, 2002; Statistics Canada, 2004; Couillard, 2004). For example, racial profiling represents a waste of scarce police resources when so many other race-neutral strategies, such as monitoring high-crime areas, can be far more effective in eliminating crime. Similarly, racial profiling undermines respect for the administration of justice, brings the justice system into disrepute, erodes public trust, contributes to urban strife, and weakens police–community relations and effectiveness.

Society generally and law enforcement agencies in particular are attempting to develop best practices to address diversity issues, including racial profiling. For example, the Ontario Human Rights Commission issued a report in 2003 in which it argued that racial profiling exists in Ontario, and recommended that strong action be taken by all government agencies (including the police) to counter it (Ontario Human Rights Commission, 2003; Toronto Police Accountability Coalition, 2003). In relation to police services across the province, the commission made two recommendations. The first recommendation was that police officers and private security guards wear name badges that are clearly displayed. The second recommendation was that cameras be installed in police cruisers to allow for monitoring of interactions between police and the public. The use of video cameras in police cruisers has been criticized on the grounds that their installation "smacks of a sentiment of not trusting the police," and that they provide a "technological fix to a problem that is much broader than what might be caught on a fixed camera" (Toronto Police Accountability Coalition, 2003).

Police services face the challenge of developing best practices and initiating innovative service models to strengthen their relationships with the increasingly diverse communities they are mandated to serve and protect, and to deal effectively and efficiently with hate crimes, and racial profiling issues. Police defensiveness and denial and closed-mindedness regarding police service evaluation are counterproductive. On the other hand, irresponsible criticism of police, selective focus on negative police conduct, and uncritical acceptance of methodologically flawed police studies and surveys do not promote positive relations between communities and the police. Trust is a two-way street. Police services and communities need mutual trust for effective community policing. A paradigm shift needs to occur for the prevention of hate crime, propaganda, terrorism, and racial profiling. All communities, their leaders, and their members need to love life more than they hate their adversaries and perceived enemies. All communities, their leaders, and their members need to establish strong ties to Canada, identify themselves as Canadian first, and embrace the Canadian values of democracy and "one law for all." Canadian citizens and foreign nationals, irrespective of their diversity, race, ethnicity, and faith, need to see the good in police services and police officers themselves rather than be preoccupied and consumed just with the bad and the ugly. Table 7.3 lists dos and don'ts related to diversity-motivated police conduct.

TABLE 7.3   Dos and Don'ts of Diversity-Motivated Police Conduct

Dos	Don'ts
■ Recognize diversity-motivated police misconduct.	■ Don't close your eyes to diversity-motivated police misconduct.
■ Unlearn racist stereotypes while relearning or embracing an anti-racist attitude for life and others around you.	■ Don't be a tool of racism.
■ Partner with people of diversity to fight crime and to secure law, order, and safety.	■ Don't practise diversity profiling.
■ Be inclusive, impartial, and just.	■ Don't condone diversity-motivated hate activity by failing to act on it.
■ Recognize that you may not see events in the same way that another person may see them.	■ Don't let anyone's diversity cloud your integrity.
■ Support initiatives to eliminate diversity-motivated hate activities without violating people's constitutional rights.	
■ Prevent hate crimes.	

CHAPTER SUMMARY

Diversity-motivated beliefs and practices are serious social and policing issues. Even though racism and racial profiling among police officers and police services are the exception rather than the rule, such practices are damaging to the police and their relations with the community.

There are two basic approaches to dealing with diversity-motivated beliefs and practices. The external, reactive approach relies on royal commissions and task forces to dictate to police what to do. The internal, proactive, and preferred approach enables police to work with people of diversity in partnership to develop a police service that fights crime effectively, is tough on police officers who discriminate, and takes pride in treating all members of the public fairly. Communities, in turn, have the civic and moral responsibility to embrace the Canadian values of democracy and "one law for all," and support their police services and police officers in their mandate to fight racism, racial profiling, and terrorism.

KEY TERMS

diversity-motivated beliefs and practices   racism

prejudice   systemic racism

stereotyping   hate crime

bullying   hate propaganda

discrimination   racial profiling

REFERENCES

Bailey, I. (1998, January 16). Crackdown urged on Internet hate. *The London Free Press*, p. A9.

Biles, J., & H. Ibrahim. (2002). After September 11, 2001: A tale of two Canadas. Paper presented at the 7th International Metropolis Conference in Oslo, Norway. http://www.international.metropolis.net.

Canadian Charter of Rights and Freedoms, part I of the *Constitution Act, 1982*, RSC 1985, app. II, no. 44.

Canadian Human Rights Act, RSC 1985, c. H-6, as amended.

Canadian Heritage (2006). *Annual report on the operation of the Multiculturalism Act: 2004-2005*. http://www.pch.gc.ca/multi.

Canadian Race Relations Foundation (2003, April 16). The CCRF welcomes Ontario Court's historic ruling on racial profiling. http://www.crr.ca.

Commission on Systemic Racism in the Ontario Criminal Justice System. (1994). *Report on youth and street harassment: The police and investigative detention*. Toronto: Queen's Printer for Ontario.

Couillard, D. (2004, Fall). Managing hot-button issues in policing. *Canadian Police Chief Magazine*, pp. 9–11.

Fernandes, C., & D. Costanza. (1996). *Hate activity: Communities can respond.* Toronto: Municipality of Metropolitan Toronto, Access and Equality Centre.

Gillespie, I. (2006, August 26). Figures on police shootings more than just black and white. *The London Free Press*, pp. B1–B2.

Gillis, C. (1993, June 3). Hecklers spur anti-hate action. *The London Free Press.*

Hannan, P. (1993, May 15). How widespread is hate crime? *The Hamilton Spectator.*

Harris, D. (2002). *Profiles on injustice: Why racial profiling cannot work.* New York: New Press.

Human Rights Code. RSO 1990, c. H.19, as amended.

Glaser, K., & S.T. Possony. (1979). *Victims of politics: The state of human rights.* New York: Columbia University Press.

Kallen, E. (2003). *Ethnicity and human rights in Canada* (3rd ed.). Toronto: Oxford University Press.

Kazarian, S.S. (1997). The Armenian psyche: Genocide and acculturation. *Mentalities* 12: 74–87.

Leighton, B. (1993). Community-based policing and police/community relations. In J. Chacko and S.E. Nancoo (Eds.), *Community policing in Canada* (pp. 245–50). Toronto: Canadian Scholars' Press.

McIntyre, D. (1992). Race relations and policing. In K.R.E. McCormick & L.A. Visano (Eds.), *Policing in Canada* (pp. 647–55). Toronto: Canadian Scholars' Press.

Mordin, J.W., J.K. Laskin, & K. Feldman. (2003, April 16). Ontario Court of Appeal: R v. Decovan Brown.

Office of the United Nations High Commissioner for Human Rights. (1948). *Universal Declaration of Human Rights.* http://www.ohchr.org/english.

Office of the United Nations High Commissioner for Human Rights. (1969). *International Convention on the Elimination of All Forms of Racial Discrimination.* http://www.ohchr.org/english/law.

Office of the United Nations High Commissioner for Human Rights. (1976). *International Covenant on Civil and Political Rights.* http://www .ohchr.org/english/law.

Ontario Human Rights Commission. (2003). *Paying the price: The human cost of racial profiling.* News release. http://www.ohrc.on.ca.

Pruegger, V. (2003). *Community and policing in partnership.* Paper developed for Policing in a Multicultural Society conference. Ottawa. www.canadianheritage.gc.ca/progs/multi/pubs/police/partner_e.cfm.

Report of the Commission on Systemic Racism in the Ontario Criminal Justice System. (1995). Toronto: Queen's Printer for Ontario.

Simpson, G.E. & J.M. Yinger. (1972). *Racial and cultural minorities: An analysis of prejudice and discrimination* (4th ed.). New York: Harper & Row.

Statistics Canada. (2004). *Pilot survey of hate crime.* http://www.statcan.ca/ menu-en.htm.

Sun Media Newspapers. (1998, February 17). More hate groups on Net. *The London Free Press*, p. A8.

Swainson, G., & P. Small. (1993). Province looks at tougher laws after London cross-burning. *The Toronto Star*, p. A10.

Toronto Police Accountability Coalition. (2003, December 1). *Racial profiling— again.* Toronto Police Accountability Bulletin Number 6. http://www.tpac .ca/bulletins.cfm.

Wortley, S. (1994). *Perceptions of bias and racism within the Ontario criminal justice system: Results from a public opinion survey.* Toronto: Commission on Systemic Racism in the Ontario Criminal Justice System.

EXERCISES AND REVIEW

Personal Reflection

Read each statement below and circle whether you agree or disagree with it.

1. Police are not bigots. They never let their values, biases, and prejudices colour their treatment of the people they police.

   AGREE   DISAGREE

2. Society expects police to treat people of diversity more leniently because of their past experiences with police in their countries of origin.

   AGREE   DISAGREE

3. Individuals who have had bad experiences with police in their countries of origin can learn to trust police here because the police in this country show professionalism.

   AGREE   DISAGREE

4. Although to be prejudiced is only human, police shed their biases and prejudices as soon as they put on their uniforms.

   AGREE   DISAGREE

5. When I see a white man in a police uniform, a white woman in a police uniform, and a member of a minority group in a police uniform, I still see a "police officer."

   AGREE   DISAGREE

6. Because we are all created the same and have equal opportunities in life, it bothers me when some people get handouts to enter the police force because of their sex, culture, race, or sexual orientation.

   AGREE   DISAGREE

7. History teaches us that not all people have had equal opportunities to participate in the economic, political, and social life of a pluralistic society.

   AGREE   DISAGREE

8. Institutional racism in policing is the myth of the 21st century.

   AGREE   DISAGREE

9. It is natural for us to dislike or have a hard time understanding or accepting those who are visibly different from us or those who do things differently from the way we do things.

   AGREE   DISAGREE

10. Labelling people—for example, calling them squaws or faggots—plays a critical role in treating them as less than human beings.

    AGREE   DISAGREE

SCORING: This exercise does not require scoring. Nevertheless, consider holding a class discussion of the attitudes expressed in the statements.

Diversity IQ: Multiple-Choice Questions

Circle the best answer.

1. Which of the following is true about stereotyping?

   a. it involves the use of glorifying labels

   b. it is a way of subjugating others

   c. it is a way of establishing social equality

   d. all of the above

2. Racial profiling among police

   a. can be proved with anecdotal evidence

   b. can be proved with evidence from government task forces and commissions

   c. is recognized by police services themselves

   d. all of the above

3. Which of the following is a negative consequence of racial profiling?

    a. poor police–community relations

    b. potential for urban strife

    c. waste of police resources

    d. all of the above

4. Racial profiling and racism in policing are exemplified in

    a. equal treatment of people of diversity

    b. differential police treatment of people of diversity

    c. failure to use differential physical force

    d. all of the above

5. Which of the following needs to be considered to address racism in policing?

    a. public accountability for police services

    b. police workforce diversity

    c. race relations training for police

    d. all of the above

6. Which of the following is true about diversity-motivated beliefs and practices in policing?

    a. the majority of officers are bad apples

    b. the minority of officers are bad apples

    c. there are no bad apples in law enforcement

    d. all of the above

7. A hate crime refers to

    a. promoting expressions of hatred against people of diversity

    b. participating in hateful acts against people of diversity

    c. promoting hateful acts against people of diversity

    d. all of the above

8. Hate propaganda

    a. is a criminal offence

    b. is legal

    c. harms no one

    d. benefits everyone

9. Which of the following is true about hate crimes?

    a. they are taken seriously by police

    b. they are very easy to track and record

    c. their motivational basis is easy to establish

    d. all of the above

10. Which of the following is offered as an explanation for race-based differential use of force?

    a. police subculture

    b. high-crime neighbourhoods

    c. racial animosity

    d. all of the above

Diversity IQ: True or False?

_____ 1. Police today are more knowledgeable about racism than in the past.

_____ 2. Disliking someone because of the person's skin colour represents prejudice.

_____ 3. Racism is race-based prejudice and discrimination.

_____ 4. Prejudice can be discerned through stereotyping, bias, bullying, and discriminatory behaviour.

_____ 5. Discrimination is against the law even though the illegality of prejudice is still in question.

_____ 6. Police cannot be a target for prejudice.

_____ 7. Racism does not exist in the criminal justice system.

_____ 8. Racial profiling refers to criminalization based on race.

_____ 9. Hate crimes are committed by whites only.

_____ 10. Hate crimes can increase in response to national and international events.

Application Now

1. The following is a partial list of known hate groups:

    - Heritage Front

    - Knights of the Invisible of the Ku Klux Klan

    - Northern Hammerskins

    - Aryan Resistance Movement

    a. Add any hate groups known to you or others. Do independent research on any (or all) of these groups from the perspective of racism. What diversities do the groups target? What similarities or differences are there among these groups? What are their methods of operation?

    b. What effect do you think perpetrators of hateful deeds against people of diversity and revisionists such as deniers of the Holocaust and other genocides have on society generally and policing in particular?

    c. What concrete suggestions can you offer to society and police services to deal with hate crimes without violating the constitutional rights and freedoms of individuals?

        Suggestions to society

Suggestions to police services

2. In 1996, the BC attorney general, Ujjal Dosanjh, established a provincial hate crime team to prevent and prosecute hate-motivated crimes. The team included representatives from the Royal Canadian Mounted Police (RCMP), the Vancouver Police Department, a Crown counsel, and staff from the Ministry of the Attorney General and Multiculturalism BC. Research how effective this team has been in dealing with hate crimes. You may also want to research other models for hate crime intervention and prevention and report your findings to the class. Consider researching hate crime initiatives in other Canadian provinces and in such countries as Australia, Germany, Britain, and the United States.

Food for Thought

1. Which of the following constitute actionable race-motivated behaviours? Circle R if you consider the behaviour to be race-based. Circle NR if you consider the behaviour to be non-race-based.

    R   NR   racial slurs

    R   NR   jokes about people with physical disabilities

    R   NR   racial innuendoes

    R   NR   harassment of members of visible minorities

    R   NR   racial compliments

    R   NR   statements to newcomers such as, "I don't know why you people don't go back to where you came from, because you sure don't belong here"

    R   NR   humiliating or demeaning "teasing" of a bisexual person

    R   NR   graffiti of a demeaning or discriminatory nature

    R   NR   consistent treatment of a gay person in an unfavourable manner

    R   NR   racial epithets

    R   NR   ridiculing comments about a person's past psychiatric history

    R   NR   ridiculing comments about a person's religious dress

    R   NR   a work atmosphere that is poisonous for some employees

    R   NR   derogatory names (savage, redskin) aimed at an aboriginal man

    R   NR   derogatory names (squaw, primitive) aimed at an aboriginal woman

    R   NR   police detainment of blacks for no apparent reason

2. Which of the following factors contribute to diversity profiling among some police? Circle Y if you believe a factor contributes to racial profiling and N if you do not believe it does.

    Y   N   violent acts (real or perceived) against police officers

    Y   N   police isolation and alienation from the community

    Y   N   cynicism

    Y   N   prejudice

    Y   N   racism

    Y   N   job satisfaction

    Y   N   understanding of the role of a police officer

Y	N	application of the policing philosophy "compliance through pain"
Y	N	high morale in the police services
Y	N	poor conflict and dispute-resolution skills
Y	N	personal problems off-duty
Y	N	fatigue
Y	N	getting "pumped up" for a police call
Y	N	good physical health
Y	N	exposure to homicide, domestic violence, and fatal traffic accidents

3. What personal measures should police officers, police administrators, and the community take to prevent racial profiling by police? If you believe that law enforcement agencies should have a policy on racial profiling, what should that policy entail? Would your policy include the installation of video cameras in police cars?

4. Identify the impact of cultural and community organizations on how specific groups interact with the justice system.

From Thought to Action

1. Read each of the following real-life scenarios. Analyze whether the actions and feelings of the individuals (citizens and police) were justified, and how the police might have handled the situations differently. After analyzing the scenarios, consider role-playing them.

    a. I was walking with my date when three men started harassing us and calling us "butt-fuckers, faggots, and queers." I lost my patience and flicked my cigarette butt at their car. When the men got out of the car, I apologized but told them that they had no right to act the way they did. The men jumped me and then fled in their car. I was rushed to hospital badly bruised and needed I 16 stitches to my lips. The police officer who came to the hospital to take my statement hinted that this had all happened because I flicked the cigarette. I was furious.

Source: Adapted from Fernandes and Costanza (1996).

Citizens

Police

Solution

b. I am an 18-year-old black male. I was stopped for the first time by the police, who said that I was disturbing the peace. My younger brother and I were coming from our church's youth basketball game. We were standing at a busy intersection when a police car drove by. I waved a peace sign because I thought it was the officer I usually say hello to. The car made a U-turn and stopped in front of us. Two officers got out and asked what I'd meant. I explained. The officer told me that I had picked the wrong officer to mess with, and then asked me to show him my ID. I asked if I was being arrested. My brother pointed out that I didn't have to show any ID. The next thing I knew, I was being thrown against the police car. There was a struggle. One officer handcuffed me while I yelled, "What's going on?" I was taken away to the station, where I was charged with resisting arrest, assault, mischief, and disturbing the peace.

I feel I was harassed because of my race, class, clothes, and sex. I used to trust police, but now I feel that they don't serve and protect me or other black people. When I said that the police are supposed to protect me, the officer told me, "We don't serve or protect people like you."

Source: Adapted from Commission on Systemic Racism
in the Ontario Criminal Justice System (1994).

Citizens

Police

Solution

c. I am a 50-year-old Chinese woman and a nurse. I speak English well but with an accent. One evening, around 7 p.m., I was driving with a co-worker from the hospital on our way for a dinner break in Chinatown when we were pulled over by two police officers (one male and one female). They checked my licence and ownership, but took a long time and giggled. I was in a hurry since I still had to return to work. I approached the police car to explain and to ask for my licence back. I was thrown into the back of the cruiser by the policewoman and suffered head and other injuries. She swore at me when I tried to ask questions, explain, and stand up for my rights. They gave me a ticket for an expired licence sticker, told me I was charged with assault and disturbing the peace, and took me to the station. I was kept there for several hours, not allowed a phone call, not given a chance to file a complaint despite making repeated attempts to explain to the booking

officer, and only taken to the hospital after making repeated
complaints that I'd suffered a head injury. Finally, I was released.

Source: Commission on Systemic Racism in the
Ontario Criminal Justice System (1994).

Citizens

Police

Solution

2. I am a 19-year-old East Indian. I was stopped by a police officer while
driving to work. When I told her that she had stopped me because I am
Indian, she said, "That may have been your experience in the past, but the
reality is that you were driving 30 kilometres an hour over the speed
limit." I apologized to the officer and told her I was late for work. She gave
me a ticket for driving only 15 kilometres an hour over the speed limit.

Citizen

Police

Solution

3. Which of the following actions would you consider when an incident occurs in which a police officer has used deadly force against a person of diversity? Explain your choice(s). Can you suggest any other approaches?

   - Ensure that both the police and the community have all the available information.

   - Ensure that good communication is maintained between the police and the victim's family and community.

   - Provide a forum for public discussion of the incident specifically and police–community relations in general.

   - Identify necessary steps to avoid future similar incidents.

   - Commit to developing programs for repairing and promoting police–community relations.

Source: Based on Leighton (1993).

4. Ontario Provincial Police released a video camera tape showing that a Toronto police officer punched a visible minority youth in the face after the youth broke up a fight in a parking lot. Contrary to a previous police statement that the youth had been injured in a fight and then attacked an officer, leading to the youth being charged by police with assaulting an officer, the video clearly showed that until being punched in the face by the officer, "the youth was not injured, and had not made any attempt to approach or go after the officer." On the basis of what you have learned in this course, what inferences would you make and what courses of action would you take?

Source: Based on Toronto Police Accountability Coalition (2003).

5. Critique the list of dos and don'ts in table 7.3 (on p. 207). What do you think should be deleted from the list and what should be added?

Lessons from History

Following are some indicators of diversity-motivated beliefs and practices in policing. Read each indicator and identify ways to correct it. You may have to do some research on some of the items.

1. Using excessive deadly or physical force.

2. Stopping non-white young people for no reason.

3. Harassing homeless mentally ill people, young people, gays and lesbians, and members of racial minorities (for example, using the stop-and-frisk and harshly enforcing petty offences).

4. Arresting a disproportionately higher number of non-white people.

5. Treating with hostility people apprehended from certain age, cultural, racial, or sexual orientation groups.

6. Verbally abusing members of the public, including using racist, sexist, and homophobic slurs.

7. Using discriminatory non-enforcement of the law—for example, not responding effectively to calls in low-income neighbourhoods or half-heartedly investigating sexual assaults or hate crimes.

The Great Debate

Some people claim that police practise racial profiling, while police claim that they treat everyone the same.

Debate this topic by having one group take the position that police racial profiling is impossible because the police treat everyone the same when they put their uniforms on. Have the second group take the position that racial profiling is likely because it is impossible for the police to treat everyone the same. Back your arguments with facts.

CHAPTER 8

Policing with Diversity Competency

CHAPTER OBJECTIVES

After completing this chapter, you should be able to:

- Describe police self-perceptions and community perceptions of police.

- Identify four forms of anti-racism initiatives in pluralistic societies.

- Understand the importance of police training in race relations, cultural sensitivity, and diversity.

- Develop policing strategies, structures, and skills for cultural and diversity competence.

PREVIEW SCENARIO

In 1998, Detective Sergeant David Perry was in charge of 42 Division Detective Office in the heart of Scarborough, Ontario, which had an extremely large and diverse community. At the time, the Tamil community was growing rapidly. However, the law-abiding Tamil people who immigrated to Canada were followed by a criminal element, who began to perpetrate crimes against their own people. Frequent, violent clashes between rival Tamil gangs, who often used AK 47 assault rifles in their attacks on each other, endangered both police and the public, and culminated in a number of deaths. Consequently, a joint forces project was established to eradicate the problem with the Tamil gangs. The development of enforcement initiatives and the tireless work of Superintendent Gary Ellis and a team of officers helped police identify the true leaders of the Tamil community. At the same time, police were cultivating their relationships with community leaders behind the scenes. While police were forging a sound relationship with the Tamil community, the joint task force was preparing to conclude their initiative with mass arrests of Tamil gang members across the Greater Toronto Area. As Detective Sergeant David Perry put it, "The problem we faced was making the arrests, which generated a tremendous amount of media attention, while maintaining our relationship with the Tamil community." The dilemma was resolved by developing a plan that assured leaders that the arrests of gang members, who comprised a small percentage of the Tamil community, would not damage the reputation of the entire Tamil community. Just after the search warrants were executed but before the media were alerted and began reporting the arrests, Tamil community leaders were invited to attend an emergency meeting at 42 Division to help craft the division's news release, and to be present at the news conference to speak on behalf of the Tamil community. Images of the Tamil community and police united in their efforts to stamp out gang violence overshadowed the images of the gang members being handcuffed and arrested. (Perry, 2004)

INTRODUCTION

Police and the community share common goals—both want crime-free neighbourhoods and safe streets, and both strive for an improved quality of life. A police officer who is a friend of the people is more effective in fighting crime and apprehending suspects than an officer who is perceived as an enemy of the people. When people respect the police, they are more prone to assist them when required.

The changing face of Canada has been driving police services to rethink how they can competently respond to the growing diversity in the country, and ensure that police organizations are "internally welcoming, reflective, and knowledgeable in facing this challenge" (cited in Taylor, 2004). This chapter focuses on police self-perceptions and community perceptions of police. It discusses diversity strategies, structures, and skills in policing, efforts to make police organizations more culturally inclusive and responsive, and the role of diversity in enhancing public safety.

POLICE–COMMUNITY PERCEPTIONS

The quality of the administration of justice is a critical factor in determining the health of a free society. The police are the one segment of the criminal justice system that has a direct relationship with the community. Understanding the role of the police and the effectiveness of that role requires consideration of two elements: police perception of themselves and community perception of police.

Self-Perception of Police

The three police self-images that have evolved over time can be represented by the acronym ZAC—zookeeper, avenger of the lord, and champion of the people. The first two images are historical. The zookeeper self-image is a result of police seeing the community as "a large zoo where the ferocious animals must not only be fed and watered but also must be watched every moment and allowed only that limited freedom which the zoo keeper's security can stand" (Steinberg & McEvoy, 1974, p. 149). In describing the image of the police as avengers of the lord, Reverend Billy Graham has commented that police are "the sword of the Lord, avenging the wickedness of this world" (Steinberg & McEvoy, 1974, p. 148).

These historical images are not in keeping with contemporary realities. Lewis (1993) indicates that approximately 80 percent of an Ontario police officer's time is spent serving people. Thus, the self-image of police as champions of the people most reflects reality.

Community Perception of Police

Police officers are not in the business of policing to win popularity contests. They do, nevertheless, care about their public image. A positive public image enhances police self-respect, effectiveness in combatting crime, police safety, job satisfaction, and social contribution. Although in general the role of police in society is recognized and honoured, and most people are satisfied with the police most of the time, some unfavourable community perceptions of police persist, particularly in the context of relations between police and people of diversity.

Wortley (1994) assessed community satisfaction with police services in Metropolitan Toronto. His findings are summarized in table 8.1. As you can see, satisfaction rates across all three groups are less than perfect. Satisfaction and dissatisfaction rates are also culturally dependent, with blacks showing the highest dissatisfaction ratings and whites showing the highest satisfaction ratings.

Wortley's findings highlight the importance of assessing community perceptions of police services, a requirement legislated in 1999. Ontario regulation 3/99, also known as the Adequacy Standards Regulation, requires police services to consult with their respective communities to determine their level of satisfaction with policing and to solicit their recommendations regarding police service delivery.

Although many variables contribute to the public's perception of the police and satisfaction with their performance, a fundamental factor is the interpersonal encounters between the public and the police. Positive police attitudes toward the public and positive police–public interactions contribute to a positive police image in the eyes of the public. Similarly, positive public attitudes toward the police and

TABLE 8.1   Community Satisfaction with Police Services*

Satisfaction	Blacks (%)	Chinese (%)	Whites (%)
Police enforcing the law	66.9	56.2	80.9
	8.9	**5.7**	**5.7**
Police being approachable/easy to talk to	33.3	59.3	80.5
	17.5	**10.4**	**5.3**
Police sharing information or ways of reducing crime	57.6	61.4	76.1
	24.5	**17.8**	**11.3**
Police making neighbourhoods safe	82.0	76.5	84.6
	9.6	**8.9**	**6.2**

 * Non-bold figures represent rates of satisfaction (combined ratings of an average job and a good job). Bold figures represent rates of dissatisfaction (a poor job).

Source: Wortley (1994).

positive police–public interactions foster a positive image of the public in the eyes of the police. The reciprocal relationship between police–public encounters and perceptions forms a feedback loop that either makes or breaks police–community relations. Negative encounters that generate negative perceptions are self-defeating—negative police perceptions of the community are reciprocated by the community, and vice versa (Coffey, 1990).

On the other hand, it can be argued that the functions police perform are by necessity coercive (Rodelet and Carter, 1994). This adversarial nature of the police–community relationship creates an inherent conflict and precludes positive encounters. While the view of police and public as adversaries may be justified in certain contexts—for example, when police deal with certain types of criminals or in tough, urban neighbourhoods—Banton (1963; cited in Rodelet & Carter, 1994, p. 229) rejects the view of police and public as adversaries on three grounds:

1. The police officer spends very little time "chasing people or locking people up." Instead, he or she spends most of his or her time helping citizens in distress.

2. It is misleading to describe a police officer's job as law enforcement. An officer's activities "are governed much more by popular morality than they are by the letter of the law."

3. Even criminals recognize the moral authority, as opposed to the power, of the police. When people grumble at the police, they are really "trying to make their violations seem excusable to still their own conscience."

The majority of people view police as champions of the people rather than as overprotective zealots. Nevertheless, effective police–community alliances can be tarnished by police conduct that is rude and authoritarian. Rudeness is one of the most common complaints expressed against police officers. Interestingly, accusations of police rudeness are rarely made by people arrested for serious crimes. Rather, such accusations come from citizens involved in traffic stops, those reporting crimes to police, or those simply seeking directions from police. **Authoritarianism** is "badge-heavy" conduct that demands obedience to authority. While police must be prepared for violence, and while an *authoritative* approach is required in a variety of situations—for example, interrogating a suspect, handling a crime scene, conducting an investigation, and resolving a domestic dispute—authoritarian conduct is unproductive in situations that require cooperation, compromise, and capitulation and creates an obstacle to police–community alliances.

Visibility, accessibility, client-centredness, the ability to solve problems, fairness, and openness to partnership are the core values that communities expect from police.

authoritarianism
conduct that demands obedience to authority

DIVERSITY INITIATIVES IN CANADIAN SOCIETY

The Department of Canadian Heritage lists the following as priority areas for its multiculturalism program (Canadian Heritage, 2006):

- Fostering cross-cultural understanding by supporting programs and initiatives that facilitate understanding of cultural differences, fostering an appreciation of the value of diversity, and promoting ties among all sectors of society including urban–rural connections.

- Combatting racism and discrimination by engaging the diverse communities and the broader public in informed dialogue and sustained action to fight racism and discrimination.

- Promoting civic participation by developing among the country's diverse population active citizens who have both the opportunity and the capacity to participate in shaping Canadian society.

- Making Canadian institutions more reflective of the country's population by assuming a leadership role to help federal institutions develop policies, programs, and services that are responsive to and reflective of the country's demographic diversity.

POSITIVE DIVERSITY MANAGEMENT IN POLICING

In the past three decades there has been an increasing focus on processes, outcomes, and programs related to diversity-based recruitment, promotion, and retention, and on staff diversity training programs in policing.

Diversity as a Strategic Advantage in Policing

Police services across Canada have begun to see that diversity is a key component of effective law enforcement rather than a liability. Police are increasingly supporting initiatives to ensure that their organizations are reflective of and responsive to the needs of the diverse communities they serve and protect, and offer equal opportunities for the recruitment, promotion, and career development of people of all backgrounds (Laws, 2005). In fact, the globalization of business, changing demographics and market forces in Canada, and the imperatives of national security and public safety have made diversity in law enforcement not just a strategic advantage but a necessity.

Police are making diversity a strategic advantage by encouraging and supporting a diverse police workforce through two processes: the identification and removal of organizational barriers and the development of human resource initiatives to recruit, retain, and promote the most qualified individuals. Diversity as a strategic advantage is different from the traditional employment equity program legislated in federal and provincial jurisdictions. Whereas employment equity recognizes the contribution of just the legislatively designated groups, a policy that uses diversity as a strategic advantage recognizes the contributions that individuals make as individuals (Laws, 2005).

employment equity
strategy designed to make
workplaces reflect society's
diversity by encouraging
the full participation of
people of all diversities

Diversity as a strategic advantage has been more readily accepted than **employ-ment equity**, which has generated controversies and misunderstandings. Employment equity has been criticized for resembling US-style quotas and affirmative action, for creating red tape, for not using merit as the basis for hiring, for jeopardizing police safety, for amounting to reverse discrimination, and for "pandering to minority extremists by politicians who should be kept at arm's length" (McIntyre, 1992, p. 652). In reality, none of these criticisms are founded. The object of employment equity is to reflect a nation's diversity in its workforce without arbitrary quotas, reverse discrimination, or the lowering of employment standards (Redway, 1992; Samuel & Suriya, 1993; Laws, 2005).

Many police services and organizations have been proactive in instituting diversity management policies and best practices (Pruegger, 2003; Laws, 2005). The Toronto Police Service (TPS), Ottawa Police Service (OPS), Ontario Provincial Police (OPP), Durham Regional Police Service (DRPS), Halton Regional Police Service (HRPS), London Police Service (LPS), and Royal Canadian Mounted Police (RCMP) have all taken steps to institute diversity management and best practices. Some examples are given below:

- In 2002, the Toronto Police Service encouraged all Toronto citizens to provide their thoughts and insights on accusations of police of racial profiling on the TPS website.

- Ottawa Police Service launched an Enhanced Language Training Program for a Policing Career (sponsored by Citizenship and Immigration Canada, and in partnership with Graybridge Malkam) that offers advanced job-specific language training to eligible immigrants.

- In 2003, the Ottawa Police Service asked for input on how members of diverse communities could be encouraged to join police services.

- In 2003, the Ontario Provincial Police selected 102 women out of 2,500 applicants from across the province to attend OPP Bound, a five-day recruit-camp in Orillia, and then began the selection of and hiring process for 78 of the 102 women.

- In 2005, Durham Regional Police Service initiated a Diversity Strategic Plan, which includes strategic goals for the recruitment, selection, retention, and promotion of diverse talent, building bridges within the community, developing diversity competence within the DRPS, and identifying diversity as a strategic advantage.

Police Training in Race Relations and Cultural Sensitivity

The traditional model of diversity training in policing followed a stand-alone or an add-on approach in which police officers took brief race relations, cultural awareness, or cross-cultural training modules, or a combination of such packages. Contemporary diversity training models in policing regard diversity training as integral to the strategic planning of police services rather than add-ons.

RACE RELATIONS TRAINING

Race relations training is a formal, short-term program designed to prepare police to deal more effectively with race-related issues. This approach does not support the view that an understanding of cultural heritage offers immediate solutions to or addresses the serious consequences of racism in policing. Instead, this approach considers racism a social disease that requires the antidote of race relations training and education.

Early race relations training programs focused on individual police officers' attitudes toward race or on raising awareness of race-related beliefs and the requirements of the law in general, and on employment equity legislation in particular. These early efforts failed to inspire confidence among police trainees because they were seen as soft science or touchy-feely, not relevant to real police work, confrontational, and ineffective in changing police attitudes and bringing about institutional or systemic change (Rees, 1992; Ungerleider, 1992; Harris & Currie, 1994; Pruegger, 2003).

The limitations of previous race relations training programs (see table 8.2) led to a rethinking of the goals of such programs and a new strategic focus on changing police organizations rather than just the feelings and behaviours of individual police officers. Some programs combined both elements—individual and systemic—in their approach to race relations (see table 8.3).

CULTURAL AWARENESS TRAINING

Cultural awareness training is a formal, short-term program designed to prepare police to deal more effectively with cultural issues. Some cultural awareness training programs focus on both culture and race (see, for example, Hennessy, Warring, & Arnott, 1994). Table 8.4 summarizes the important differences between cultural

race relations training
training in how to deal more effectively with race-related issues, from the perspective that racism is a social disease that can be eliminated with education

cultural awareness training
training in how to deal more effectively with cultural issues, either in general or in terms of a particular culture

TABLE 8.2 Limitations of Early Police Race-Relations Training Programs

- Use of non-needs-based content (that is, the content is developed without surveying the needs of police)

- Time-limited training, which precludes meaningful integration and practice

- Passive instructional approach (one-way lectures)

- Confrontational learning environment and teaching style (for example, white bashing and assumption that all white participants are racist)

- Lack of differentiation of training programs from orientation, briefing, and education programs

- Inadequate knowledge and skill of instructors

- Programs not tailored to rank in the police organization (that is, new recruits and veterans take the same program)

- General programs provided rather than programs specific to policing structure and functions

- Lack of serious administrative support

- Absence of short- and long-term impact evaluations

TABLE 8.3   Goals of Contemporary Police Race-Relations Training Programs

- Change in the organizational structure of police services to promote employment equity and to eliminate systemic barriers to recruitment, selection, retention, and promotion of visible minorities

- Change in the police organizational climate to reduce racism and race-based conduct

- Change in the behaviour of those who work in police organizations to promote better race relations

- Change in society—for example, in socioeconomic conditions—to eradicate racism

TABLE 8.4   Cultural Awareness Training Versus Race Relations Training

Cultural awareness training	Race relations training
Personal growth Increased understanding of one's own culture	*Personal growth* Increased understanding of the dynamics of racism
Interpersonal growth Increased cognitive and emotional understanding of other cultures	*Interpersonal growth* Increased competence in combatting racially based discrimination and harassment
Interpersonal effectiveness Increased competence in cross-cultural communication	*Interpersonal effectiveness* Ability to effect structural changes in institutions to remove systemic barriers
	Ability to effect social change to eradicate racism

awareness training and race relations training. Still, it is important to remember that there is no such thing as a universal cultural awareness training program. In addition, such training may be general or may focus on a particular culture.

Cultural awareness or sensitivity training for police is justified on several grounds. First, police spend a significant amount of time interacting with people from various cultural groups in the community and in the police services. This extensive contact has the potential for misunderstandings and conflict (Triandis, 2000). Training can give police the necessary tools to deal with intercultural encounters. Second, the most common complaints levelled against police are social in nature rather than specific to law enforcement. Third, police want to be more competent in human relations. Fourth, improved police relations with multicultural groups are associated with police effectiveness and an improved quality of life.

CROSS-CULTURAL TRAINING

cross-cultural training
training in how to deal with other cultures, whether in another country or within one's own country

Cross-cultural training programs prepare individuals for living in another country or for living in their own country and dealing with people of diverse cultures (Bhawuk & Brislin, 2000). As well, such programs help people to deal with emotional experiences that arise from intercultural encounters, including clashes in cultural values, culture shock, and personal stereotypes and prejudices. Brislin and

Horvath (1997) suggest a CAB approach to cross-cultural training—cognitive (thinking), affective (emotions), and behavioural (what is actually done). The *cognitive component* focuses on changing people's thinking by increasing their knowledge of culture, cultural differences, and issues that they may face in intercultural encounters. The goal is to increase participants' understanding of people from other cultures so that participants can put themselves in others' shoes. Through cognitive cultural training, police increase the complexity of their thinking using an approach that includes multiple points of view.

The *affective component* focuses on the feelings and emotions generated in intercultural encounters. Cultural differences in habits, customs, and values, and even differences in physical features, may draw out negative emotions in police. These negative emotions may in turn contribute to negative attitudes toward people from diverse cultures. Such attitudes can interfere with police functions and contribute to police–community hostilities. The goal of affective cultural training is to help police develop effective strategies for dealing with their negative emotions.

The *behavioural component* focuses on actual behaviours in intercultural encounters. The goal of behavioural cultural training is successful intercultural interaction. Police learn appropriate behaviours for intercultural encounters.

POLICE TRAINING IN ANTI-RACISM

Anti-racism is defined as an action-oriented, educational, and political strategy for institutional and systemic change that addresses the issues of racism and social oppression (for example, sexism and classism) (see Dei, 1996 expanding on the formulations of Lee, 1985). Anti-racism training helps police become culturally sensitive and more effective. Furthermore, police officers need to understand the issues of race, class, gender identity, and representation as they pertain to community members who come into contact with the police either as suspects or complainants.

ONTARIO POLICE COLLEGE DIVERSITY TRAINING PROGRAMS

The Ontario Police College has a faculty of over 150 full-time and part-time staff members who offer a continuum of training courses for all police personnel, from recruits to police chiefs (Stephens, 2005). The college offers diversity and race relations training as part of its Race Relations and Adult Education training course. The college also offers other training programs that address diversity issues, including the Basic Constable Program, Front Line Supervisor Program, and Leadership Program.

POLICE SERVICES DIVERSITY TRAINING PROGRAMS

Diversity training in policing uses a holistic approach to prepare police and police organizations to become culturally competent and deal more effectively with the diverse communities that they protect and serve. Diversity training programs are different from traditional race- or culture-based training initiatives in four respects. First, diversity training programs are not piecemeal, as were race relations, cultural awareness, and cross-cultural training approaches, and they do not merely pay lip service to diversity in policing. Second, diversity training in policing is integral to policing organizational culture rather than an add-on. Third, diversity is regarded

diversity training
a holistic approach to preparing police and police organizations to become culturally competent

as an asset rather than an irritant to contend with. Finally, diversity training programs are highly relevant to policing work.

A best practices police diversity training program is a program that is developed as part of a police-sponsored diversity training plan and is based on the following principles: it is grounded in supportive policy, it is integrated into all aspects of policing, it provides targeted training for personnel at all levels of service, it allows on-the-job training and mentoring of cross-cultural competence, and it has an anti-racism focus (Pruegger, 2003). An example of a diversity training program recommended for the Durham Regional Police Service is provided in table 8.5. Diversity training curriculums and their modules should rely on a variety of instructional approaches, including guest speakers and role-play, to increase police diversity intelligence.

cross-cultural communication
understanding the verbal and non-verbal communicative patterns of people from diverse cultures for the purpose of effective intercultural interchange

CROSS-CULTURAL COMMUNICATION

In addition to integrative approaches to police training in diversity, policing has been focused on cross-cultural training. **Cross-cultural communication** entails understanding the verbal and non-verbal communicative patterns of people from diverse

TABLE 8.5   Recommended Components of the Diversity Training Plan for the Durham Regional Police Service

- *Valuing Diversity*: All employees learn to understand and value diversity, discuss the influences of culture on communication and behaviour, develop the knowledge, skills, and attitudes to create a more inclusive work environment, and learn to identify stereotypes, prejudices, and biases and their impact in the workplace.

- *Diversity Awareness Module*: New employees gain a basic understanding of diversity, discuss the Diversity Strategic Plan, and learn what is expected of them as members of the police service.

- *Managing Diversity*: Managers learn about the police service's commitment to provide an inclusive and barrier-free workplace, learn about human rights legislation, understand the business case for diversity, build skills for cross-cultural communication, identify characteristics of inclusive leaders, and learn strategies for identifying and accommodating differences.

- *Bias-Aware Selection*: Human resources personnel learn about the police service's commitment to provide a fair recruiting, hiring, and interviewing process; discuss the concepts of stereotype, prejudice, and personal bias and their effect on candidate selection; understand how diversity can positively or negatively affect the outcome of the interview process, build skills in cross-cultural communication, and discuss strategies for better assessing candidates from diverse backgrounds.

- *Respect in the Workplace*: To promote an environment of respect, individuals and organizations learn the definition of harassment, identify attitudes that underlie harassment and the personal and organizational repercussions of discrimination and harassment, understand the responsibilities of employees and managers regarding inappropriate behaviour in the workplace, and develop tools and strategies for creating a culture of respect in the workplace.

Source: Based on Laws (2005).

cultures for the purpose of effective communication. Communication is a critical issue for police, but especially so in a culturally diverse community. Conflict may occur as a result of misunderstandings over language and cultural behaviours. For example, Middle Eastern people tend to take time to warm up to and trust people. North Americans tend to rush right into another person's business. In some cultures, you are expected to wait for an invitation to join others in an activity. In others, you are considered aloof for not joining in.

Cross-cultural communication can be impeded by **misattribution**—a misinterpretation of a message or behaviour. For example, rap music can be misattributed. Fine (1995) explains that rap is a way of communicating a message and establishing reputation. Black and white people's understanding of rap, however, can differ. Blacks do not necessarily expect the performer to act on the words. If the rap is forceful enough, action is unnecessary. Idle boasting in black culture is called "woofin." In the absence of an understanding of "woofin," whites sometimes take the words of the rap literally. It was this lack of understanding that led some people to believe that the lyrics of "Cop Killer" by rap artist Ice T were intended to encourage young blacks to kill police. Blacks, on the other hand, were bemused by all the fuss (Fine, 1995).

misattribution
misinterpretation of a message or behaviour

Verbal Communication

Police often encounter situations in which a person's accent (or their own) or an inability to speak or understand a language are barriers to communication and police performance of duties. For example, a deaf person's failure to respond to a verbal request may be mistaken for resisting police. In other cases, a person's difficulty with English may be seen as a lack of intelligence or a sign that the person is an immigrant who is "right off the boat" and isn't trying to become Canadian. Misattribution is bound to adversely affect police judgment and may influence how police use discretion and handle cases.

Paralanguage, which refers to such features of speech as tone, loudness, speed, and use of silence, may also be a source of misattribution. Asians tend to be soft-spoken, Americans loud, and Middle Easterners even louder. Asians and aboriginal people value silence and interpret the North American rush to butt in and talk as impulsive and rude.

paralanguage
features of speech, such as tone, loudness, speed, and use of silence

Non-Verbal Communication

Non-verbal communication has been neglected in many cultural awareness training programs even though it is estimated that up to 93 percent of the social meaning of a message is delivered non-verbally (Singelis, 1994). A simple definition of non-verbal communication is communication without words (DeVito, 1989).

Kinesics refers to physical communication: look and appearance, eye contact, facial expressions, posture, body movements, and touching. Some cultures like to touch more than others. Koreans refrain from touching people they do not know because such behaviour is considered rude in their culture. Chinese people do not like to be touched on the head. Black people may become grouchy if touched when angry. French, Middle Eastern, and Latin-American people touch more than North Americans or Northern Europeans. For example, a Middle Eastern shop owner may take the arm of a customer and lead her or him around the store, explaining the merchandise.

kinesics
physical communication, including look and appearance, eye contact, facial expressions, posture, body movements, and touching

Facial display of emotions is universal. Six facial expressions of emotion are recognizable in all cultures: anger, fear, happiness, sadness, surprise, and disgust. However, the rules associated with displaying emotions are culture-specific. Thus, some cultures prohibit or discourage the public display of emotions whereas others consider it acceptable and normal. For example, Japanese people consider facial expression of emotions bad manners.

While in North America nodding your head up and down signifies agreement, in other cultures (such as Sri Lankan) shaking your head from side to side means the same thing. In North America, direct eye contact is a sign of respect and attentiveness, whereas in other cultures (for example, Laotian) downcast eyes are the norm for showing respect and attentiveness. In some cultures (for example, Japanese), closing the eyes while listening to another, especially a higher-status person, indicates intense attentiveness rather than disinterest in what is being said.

proxemics
use of space, in terms of physical distance between people, as a form of non-verbal communication

Proxemics refers to the use of space in terms of physical distance between people. Hall (1966) identified four aspects of use of space:

- Intimate distance, which characterizes comforting, lovemaking, and wrestling.

- Personal distance, in which a comfort zone of about 0.5 to 1.0 metres separates one person from another. A police officer who intrudes on this personal space evokes feelings of discomfort or even threat.

- Social distance, in which one person is far enough from another that touching cannot occur.

- Public distance, in which there is a distance of 4 metres or more between two people.

Singelis (1994) has identified several functions of non-verbal communication: replacing verbal communication (for example, gesturing instead of using words), modifying verbal communication (for example, raising your voice for emphasis), regulating social intercourse (for example, applying turn-taking and eye-contact rules in social interactions), carrying emotional messages (for example, communicating like or dislike for a person), and conveying attitudes.

Singelis has also described four pitfalls of non-verbal communication: missing signals, confusing context, misattributing, and sending wrong signals. Missing signals refers to not perceiving or not recognizing non-verbal messages—for example, failing to recognize anger in someone's tone of voice. Context confusion is the process of sending the right message at the wrong time, which can result in misunderstanding. Misattribution, in the context of non-verbal communication, is the process of misdiagnosing a non-verbal behaviour. Here are some examples of misattribution (Community Policing Consortium, 1996):

- A person's passive facial expression is seen by a police officer as a sign of deceit or obstruction.

- A person's silence is interpreted by a police officer as a sign of disrespect or an admission of guilt.

- Touching by a female police officer is mistaken as sexual by a male police officer.

- A man's loud speech and physical closeness comes across as threatening to a police officer.

- A woman's downcast eyes while being questioned by a police officer is misinterpreted as a sign of deceit and guilt.

Singelis (1994) points out that sending the wrong non-verbal signal is the other side of misattribution. He provides the example of former US president Richard Nixon's visit to Brazil in the 1950s when he was still vice-president. On his arrival, Nixon gave the "A-okay" sign without realizing that, in Brazil, putting the thumb and forefinger together in a circle and extending the other fingers is an obscene gesture. Similarly, a police officer who tries to make eye contact with Latina and Arab women will likely be seen as coming on to the women sexually.

Asynchronies in Cultural Encounters

Asynchronies in cultural encounters are "out of step" verbal or non-verbal communication styles. Fine (1995) identified four asynchronies associated with white and black people's interactions: persuasive disclosure, expressing individual feelings, eye contact, and conversational rules.

Persuasive disclosure refers to approaches people use to persuade others. Generally, Canadians of British heritage consider emotion and reason to be mutually exclusive, and emotional debate to be a sign of not exercising reason. Consequently, they tend to use a calm and rational approach to persuasive discussion: language that is careful, calculated, and unemotional; a tone of voice that is low and well modulated; polite decorum at all times; and discussion that does not use intense emotional expressions and argumentative challenges. Challenges and confrontations are perceived as signs of anger and hostility, signifying irrationality. People of Jamaican heritage, on the other hand, define self-control differently, as the ability to express anger fully without allowing the anger to escalate into violence.

To illustrate the misunderstanding and conflict that can arise when the rational persuasive approach meets the emotional persuasive approach, Fine (1995) gives the example of a staff meeting on affirmative action in which a black man, a white woman, and five white men were participants. The black man used very forceful and emotionally charged language as he accused the organization, represented by the remaining participants, of lacking commitment to affirmative action. He also became very angry when none of the participants would respond or defend the organization's actions. The discomfort level of the white participants, and their withdrawal from the discussion, increased in response to the increased level of anger displayed by the black man.

In analyzing the situation, Fine discovered significant differences in the participants' perceptions. The black man experienced fury at the failure of the remaining participants to communicate with him. The white participants, on the other hand, were furious that he was not discussing the issue calmly and rationally, felt angry that he questioned their integrity and commitment to affirmative action, and, in turn, questioned his credibility by assuming that he had a chip on his shoulder about racial issues. The misunderstanding was magnified by the different meanings ascribed by the participants to the arguments that were presented. Whereas the black man was accusing the organization of not supporting affirmative action, the white

asynchrony
state of two (or more) communication styles being out of step with each other as a result of cultural differences

persuasive disclosure
approaches people use to persuade others

people were construing his accusations as personal attacks. Fine (1995, p. 97) points out that in black culture,

> individuals are not expected to defend themselves against general accusations. When a black speaker accuses whites of racism, the speaker is indicting a system of institutional racism in which whites participate; the speaker is not accusing any particular white person, including the person or persons with whom he or she is speaking, of being racist. Denying one's guilt, therefore, is unnecessary. Individuals only need to deny specific accusations that are directed at them, and denial should be firm but not overly vehement. In black culture, a vehement denial is taken as a sign of guilt.

How *individual feelings are expressed* is a second source of misunderstanding in intercultural communication. For example, Fine (1995) indicates that in British cultures, care is taken not to offend individual *sensibilities* (matters of taste, decorum, and refinement) whereas in black culture, care is taken not to offend individual *feelings*. While whites are likely to suppress their feelings so as not to offend the sensibilities of others or even themselves, blacks assert their right to express their feelings even if such expression offends the sensibilities of others.

Eye contact is a third source of asynchrony in cultural encounters. For example, while blacks tend to maintain eye contact when they are speaking, whites tend to maintain eye contact when they are listening. This invariably leads to blacks and whites staring at each other. Fine (1995, pp. 99-100) points out that the mutual staring can heighten the sense of confrontation between blacks and whites:

> What blacks consider normal conversational interaction, therefore, is interpreted by whites as not only unusual but also angry and confrontational, which further strengthens the belief held by many whites that African Americans have "a chip on their shoulder" and are difficult to work with.

Fine also describes a pattern of eye contact that is the reverse of staring. When the white person is speaking, both sides appear to be not paying attention. White speakers break eye contact frequently, leading black listeners to think the whites don't care for them, are disrespectful, are nervous, and are being dishonest. Whites are equally likely to misunderstand the behaviour of blacks. While blacks believe it is disrespectful to maintain eye contact with a speaker, whites believe that looking away from a speaker is a sign of inattentiveness or disrespect. Needless to say, eye contact asynchrony in both of its forms—staring and inattentiveness—can have negative consequences for short-term and long-term relationships between people.

Conversational rules are a fourth source of asynchrony in cultural encounters. For example, Fine (1995) explains that whites adhere to *turn-taking rules* in conversations, while blacks are much more fluid in conversations, with speakers and listeners essentially inseparable from each other. When whites adhere to the turn-taking rules and remain silent while blacks are speaking, blacks interpret the behaviour as not listening. Conversely, when whites are the speakers, they interpret the blacks' behaviour as not listening, talking back, and otherwise interrupting.

Timeliness and Punctuality

Time is culture-bound. Timeliness and punctuality are more of a North American and Northern European preoccupation. People from other cultures are not necessarily as concerned with time. If it is God's will that they will be on time, they will be on time. If God's will is that they will be late, they will be late. Middle Eastern and Latino people may show up an hour or two later than a scheduled meeting or social event. There is no need to worry, and lots of time to be happy.

POLICING WITH CULTURAL COMPETENCY: POLICE ABILITIES, KNOWLEDGE, AND SKILLS

Police play a major role in contributing to their own safety and reputation and ensuring public safety and order. Their understanding of diversity, their competence in dealing with issues of diversity, and their partnership with people of diversity not only inspire self-satisfaction and positive police–community alliances but also nurture community respect and police protection. On the other hand, a lack of understanding of diversity and collaboration with the community will likely contribute to misunderstandings, miscommunication, tension, and conflict. Negative encounters with people of diversity have the added disadvantage of increasing personal exposure to complaints, lawsuits, and job dissatisfaction—not to mention irate taxpayers and bad press.

In the past two decades, police services have made considerable efforts to change law enforcement culture so that it is both more inclusive and more responsive to the needs of their communities (MacLeod, 2004 as cited in Taylor, 2004). Police have gration, globalization, terrorism, and the increased pluralism of the communities police serve and protect. Today, a primary goal of law enforcement organizations is to be "internally welcoming, reflective and knowledgeable" (cited in Taylor, 2004; MacLeod, 2004 as cited in Taylor, 2004; Perry, 2004). The seeds of diversity training programs were planted three decades ago and have grown into a consideration of diversity as a strategic advantage in policing. Other initiatives have followed: the establishment of human rights offices and diversity units in police services; participation in the Law Enforcement Aboriginal and Diversity Network (LEAD) and Data Collection Strategy on Hate-Motivated Crime initiatives (Canadian Heritage, 2006); the drafting of the Bias-Free Policing Policy by the RCMP; and the application of diversity principles to cross-cultural criminal investigations for increased community policing effectiveness and public safety (Pruegger, 2003; Perry, 2004; Taylor, 2004).

Supported by the Multiculturalism Program of Canadian Heritage, the Canadian Association of Chiefs of Police assumed responsibility for LEAD to help law enforcement officers across the country develop better working relationships with the ethnocultural and aboriginal communities they serve (cited in Taylor, 2004; Canadian Heritage, 2006), and to offer training and information on delivering bias-free policing services and help law enforcement institutions become more diverse through recruitment and retention. An important aspect of the LEAD initiative has been the construction of a website (www.lead-alda.ca) to provide a forum for discussion of best practices on diversity. The website also provides resources in such areas as hate crime, national crime statistics, community and police partnerships, and other issues of interest to police (Taylor, 2004).

The innovative application of diversity principles to community policing has increased the effectiveness of this form of policing and enhanced community safety.

TABLE 8.6   Dos and Don'ts of Policing with Diversity Competency

Dos	Don'ts
■ Participate in and support diversity awareness training programs.	■ Don't compromise your safety.
■ Learn the customs, values, and behaviours of people of diversity.	■ Don't avoid becoming literate about diversity.
■ Recognize that different people do or say things differently.	■ Don't treat people of diversity as if they are stupid or dangerous.
■ Recognize that non-verbal communication can be even more important than verbal communication.	■ Don't touch others if you don't have to.
■ Watch for potential misattributions in communication.	■ Don't intimidate people by staring them down.
■ Prevent conflicts from escalating or occurring in the first place.	■ Don't assume that everyone communicates in the same way.
	■ Don't assume that everyone gets the same message when communicating.

cross-cultural criminal investigation
application of diversity principles in crime investigation

Police have also recognized that diversity competency is important in cross-cultural criminal investigations. **Cross-cultural criminal investigations** require that police understand diversity issues in crime, assign police personnel to interact and gain the confidence of communities and their leaders to secure critical information, and apply policing policies that direct investigators or cultural experts to work with community leaders when an investigation is likely to have an impact on the diverse communities (Perry, 2004). An underlying assumption of cross-cultural criminal investigations is that using open and honest dialogue with community leaders to identify problems specific to their particular culture and involving them in the process of criminal investigations are conducive to the formation of long term police–community relationships.

Policing has come a long way in recognizing the value of diversity, changing its traditional "white male image," and increasing its cultural competence for the benefit of police and society. Although there is always need for improvement, police organizations need to be commended for forging ahead and professionalizing and diversifying the face of policing. Table 8.6 provides a list of dos and don'ts of policing with cultural competency.

CHAPTER SUMMARY

Positive anti-racism initiatives are required at the societal level and at the policing level. Although diversity was once considered a liability, the contemporary view of diversity is that it is an integral part of policing culture, improves police–community relations, aids in criminal investigations, and enhances public safety. Police organizations have recognized that stand-alone race relations and cultural awareness police training programs are limited in scope and effectiveness; instead, they have embraced best practices diversity training programs in policing that are part of a police-sponsored diversity training plan and are integral to police culture.

KEY TERMS

authoritarianism

employment equity

race relations training

cultural awareness training

cross-cultural training

diversity training

cross-cultural communication

misattribution

paralanguage

kinesics

proxemics

asynchrony

persuasive disclosure

cross-cultural criminal investigation

REFERENCES

Banton, M. (1963, April). Social integration and police. *Police Chief*: 10–12.

Bhawuk, D.P.S., & R.W. Brislin. (2000, January). Cross-cultural training: A review. *Applied Psychology: An International Review* 49(1): 162–91.

Brislin, R.W., & A.M. Horvath. (1997). Cross-cultural training and multicultural education. In J.W. Berry, M.H. Segal, and C. Kagitcibasi (Eds.), *Handbook of cross-cultural psychology: Social behaviour and applications.* Vol. 3 (pp. 327-69). Needham Heights, MA: Allyn and Bacon.

Calliste, A., & G.S. Die. (2000). *Anti-racist feminism: Critical race and gender studies.* Halifax: Fernwood.

Canadian Heritage. (2006). *Annual report on the operation of the Canadian Multiculturalism Act 2004-2005.* http://www.pch.gc.ca/progs/multi/pubs/index_e.cfm.

Coffey, A. (1990). *Law enforcement: A human relations approach.* Englewood Cliffs, NJ: Prentice-Hall.

Community Policing Consortium. (1996, June). *Cultural diversity* 1. http://www.communitypolicing.org/cultural/index.html.

Dei, G.S. (1996). *Anti-racism: Theory and practice.* Halifax: Fernwood.

DeVito, J.A. (1989). *The nonverbal communication workbook.* Prospect Heights, IL: Waveland Press.

Fine, M.G. (1995). *Building successful multicultural organizations: Challenges and opportunities.* Westport, CT: Quorum Books.

Hall, E.T. (1966). *The hidden dimension.* New York: Doubleday.

Harris, E.V.C., & G.A. Currie. (1994). An integrated anti-racism training model: A framework for positive action. *Crime & Justice: The Americas* 7: 11–14.

Hennessy, S.M., D.F. Warring, & J.S. Arnott. (1994). *A cultural awareness trainer's manual for law enforcement officers.* Scottsdale, AZ: Leadership Inc.

Kallen, E. (2003). *Ethnicity and human rights in Canada.* 3rd Edition. Toronto: Oxford University Press.

Laws, J. (2005, February 4). *Durham Regional Police Service (DRPS): 2005-2010 diversity strategic plan.* Graybridge Malkam.

Lee, E. (1985). *Letters to Marcia: A teacher's guide to anti-racist education.* Toronto: Cross Cultural Communication Centre.

Lewis, C. (1993). The police and the community. In J. Chacko and S.E. Nancoo (Eds.), *Community policing in Canada* (pp. 269–73). Toronto: Canadian Scholars' Press.

MacLeod, E. (2004, Fall). Message from the president. *Canadian Police Chief Magazine*, p. 7.

McIntyre, D. (1992). Race relations and policing. In K.R.E. McCormick and L.A. Visano (Eds.), *Policing in Canada* (pp. 647–55). Toronto: Canadian Scholars' Press.

Perry, D. (2004, Fall). Complexities of cross-cultural investigations. *Canadian Police Chief Magazine*, p. 22–24.

Pruegger, V. (2003, February). Community and policing in partnership. Paper developed for Policing in a Multicultural Society Conference, Ottawa.

Redway, A. (1992). *A matter of fairness: Report of the Special Committee on the Review of the Employment Equity Act.* Ottawa: Supply and Services Canada.

Rees, T. (1992). Police race relations training. *Currents: Readings in Race Relations* 7: 15–18.

Rodelet, L.A., & D.L. Carter. (1994). *The police and the community.* New York: MacMillan College Publishing.

Samuel, T.J., & S.K. Suriya. (1993). A demographically reflective workforce for Canadian policing. In J. Chacko and S.E. Nancoo (Eds.), *Community policing in Canada* (pp. 271–87). Toronto: Canadian Scholars' Press.

Singelis, T. (1994). Nonverbal communication in intercultural interactions. In R.W. Brislin and T. Yoshida (Eds.), *Improving international interactions: Modules for cross-cultural training programs* (pp. 268–94). Thousand Oaks, CA: Sage.

Steinberg, J.L., & D.W. McEvoy. (1974). *The police and the behavioural sciences.* Springfield, IL: Charles C. Thomas.

Stephens, B. (2005, February 27). Policing as a career in Ontario. Paper presented at the Hong Kong University Alumni Association. Aylmer, ON: Ontario Police College.

Taylor, N. (2004, Fall). Policing with cultural competency. *Canadian Police Chief Magazine*, pp. 14–19.

Triandis, H.C. (2000). Culture and conflict. *International Journal of Psychology* 35(2): 145–52.

Ungerleider, C. (1992). *Issues in police intercultural and race relations training in Canada*. Ottawa: Canadian Centre for Police–Race Relations.

Wortley, S. (1994). *Perceptions of bias and racism within the Ontario criminal justice system: Results from a public opinion survey*. Toronto: Commission on Systemic Racism in the Ontario Criminal Justice System.

EXERCISES AND REVIEW

Personal Reflections

Read each statement below and circle whether you agree or disagree with it.

1. Demographic diversity needs to be considered in policing.

    AGREE   DISAGREE

2. Diversity has a significant impact on policing.

    AGREE   DISAGREE

3. Differences in communication styles have an impact on police–community relations.

    AGREE   DISAGREE

4. Diversity training programs benefit police working the street.

    AGREE   DISAGREE

5. Police with high cultural competence are more likely to gain the respect of the diverse communities they serve and protect.

    AGREE   DISAGREE

6. Police organizations that invest time and energy in diversity training contribute to police safety and public safety.

    AGREE   DISAGREE

7. Police training programs in diversity are nothing but cop-bashing sessions.

    AGREE   DISAGREE

8. Police who learn about diversity are likely to do a better policing job.

    AGREE   DISAGREE

9. Police need to see diversity as a positive principle rather than a problem or irritant.

    AGREE   DISAGREE

10. Cross-cultural communication training has little relevance to crime investigations in diverse communities.

AGREE   DISAGREE

SCORING: Give yourself one point for agreeing with each of the following statements: 1 to 6, 8, and 9. Give yourself one point each for disagreeing with 7 and 10. The higher the score, the more favourable your attitude toward diversity training in policing. Compare your score with a classmate's and try to reconcile any differences in opinion.

Diversity IQ: Multiple Choice

Circle the best answer.

1. Which of the following is a traditional image of police?

   a. zookeeper

   b. James Bond

   c. curator

   d. Lone Ranger

2. Which of the following is true about a diversity strategic plan?

   a. it is irrelevant to police work

   b. it is an add-on training package

   c. it is grounded in policing policy

   d. none of the above

3. Which of the following is an aspect of best practices police training in diversity?

   a. management of diversity

   b. understanding of the concept of diversity

   c. anti-discrimination

   d. all of the above

4. Which of the following is a component of race relations training programs for police?

   a. raising awareness of racist inclinations in white police officers

   b. activism for organizational change

   c. a and b

   d. none of the above

5. Non-verbal communication

    a. regulates interpersonal interactions

    b. complements verbal communication

    c. sends important emotional messages

    d. all of the above

6. Which of the following non-verbal messages may be misinterpreted?

    a. eye contact

    b. head movements

    c. hand gestures

    d. all of the above

7. The rational persuasive approach involves

    a. separating emotions from opinions

    b. expressing opinions in an argumentative way

    c. verbal confrontation

    d. all of the above

8. Which of the following is likely to contribute to intercultural misunderstanding?

    a. mismatch in conversational rules

    b. differences in patterns of eye contact

    c. differences in expressing emotions

    d. all of the above

9. Which of the following is a possible pitfall of communication?

    a. missing signals

    b. misattribution

    c. context confusion

    d. all of the above

10. Which of the following is an outcome of police training in diversity?

    a. insensitivity to diversity

    b. incompetence to deal with diversity

    c. diversity competence

    d. all of the above

Diversity IQ: True or False?

_____ 1. Police may develop a negative view of a community because of negative experiences with its members.

_____ 2. The view of police and public as adversaries is always justified.

_____ 3. Police services that support and implement diversity training programs are acting in their own interests.

_____ 4. Authoritarianism in policing represents "badge-heavy" police conduct.

_____ 5. Cultural awareness training programs for police focus on refining police skills in intercultural encounters.

_____ 6. Diversity awareness training programs for police are a waste of police time and energy.

_____ 7. A person with limited competence in the English language is most likely not too bright.

_____ 8. Direct eye contact is a sign of respect in one culture and a sign of disrespect in another culture.

_____ 9. A criticism of anti-racism training programs is that the training is sometimes used for "white bashing" or "cop bashing."

_____ 10. Anti-racism initiatives aim at removing barriers that prevent people of diversity from fully participating in the economic, social, and political domains of society.

Application Now

1. This chapter discussed some anti-racism initiatives. Research initiatives in the area of anti-sexism, anti-ageism, or anti-monoculturalism, and describe your findings.

2. Research the topic of cultural intelligence and its relevance to policing.

3. Imagine that you are a police officer. Underrepresentation of Arab/Muslim officers is problematic in your community. Some members of the Arab/Muslim community will not call police if there is a problem because they are not comfortable talking with non-Arab, non-Muslim officers. What actions would you take to address this issue from a diversity community policing perspective?

Food for Thought

1. Role-play situations in which a police officer is questioning a member of the public, using each of the following situations. After your role plays, have players describe what happened, how they feel about what happened, and the degree to which they liked or disliked the person with whom they were interacting.

    The two participants maintain eye contact at all times.

    The two participants avoid eye contact at all times.

    One participant follows turn-taking rules while the other does not.

From Thought to Action

1. Role-play each of the following situations in class. Have observers watch the verbal and non-verbal communication of the participants. First, role-play the situations according to the scripts provided in a, b, and c below. After feedback from the class, re-enact them with the "police officers" using culturally competent verbal and non-verbal communication.

   Observe the responses of the role players in relation to:

   - tone of voice
   - facial expression
   - eye contact
   - body posture and movement
   - physical distance

   - hand gestures, including touching
   - turn-taking rules
   - expression of emotions
   - empathy
   - persuasive disclosure

   a. Police officer stops a teenager on the street.

      Black teenager to police officer: "I was doing nothing wrong."

      Police officer: "Listen, boy, with that attitude of yours you're going to be a loser for the rest of your life."

   b. Police officer to white woman involved in argument with another white woman: "You better shape up, bitch, or else I'm going to lock you in the slammer for good."

   c. Police officer called to school to deal with an incident in which a straight student called a gay student a "fag." Police officer to gay student: "What's the big fuss, boy? You have to stop carrying a chip on your shoulder and learn to get along with all the straight kids in school."

d. A 14-year-old has called police because his father slapped him in the face for getting home after his 2 a.m. curfew. Police officer to father: "You may slap your son in your country, but here in my country we do things differently."

e. A 13-year-old Arab teenager calls the police and complains that her father is not allowing her to go out on a date with a 16-year-old from the neighbourhood. Police officer to father: "This is not the Middle East. When are you going to do things our way?"

f. A group of Arabs and Muslims requests a meeting with police to express their concern that members of their community are being harassed and subjected to racial profiling following news reports on terrorism. One of the community leaders says in the meeting, "We are being wrongly categorized as dangerous, as terrorists. We are law-abiding citizens. We will not do harm to our fellow citizens or violate Canadian laws. We want our civil rights to be protected. We want the phenomenon of 'traveling while Arab/Muslim' to stop."

2. Critique the list of dos and don'ts in table 8.6 (on page 240). What do you think should be deleted from the list; what should be added?

Lessons from History

The last victim of a serial rapist who was attacking women in Don Mills, Ontario provided detailed descriptions of her attacker and identified him as being Filipino. The victim was a white female whose boyfriend was from the Philippines, so she was familiar with Philippine culture. The Philippine community complained loudly when police issued a statement to the media saying that the suspect was believed to be from the Philippines. They claimed that the racial description was racist. The police broke with tradition. When police met with the Philippine community leaders and heard information sensitive to the investigation and the victim's knowledge and ties to their community, they were satisfied with the police explanation. Police also promised to provide a public explanation for the release of the racial description once the suspect was apprehended. Police were able to make good on their promise. The suspect was in fact a recent arrival from the Philippines (Perry, 2004).

How can police benefit from the non-traditional criminal investigation approach taken in this case?

The Great Debate

Perry (2004) has argued that police can become "culturally sensitive to a fault" such that in some cases diversity sensitivity can become "a roadblock between police and the diverse communities … . [T]oo much attention can be paid to those who speak the loudest but who don't necessarily represent the views of their communities." Debate the dilemma facing modern-day policing: diversity sensitivity versus public safety.

PART IV

Special Diversity Considerations

CHAPTER 9

Policing Family Violence

CHAPTER OBJECTIVES

After completing this chapter, you should be able to:

- Discuss diversity issues as they relate to family violence.

- Identify strategies that enable police to work with diverse groups in the community to address family violence issues.

> ### PREVIEW SCENARIO
>
> Jennifer and Jenny met at a party. Jennifer saw Jenny's intelligence, beauty, and wonderful sense of humour. Their relationship developed rapidly, and Jennifer felt that she had never experienced such closeness before. At the beginning, Jenny's abuse of Jennifer was subtle. Jenny would criticize Jennifer's cooking and call her names during arguments. Jennifer did not think of these incidents as signs of abuse. Instead, she linked them to recent stressors in Jenny's life. Jenny had recently lost custody of her daughter to her ex-husband and subsequently attempted suicide. Jenny supported Jennifer when Jennifer's family disowned her because she was a lesbian. However, Jenny insisted that the car Jennifer bought be put in Jenny's name. Jenny's bouts of drinking and drug use increased, as did the arguments between her and Jennifer. At one point, Jenny was arrested for possession of drugs and driving under the influence, and insisted that Jennifer submit to drug testing in her place. When Jennifer resisted, Jenny threatened to squeal on her and tell her employer that she was a lesbian. Jennifer kept telling herself that things would get better, but they never did. Jenny carried on a pattern of falsely accusing Jennifer of being unfaithful. Jenny even raped Jennifer on one occasion after accusing Jennifer of flirting with a supermarket cashier. The abuse escalated to other physical violence. Jennifer asked Jenny to go with her to counselling. Even though things felt worse to Jennifer, the therapist assessed the situation as normal and advised them to continue their relationship. Jennifer went through a period of blaming herself and thinking that the relationship might improve

if she improved. When Jenny pulled a knife on her, Jennifer realized that things were only getting worse. She called a crisis line. The counsellor's suggestion that she was experiencing family violence was a shock to Jennifer. It had never occurred to her that she was in an abusive relationship because she and Jenny were both women. Jennifer left Jenny, the hardest thing she had ever done. Jennifer is still in occasional contact with Jenny because her car is still in Jenny's name. Jenny is still verbally abusive. Jennifer is still coming to grips with four realities: first, women can abuse women; second, violence is not caused by alcohol, drugs, anger, depression, or stress; third, abuse is a choice the abuser makes; fourth, Jennifer is not to blame. (MINCAVA, 1998)

INTRODUCTION

Everyone has the right to a safe home environment that is free from neglect and economic, physical, psychological, and spiritual abuse. In the absence of such an ideal, people who are exposed to neglect, intimidation, domination, and physical or sexual assault have the right to protection and assistance. Similarly, perpetrators of family neglect and abuse have the right to receive help in learning to coexist with others peacefully.

This chapter discusses family violence from the perspective of diversity policing. It emphasizes that all people, regardless of their age, gender, ethnicity, level of education, socioeconomic status, occupation, race, religion, sexual orientation, or physical or mental abilities, can experience family violence. The chapter also describes the often devastating consequences of family violence for victims. Finally, it discusses past and present policies on how police respond to calls involving family violence, especially those involving immigrant and refugee women, who are particularly vulnerable.

DEFINITION OF FAMILY VIOLENCE

family violence
behaviour that causes one partner in a relationship to be afraid of and controlled by the other, or that is caregiver abuse of children or abuse of caregiver by children

In the past, "family dispute," "family trouble," and "husband and wife spat" have been used as euphemisms for family violence. **Family violence** is a term that includes the many different forms of abuse, mistreatment, or neglect that adults or children may experience in their intimate, kinship, extended, or dependent relationships (Department of Justice Canada, 2006). Although family violence typically involves behaviour that causes one partner in a relationship to be afraid of and controlled by the other, it can also entail abuse of the caregiver by the children.

Abuse may take a variety of forms, including infanticide, physical assault, physical neglect, sexual assault, sexual exploitation, emotional and psychological abuse, financial abuse, and spiritual abuse. Physical assault may range from bruising to murder. Sexual assault may range from unwanted sexual touching to rape. Psychological abuse may range from emotional or mental violence (verbal abuse, put-downs, humiliation, threats, property damage, and destruction) to excessive possessiveness, forced isolation from friends and family, and harassment. Financial abuse may entail withholding money to buy food or medical treatment, creating a financially dependent relationship, controlling a person's bank accounts, denying a person access to finances, and preventing a person from working. Finally, spiritual abuse may involve putting a person's religious beliefs and practices down or not allowing that person's spiritual needs to be met.

FAMILY VIOLENCE AND THE LAW

Family violence is against the law in Canada. Ontario's *Child and Family Services Act* protects the well-being of children and provides for services to children and their families in a manner that respects their "cultural, religious and regional differences" (section 1(a)). Similarly, the *Criminal Code* and the *Canada Evidence Act* include provisions to deter and prevent family violence and are amended periodically to better address family violence issues including rising concerns over child pornography, Internet luring, child sex tourism, and the testimony of child victims and witnesses (Department of Justice Canada, 2006a).

Although the *Criminal Code* does not make specific reference to family violence offences, those who engage in family violence can be charged on a number of grounds under the Code:

- failure to provide the necessaries of life (s. 215);

- abandoning a child (s. 218);

- assault, including assault causing bodily harm, assault with a weapon, and aggravated assault (ss. 265-268);

- sexual assault, including sexual assault causing bodily harm, sexual assault with a weapon, and aggravated sexual assault (ss. 271-273);

- sexual offences against children and youth, including sexual interference (s. 151), invitation to sexual touching (s. 152), sexual exploitation (s. 153), incest (s. 155), parent or guardian procuring sexual activity (s. 170), householder permitting sexual activity (s. 171), and corrupting children (s. 172);

- child pornography (s. 163.1);

- criminal harassment or stalking (s. 264);

- uttering threats (s. 264.1);

- kidnapping and forcible confinement (s. 279);

- abduction of a young person (ss. 280-283);

- mischief (s. 430);

- intimidation (s. 423);

- trespassing at night (s. 177);

- breach of court order (s. 127(1)), peace bond (protective order) (s. 811), or probation order (s. 773.1(1)); and

- murder, attempted murder, infanticide, and manslaughter (ss. 229-239).

HOW BIG A PROBLEM IS FAMILY VIOLENCE?

Several studies initiated since the 1980s suggest that family violence in Canada is a pervasive social and policing problem (Committee on Sexual Offences Against Children and Youth, 1984; Rodgers, 1993; Canadian Panel on Violence Against Women, 1993; Statistics Canada, 2000; Health Canada, 2001; Statistics Canada, 2005).

Abuse Among Adults

spousal abuse
violence or mistreatment experienced by a man or a woman at the hands of a marital, common-law, or same-sex partner

Spousal abuse is violence or mistreatment that a woman or a man experiences at the hands of a marital or common-law partner. It can occur between opposite-sex or same-sex partners. Adult abuse includes spiritual, emotional, psychological, economic, and physical abuse in intimate relationships (Canadian Panel on Violence Against Women, 1993). In the 2004 General Social Survey, close to 7 percent of Canadian adults (about 653,000 women and 546,000 men) indicated that they had experienced some form of abuse in their marital or common-law relationships in the past five years (Statistics Canada, 2005).

Abuse of Children and Youth

child abuse
physical and psychological maltreatment of children by adults

Child abuse describes a broad category of maltreatment of children below the age of 14, including physical and psychological abuse. *Psychological abuse* involves emotionally damaging acts of omission and commission—rejection, isolation, exploitation, and poor socialization. It is important to differentiate between the harm that children experience as a result of acts that are prohibited, deliberate, and preventable and harm that is due to economic disadvantage—for example, poverty.

child sexual abuse
sexual exploitation and maltreatment of dependent and developmentally immature children and adolescents

Child sexual abuse refers to the sexual exploitation of dependent and developmentally immature children who are made to participate in "sexual activities they do not fully comprehend, are unable to give informed consent to, and that violate the social taboos of family roles" (Schecter & Roberge, 1976). The psychological and behavioural consequences of child sexual abuse include post-traumatic stress disorder and disturbed interpersonal relations.

A total of 135,573 child maltreatment investigations were conducted in Canada in 1998: 21 percent for physical abuse, of which 34 percent were substantiated; 10 percent for sexual abuse, of which 38 percent were substantiated; 40 percent for neglect, of which 43 percent were substantiated; and 19 percent for emotional maltreatment, of which 19 percent were substantiated. (Note that in many cases, more than one type of abuse was investigated.)

The majority of the substantiated cases of physical abuse involved inappropriate punishment (69 percent), followed by shaken baby syndrome (1 percent), and other forms of physical abuse (31 percent).

The most common forms of substantiated sexual abuse were touching and fondling of a child's genitals (68 percent), followed by attempted and completed sexual activity (35 percent), and adults exposing their genitals (12 percent).

The most common forms of substantiated neglected were failure to supervise leading to physical harm (48 percent), followed by physical neglect (19 percent), permitting criminal behaviour (14 percent), abandonment (12 percent) and educational neglect (11 percent). Finally, the most common forms of substantiated emotional maltreatment were exposure to family violence (58 percent), followed by emotional abuse (34 percent), and emotional neglect (16 percent) (Health Canada, 2001).

Police reports for 2003 indicate that 61 percent of all sexual assault victims are children and youth (14-18 years old), and that parents are responsible for 32 percent of the sexual assaults against these children and youth (Department of Justice Canada, 2006a).

Abuse of Older Adults

Elder abuse is the physical, sexual, emotional, or psychological abuse or neglect, or the financial exploitation (fraud and theft) of an older person by a caregiver (spouse or partner, adult child, or relative) or institutional staff member, including staff in a nursing home. The psychological outcomes of elder abuse include feelings of shame, embarrassment, guilt, and inadequacy. In 1999, 2 percent of all victims of violent crime were 65 years and older (Statistics Canada, 2000).

elder abuse

physical, sexual, emotional, or psychological abuse or neglect, or financial exploitation, of an older person by a caregiver

COST OF FAMILY VIOLENCE

Family violence has severe economic, physical, social, and psychological costs to society generally and to victims, abusers, and witnesses of abuse in particular.

Consequences for Society

In Canada, it has been estimated that violence against women costs the nation $4.2 billion (Greaves & Hankivsky, 1995) each year. The immediate costs of medical and dental treatment and time lost from work have been estimated to be $45.2 million (Day, 1995).

Consequences for Victims

Victims of family violence can suffer bruises, broken bones, back and head injuries, loss of hearing, impaired eyesight, malnutrition, burns, disfigurement, reproductive damage, and death. In terms of the psychological costs, victims of family violence may experience terror, depression, severe anxiety, post-traumatic stress disorder, loss of self-esteem and sense of control over their own lives, and feelings of hopelessness, helplessness, guilt, shame, and isolation. In some cases, victims of family violence attempt suicide. Contrary to popular belief, battered women are not safe after separation from the batterer (Cantin, 1998; Hotton, 2001). Many batterers track down their ex-partners and commit further violent assaults.

Consequences for Abusers

Family violence has consequences for abusers as well. The abuse and the abusers' need for power and control over others are likely to destroy their relationships with the very people they love and involve them in the criminal justice system. Although some abusers recognize that they have a problem and attempt to change their behaviour, others see the victims as the source of the problem and may eventually destroy the victims and themselves.

Consequences for Witnesses of Violence

The quality of life of children who witness family violence is seriously compromised (Jaffe, Suderman, & Reitzel, 1992; Jaffe & Suderman, 1995; Dauvergne & Johnson, 2001). In addition to physical illness, children who witness family violence are likely to live in a constant state of fear and shame, to blame themselves for the violence, to be preoccupied with safety issues, and to exhibit a variety of symptoms and behaviours, including post-traumatic stress disorder.

Of considerable concern is the potential effect that violence has on the socialization of child witnesses. Violent homes rob children twice: first by robbing them of their innocence, and second by robbing them of their childhood. Violent homes also imprint in children scripts on the family life of wives and husbands. The first script is that the husband has power over the wife that he can exploit. The second script is that it's okay for the husband to hit the wife or use other means of violence to get what he wants. In this script, the man is a bully who pushes the woman around and terrorizes the household. The third script is that a man who is sensitive and considerate is a sissy. The goal is to be a "manly" man. The fourth script is the wife hiding her victimization and keeping it a secret. The fifth script is that the children of this couple trust no one. The sixth script is that what is good for the husband is good for the son, and that what the wife deserves the daughter also deserves. It is reported that 25 percent of children in one shelter for battered women in Canada felt that it is appropriate for a man to strike a woman if the house is messy.

DIVERSITY AND FAMILY VIOLENCE

People of all backgrounds, regardless of their age, gender, ethnicity, education, cultural identity, socioeconomic status, occupation, race, religion, sexual orientation, or physical or mental abilities, can experience family abuse (MacLeod & Shin, 1990; Green, 1996; Chesley, MacAulay, & Ristock, 1998; Biesenthal et al., 2000; Law Commission of Canada, 2001). Family violence tends to be kept secret in many cultures. People are embarrassed by it and do not want to talk about it. As a result, no one really knows exactly how many people are victims or survivors of this violence. Table 9.1 lists some myths associated with family violence.

Sex and Family Violence

While women and men experience similar rates of both violence and emotional abuse in their relationships, the violence experienced by women tends to be more severe and more often repeated than the violence directed at men (Statistics Canada, 2005). Women are six times more likely to report being sexually assaulted, five times more likely to report being choked, five times more likely to require medical attention as a result of an assault, and three times more likely to be physically injured by an assault (Statistics Canada, 2005).

TABLE 9.1 Myths About Family Violence

- Family violence is rare.
- Family violence is confined to the lower socioeconomic classes.
- Family violence happens only in heterosexual relationships.
- People with disabilities are immune from family violence.
- Substance abuse is the real cause of family violence.
- Victims of family violence have masochistic personalities.
- Victims of family violence exaggerate the abuse.
- Abusers cannot control their abusive behaviours.
- Victims of family violence provoke the abuse.
- Victims of family violence consider abuse a sexual turn-on.
- Diversity (for example, culture, disability) is the root cause of family violence.

The notion that there is a typical man who abuses is a myth. However, male abusers are often described by their partners as having Jekyll and Hyde personalities. These men can be charming and caring, but they can also turn vicious and violent. Men who abuse women also tend to hold beliefs that act as catalysts to abusive behaviour. These include viewing women as objects that men possess rather than as people, feeling powerless, believing that other people or circumstances are to blame for their actions, and feeling extremely jealous.

Sexual Orientation and Family Violence

Family violence is not limited to heterosexual relationships (Chesley, MacAulay, & Ristock, 1998). Family violence occurs in gay and lesbian relationships, where it has been described as a "closet within the closet." The secrecy surrounding violence in gay and lesbian relationships is attributed to a homophobic society and the media portrayal of gays and lesbians as sexual beings rather than as people who have real relationships. The rate of family violence (one in four) in gay, lesbian, bisexual, and transgendered couples is about the same as that in straight couples (Page, 1999).

Immigrants and Refugees and Family Violence

Immigrants and refugees have unique experiences, fears, needs, and hopes that complicate the reality of family violence. Western conceptions of abuse may be different from those of other cultures. Denying girls an education and setting up arranged marriages for both boys and girls can be considered abuse in Western cultures, where their consent was not given and they are below the provincial legal age for marriage, but are culturally accepted practices in some non-Western cultures. While it is important in all cases to expect all cultural and ethnic groups to respect the laws of Canada, it is also important to recognize cultural practices that do not constitute child abuse under Canadian law but can, nevertheless, be mistaken for it. Allegations of child abuse that stem from cultural ignorance can have devastating consequences for parents, including suicide.

Coining, pinching, and cupping are practices that are often mistaken for abuse. *Coining* involves rubbing an area of the body with a metal object, usually a coin or spoon, until the skin becomes red. It is used by some cultures to treat headaches, colds, fevers, stomach aches, dizziness, and fatigue. Which part of the body is rubbed depends on the problem or symptom—for example, the forehead is rubbed in the case of a headache. *Pinching* the skin between the eyebrows until it becomes red is done for similar reasons. Finally, *cupping* entails burning paper or cotton in a glass cup, removing the paper or cotton, and immediately placing the cup on the skin of the back for suction. One or more cups may be used to relieve a fever, a cold, or high blood pressure. The back is covered with a towel for a few minutes and then the cups are removed. Cupping is usually followed by rubbing the treated parts of the body with alcohol. Coining, pinching, and cupping cause bruising of the treated areas and may be mistaken for abuse.

On the other hand, immigrants and refugees may bring with them cultural beliefs and practices that are at odds with Canadian law and constitute abuse. Immigrants and refugees may come from cultures in which women have less political power, lower legal status, and lower social status than women in Canada. They may import practices such as honour killings, honour suicides, and female genital mutilation (FGM), which may have been sanctioned in their cultures or countries of origin or considered light crimes, but are serious criminal offences in Canada.

Honour killing is the murder of a female family member by a male family member, usually a brother, for allegedly sullying her family's honour. A woman may stain her family's name by engaging in sexual relations out of wedlock, refusing an arranged marriage, or trying to escape an abusive relationship.

Honour suicides occur when a daughter who is felt to have disgraced or dishonoured her family is pressured to commit suicide and given the means to do so by the family. For example, the family may lock their daughter in a room and provide her with lethal weapons—rat poison, a pistol, or a rope—and tell her that her death is the only thing resting between her disgrace and redemption (Bilefsky, 2006). The offending act may range from wearing a short skirt, to expressing a desire to go to the movies, to having been raped by a stranger or a relative. Honour suicides are honour killings in disguise. Instead of having a son kill the daughter and risk imprisonment, the family pressures the daughter to kill herself, thus sparing the son.

The dislocation of families from rural villages to cities appears to be a contributory factor in honour suicides. Tension develops within families when young women who were raised in protective families with strict familial and religious moral strictures are suddenly placed in a secular environment and embrace secular and Western values and practices. Families who believe that their daughters have brought dishonour on the family may encourage honour suicides to restore the family name (Bilefsky, 2006).

Families and young women from cultures that practise honour killings and honour suicides who immigrate to Western host countries such as Canada may experience a tension between the host countries' secular institutions and their religious upbringing, and between Western values and their traditionalist values. Such tensions contribute to familial stress generally and vulnerability to family violence in particular.

Female genital mutilation refers to the removal of part, or all, of the female genitalia. The most severe form is infibulation in which part or all of the external genitalia are removed and the labia are partially stitched together. Female genital mutilation is most common in Africa, Asia, and the Middle East. An estimated 15 percent of all mutilations in Africa are infibulations. The procedure consists of a clitoridectomy (where all, or part, of the clitoris is removed), excision (removal of all, or part, of the labia minora), and cutting of the labia majora to create raw surfaces, which are then stitched or held together in order to form a cover over the vagina when they heal. A small hole is left to allow urine and menstrual blood to escape. In some less conventional forms of infibulation, less tissue is removed and a larger opening is left.

The vast majority (85 percent) of genital mutilations performed in Africa consist of a clitoridectomy or an excision. The least radical procedure consists of the removal of the clitoral hood. In some traditions a ceremony is held, but no mutilation of the genitals occurs. The ritual may include holding a knife next to the genitals, pricking the clitoris, cutting some pubic hair, or light scarification in the genital or upper thigh area (Amnesty International, 2005).

EXPLANATIONS FOR FAMILY VIOLENCE

Popular explanations for family violence fall into four categories. The *personal view* points the finger at women and suggests that they provoke men into abusing them. The *chemical view* blames abusive behaviour on the use of alcohol and illicit drugs. Blaming these for the abuse is just an excuse. The *social view* points the finger at several factors: stress, economic hardship, men's hunger for control and power, women's fear of disclosure (Champagne, Lapp, & Lee, 1994), and society's lax attitude toward abusers. However, the social view identifies patriarchy as the main culprit, arguing that patriarchal societies institutionalize social control of women and sustain their unequal power status in relation to men. The *divine view* blames abusive behaviour on lack of spirituality or misguided spirituality. Some religions promote the view that gender is destiny and may condone the practice of gendered apartheid. **Gendered apartheid** considers women as less than human beings and morally unequal to men, and treats women as a subordinate class (Okin, 1999). Gendered apartheid is inconsistent with feminism and with Canadian law, which views women and men as equal in morality and human dignity, and promotes a culture in which women have the same advantages as men and the same opportunities to live a fulfilling life.

gendered apartheid
viewpoint that considers women unequal to men and treats women as a subordinate class

The reality is that family violence is a complex social issue and there are many factors that increase the likelihood that a person will abuse a family member. A person may be more likely to abuse a family member if he or she

- belongs to a group that was colonized, such as the aboriginal peoples of Canada;

- has been separated or dislocated from his or her culture, community, family, and language;

- has been the victim of racism, sexism, or homophobia; or

- lives in poverty.

BARRIERS TO LEAVING VIOLENT RELATIONSHIPS

Women who remain in abusive relationships do not stay because they get a kick out of it. Complex factors contribute to their decision to stay in the relationship:

- some come from a culture of silence, where they are expected to stay silent and endure the abuse;

- some feel a deep sense of shame and embarrassment and fear the abuse will be exposed if they leave;

- some are pressured by relatives to keep up appearances and stay in the relationship;

- some fear that their abuser will seek reprisals or harm the children;

- some are financially dependent on their abuser; and

- some fear they will be shunned by relatives and friends if they leave and will become socially isolated.

This is only a partial list; there are many other reasons why women stay. Whatever the reason, it is important to remember that women stay in hell not because of their love of the inferno but because of their fear of the road to paradise.

SOCIAL RESPONSES TO FAMILY VIOLENCE

All nations have the obligation to support a policy of zero tolerance for all types of violence. Zero tolerance dictates that all perpetrators of violence face appropriate consequences from the criminal justice system, that victims receive necessary protection from the criminal justice system, and that victims and survivors of violence are provided with diversity-sensitive supports and services in their communities.

In the past, community supports and services for victims and survivors of family violence, such as shelters for battered women, gave little thought to the issue of diversity. This tradition is changing as programs gradually become more diversity-oriented. Specialized community-based programs are following a support and service philosophy that respects diversity, individual autonomy, and safety; supports a community-wide response to reduce violence against women; and promotes systemic change in legal, medical, and social institutions to better protect and respond to the needs of victims.

Supports and Services

Community supports and services are essential for an effective response to family violence. Typical support services include:

- Victim Crisis Assistance and Referral Service (VCARS)—This is a community-based service that assists police in providing short-term emotional support and practical assistance to victims of crime.

- Victim/Witness Assistance Program (V/WAP)—This service provides direct support to victims going through the court process.

- Shelters—Shelters provide 24-hour emergency short-term housing assistance to victims of domestic violence (currently available for female victims and their children only).

- Hospitals—hospital-based regional sexual/domestic assault treatment centres are available 24 hours a day.

- Victim Support Line (VSL)—This is a toll-free, province-wide 24 hour information line that provides victim referrals to local services.

- Sexual Assault/Rape Crisis Centres (SAC)—there are 33 SACs across Ontario including French language centres.

Such organizations need to embrace the value of diversity in the provision of their supports and services. For example, gay and lesbian victims of family violence can feel ill at ease in mainstream shelters because of prevailing homophobia.

Abused immigrant and refugee women have unique vulnerabilities that require special consideration (MacLeod & Shin, 1990, 1994; Kazarian and Kazarian, 1998). Chief among them are worries about their immigration status (for example, their lack of permanent status or the threat or actual withdrawal of sponsorship by their abuser), their work permits, or deportation; reluctance to relive possible trauma they endured before, during, and following migration; lack of knowledge of host country laws (for example, that wife assault is a criminal act) and personal rights and freedoms; lack of familiarity with available community supports and services; and language barriers. MacLeod and Shin (1990) have identified the primary needs of abused immigrant and refugee women, which are listed in table 9.2.

TABLE 9.2   Primary Needs of Abused Immigrant and Refugee Women

- Information about basic rights and freedoms and the laws related to immigration and wife assault.

- A supportive network that conveys understanding, caring, a sense of greater freedom, and confirmation that the woman is not alone.

- An opportunity to talk about issues of violence with people who understand their language and culture.

- Subsidized language training with training allowances and free daycare facilities.

- Sensitive, multicultural, multilingual, and multiracial childcare facilities to overcome isolation.

- Job training.

- Affordable housing.

- Culture-sensitive and language-specific services to address legal, economic, safety, and support needs.

Source: MacLeod & Shin (1990).

POLICE RESPONSE TO FAMILY VIOLENCE

mediative police response
aims to avoid the arrest of the abuser; police officers responding to family violence calls take a hands-off approach

There are three major police response policies regarding family violence. The **mediative police response** aims to avoid the arrest of the abuser. Police officers responding to family violence calls take a hands-off approach. They try to get everyone in the household to calm down and leave it to them to resolve their difficulties, or, if they deem it necessary, they refer the offender or victim to the appropriate social agencies. Historically, police have not considered violence in intimate relationships a real crime and have used the mediative policy. They have also followed the mediative non-arrest approach because of two major themes: the practical and the patriarchal. Officers chose not to arrest abusers for very practical reasons—for example, the victim did not want the offender arrested; the offence was culturally acceptable; the officer was concerned that the abuser would harm the victim after he or she was released; the officer felt that arresting the abuser would ultimately break up the relationship; or the officer believed that the victim would choose not to prosecute and the court would dismiss the charges. In other cases, police chose not to arrest husbands who had abused their wives because they viewed families as patriarchies in which the man rightly holds power and control over the other family members. They had little interest in enforcing the law in such cases because it conflicted with their deeply held views.

pro-arrest policy
encourages arrest in family violence cases but the decision to arrest is at the discretion of the officer

mandatory arrest policy
a policy to lay criminal charges in family violence cases; arrest must take place whenever probable cause exists, even for less serious offences

Major policy shifts since the mid-1970s have changed the way that police respond to family violence calls. Two additional policies have prevailed. The **pro-arrest policy** encourages arrest in family violence cases but the decision to arrest is still at the discretion of the officers. The **mandatory arrest policy**, on the other hand, dictates that arrest must take place whenever probable cause exists, even for less serious offences. Police services in many countries have adopted a policy to lay criminal charges in family violence cases, but many police still underenforce the law in these cases. Ontario police follow a mandatory arrest policy for domestic violence incidents.

DIVERSITY AND FAMILY VIOLENCE: POLICE ABILITIES, KNOWLEDGE, AND SKILLS

A number of key players, including police, Crown attorneys, judges, probation officers, victim-witness assistance personnel, and correctional personnel are involved in the provision of sensitive and appropriate supports and services in the area of family violence, and the development of resources (Department of Justice Canada, 2006c).

Policing is becoming more responsive to family violence issues. Police executives are attending national forums on family violence to learn about new initiatives, explore different approaches to dealing with family violence, and improve police and community responses to family violence, and develop networks with other police chiefs, professionals, and government agencies (Department of Justice Canada, 2006c).

In addition, police are becoming more effective in responding to family violence calls. Most have shifted from a victim-blaming approach to an abuser-accountability approach. Police officers with traditional victim-blaming attitudes were failing the victim by not interceding against the abuser, and were also revictimizing the victim by giving tacit approval to the abuse.

TABLE 9.3   Dos and Don'ts of Policing Family Violence

Dos

- Treat family violence as a crime.
- Recognize the diversity issues in cases of family violence.
- Lay charges against abusers.
- Provide a shield of safety to victims and their children.
- Work collaboratively with community supports and services.
- Collect evidence and all the facts.
- Support initiatives for preventing family violence.
- Recognize the potential for family violence in your own home.

Don'ts

- Don't take a hands-off, victim-blaming attitude.
- Don't compromise the safety of victims and their children.
- Don't give tacit approval to abusers by letting them off the hook.

Police are also recognizing that they can no longer try to fight family violence alone, and that forming alliances with community supports is a more effective strategy. To effect positive changes, some police services have established specialized family-response teams, mapped at-risk households, and instituted family-violence training programs.

Finally, police themselves are recognizing that they are not immune to family violence. Police departments are recognizing the vulnerability of their own members to the problem and the need for internal initiatives to address the issue.

A list of dos and don'ts of policing family violence is provided in table 9.3.

CHAPTER SUMMARY

Family violence is a serious problem for society and policing. Most perpetrators of family violence are men, and most of its victims are women. Effective policing requires that police see this violence as the criminal act that it is, understand the unique experiences and needs of people of diversity who experience family violence, and partner with community supports and services.

KEY TERMS

family violence	gendered apartheid
spousal abuse	mediative police response
child abuse	pro-arrest policy
child sexual abuse	mandatory arrest policy
elder abuse	

REFERENCES

Amnesty International (2005). An information kit. http://www.amnesty.org/ actforwomen/index-eng.

Biesenthal, L., L.D. Sproule, M. Nelder, S. Golton, D. Mann, D. Podovinnikoff, I. Roosendaal, S. Warman, D. Lunn. (2000). *The Ontario rural woman abuse study—final report.* Ottawa: Department of Justice Canada.

Bilefsky, D. (2006, July 16). How to avoid honor killing in Turkey? Honor suicide. *The New York Times.* http://www.nytimes.com.

Canadian Centre for Justice Statistics. (2000). *Family violence in Canada: A statistical profile.* Ottawa: Statistics Canada. Catalogue no. 85-224-XPE.

Canadian Panel on Violence Against Women. (1993). *Changing the landscape: Ending violence—achieving equality.* Ottawa: Minister Responsible for the Status of Women.

Cantin, P. (1998, February 19). Family violence victims face "maze," inquest told. *The London Free Press,* p. A7.

Champagne, C., R. Lapp, & J. Lee. (1994). *Assisting abused lesbians: A guide for health professionals and service providers.* London, ON: London Battered Women's Advocacy Centre.

Chesley, L.C., MacAulay, D. & Ristock, J.L. (1998). *Abuse in lesbian relationships: Information and resources.* Ottawa: Minister of Public Works and Government Services.

Child and Family Services Act, RSO 1990, c. C.11, as amended.

Committee on Sexual Offences Against Children and Youth. (1984). *Sexual offences against children in Canada: Report of the Committee.* Ottawa: Supply and Services Canada.

The Copenhagen Post. (2006, June 30). Honour killing guilty verdict puts family of nine behind bars. http://www.cphpost.dk/get/96430.html.

Criminal Code, RSC 1985, c. C-46, as amended.

Dauvergne, M., & H. Johnson. (2001). Children witnessing family violence. *Juristat:* 21(6). Ottawa: Canadian Centre for Justice Statistics. Statistics Canada catalogue no. 85-002-XIE.

Day, T. (1995). *The health-related costs of violence against women: The tip of the iceberg.* London, ON: Centre for Research on Violence against Women and Children.

Department of Justice Canada. (2006a). About family violence in Canada. http://www.justice.gc.ca/en/ps/fm/about.html.

Department of Justice Canada. (2006b). Family violence: A fact sheet from the Department of Justice Canada. http://www.justice.gc.ca/en/ps/fm/index.html.

Department of Justice Canada. (2006c). Projects funded by the Department of Justice Canada under the Family Violence Initiative (April 2002-March 2003). http://www.justice.gc.ca/en/ps/fm/grants.html.

Gannon, M., & K. Mihorean. (2005). Criminal Victimization in Canada, 2004. *Juristat*: 25(7). Ottawa: Canadian Centre for Justice Statistics. Statistics Canada catalogue no. 85-002-XPE.

Greaves, L., & O. Hankivsky. (1995). *Selected estimates of the costs of violence against women.* London, ON: Centre for Research on Violence Against Women and Children. 2.

Green, K. (1996). Family violence in aboriginal communities: An aboriginal perspective. Information from the national clearinghouse on family violence. Ottawa: Health Canada.

Health Canada. (2001). Canadian incidence study of reported child abuse and neglect: Final Report. Ottawa: Minister of Public Works and Government Services Canada. www.phac-aspc.gc.ca/cm-vee/cishl01/index.html.

Hotton, T. (2001). Spousal violence after marital separation. *Juristat*: 21(7). Ottawa: Canadian Centre for Justice Statistics. Statistics Canada catalogue no. 85-002-XPE.

Jaffe, P.G., & M. Suderman. (1995). Child witnesses of women abuse: Research and community responses. In S. Stith and M.A. Straus (Eds.), *Understanding partner violence: Prevalence, causes, consequences and solutions.* Minneapolis, MN: National Council on Family Relations.

Jaffe, P.G., M. Suderman, & D. Reitzel. (1992). Child witnesses of marital violence. In R.T. Ammerman and M. Hersen (Eds.), *Assessment of family violence: A clinical and legal handbook* (pp. 313–31). New York: Wiley.

Kazarian, S.S., & L.Z. Kazarian. (1998). Cultural aspects of family violence. In S.S. Kazarian and D.R. Evans (Eds.), *Cultural clinical psychology: Theory, research and practice* (pp. 316–47). New York: Oxford University Press.

Law Commission of Canada. (2000). *Restoring dignity: Responding to child abuse in Canadian institutions.* Ottawa: Minister of Public Works and Government Services.

MacLeod, L., & M. Shin. (1990). *Isolated, afraid and forgotten: The service delivery needs and realities of immigrant and refugee women who are battered.* Ottawa: Health and Welfare Canada.

MacLeod, L., & M. Shin. (1994). *Like a wingless bird: A tribute to the survival and courage of women who are abused and who speak neither English nor French.* Ottawa: Health Canada.

Minnesota Center Against Violence and Abuse (MINCAVA). (1998, October 6). Jennifer's story. *Annual report on lesbian, gay, bisexual, transgender family violence.* http://www.mincava.umn.edu/documents/glbtdv.html.

Okin, S.M. (Ed.). (1999). *Is multiculturalism bad for women?* Princeton, NJ: Princeton University Press.

Page, K. (1999, October 14). Homosexual couples report family abuse. *The Badger Herald* (University of Wisconsin).

Rodgers, K. (1993). Wife assault: The findings of a national survey. *Juristat*. 14(9). Ottawa: Canadian Centre for Justice Statistics. Statistics Canada catalogue no. 85-002.

Schecter, M.D., & L. Roberge. (1976). Sexual exploitation. In R.E. Helfer and C.H. Kempe (Eds.), *Child abuse and neglect: The family and the community* (pp. 127–42). Cambridge, MA: Ballinger.

EXERCISES AND REVIEW
Personal Reflections

Read each statement below and circle whether you agree or disagree with it.

1. Family violence is a serious national problem.

   AGREE   DISAGREE

2. Police should treat family violence as a crime.

   AGREE   DISAGREE

3. Women of all diversities are vulnerable to family violence.

   AGREE   DISAGREE

4. A woman's job is to bear children and cook food.

   AGREE   DISAGREE

5. Their immigrant status and the economic and social realities of some women may prevent them from leaving an abusive relationship.

   AGREE   DISAGREE

6. Police who investigate family violence should always ask a woman victim, "Why don't you just leave?"

   AGREE   DISAGREE

7. Police can help an abused woman by charging her abusive partner, even if the woman does not want the police to arrest him.

   AGREE   DISAGREE

8. Police should treat family violence as a family issue that should be dealt with solely by those involved.

   AGREE   DISAGREE

9. Police need to send a strong message to the community that family violence won't be tolerated.

   AGREE   DISAGREE

10. Police are not immune to family violence in their homes.

    AGREE   DISAGREE

SCORING: Give yourself one point each for agreeing with the following statements: 1, 2, 3, 5, 7, 9, and 10. Give yourself one point each for disagreeing with the remaining statements. Higher scores reflect higher acceptance of the reality of family violence. Compare your score with a classmate's, and try to reconcile any differences of opinion.

Diversity IQ: Multiple Choice

Circle the best answer.

1. Family violence

   a. crosses all diversity boundaries

   b. occurs only among the poor

   c. is an immigrant and refugee problem

   d. is a heterosexual problem

2. Which of the following is a myth about family violence?

   a. drinking causes men to beat their wives

   b. diversity causes men to beat their wives

   c. women provoke and enjoy being beaten

   d. all of the above

3. Which of the following cultural practices are mistaken for child abuse?

   a. coining

   b. pinching

   c. cupping

   d. all of the above

4. Which of the following is a psychological consequence of child sexual abuse?

   a. post-traumatic stress disorder

   b. self-confidence

   c. intimacy

   d. high self-esteem

5. Which of the following is a potential victim of family violence?

    a. a heterosexual person

    b. a gay or lesbian person

    c. a person with a physical or mental disability

    d. all of the above

6. Which of the following contributes to keeping family violence in the closet?

    a. the view that the government has no right to dictate what families may or may not do in their own homes

    b. the view that violence is not the crime; rather, the woman abandoning her husband is the crime

    c. the view that it is acceptable to beat a wife if she does not fulfill her duties as a wife

    d. all of the above

7. Which of the following is a primary need for immigrant and refugee women who are abused?

    a. a job

    b. information about where to learn English

    c. culture-appropriate support and services

    d. all of the above

8. Police officers

    a. cannot lay charges of assault unless the victim consents to them

    b. can lay charges of assault based on reasonable and probable grounds

    c. should allow the partners to sort out their problems once the crisis is over

    d. should not be in the business of responding to domestic calls

9. Which of the following is a criminal offence?

    a. consensual lovemaking

    b. battering a partner

    c. teasing another person

    d. all of the above

10. Which of the following is an effective police response to family violence?

    a. scolding the victim for calling

    b. complimenting the abuser on a job well done

    c. recognizing the compounding effect of diversity on the abusive situation

    d. all of the above

Diversity IQ: True or False?

_____ 1. Police officers should take a solo approach to responding to family violence.

_____ 2. Arresting the perpetrator of violence is the primary enforcement strategy in family violence cases.

_____ 3. Police need to provide help that meets the special needs of people of diversity who are in abusive relationships.

_____ 4. The diversity policing approach to family violence means compromising the laws of the country.

_____ 5. Police can increase their effectiveness when responding to family violence calls by understanding the victim's perspective.

_____ 6. Police should consider a hands-off approach to family violence.

_____ 7. Family violence is best viewed as a power and control issue.

_____ 8. Immigrant and refugee women in abusive relationships fear deportation and loss of their children.

_____ 9. Partner abuse does not happen in lesbian relationships.

_____ 10. Everyone has a right to a safe home environment.

Application Now

1. What implication does the view that family violence is an issue for some diversity groups but not others have on police responses to perpetrators and victims?

    Perpetrators

    Victims

2. List strategies that would enable police to help people in a community deal with family violence in their respective diversity groups.

Food for Thought

1. Identify factors that police should consider when responding to a new immigrant who is in an abusive relationship.

2. List factors that need to be considered in creating a safety plan for victims of family violence and their children.

3. Identify diversity groups in your community in which family violence is a serious issue. What are relations like between these groups and the police? Suggest solutions to family violence that police and the groups could work on collaboratively.

From Thought to Action

1. As a police officer, what would you do in the following situation? Role-play the scenario, demonstrating a diversity-competent approach to responding to family violence calls. Be aware of your verbal and non-verbal messages.

    I am a physically disabled newcomer to this country. My husband has sponsored me and my three children. I have no one here other than my husband and my children. I have been beaten, as have my children, and I am scared. I finally had the courage to call the police to help me. They are my only hope. Please help me.

2. Read the list of dos and don'ts in table 9.3 (on p. 265). What do you think should be deleted from the list and what should be added?

Lessons from History

In 2006, the High Court of Eastern Denmark jailed a Pakistani man for ordering his son to kill his daughter, Ghazala Khan, who had married a man the family did not approve of. The brother admitted to shooting Ghazala, who died, and her husband, who survived. The verdict is considered a landmark ruling because seven other relatives were also found guilty for their part in conspiring to kill the woman. A group of uncles, aunts, and acquaintances were involved in a plot to lure Ghazala and her husband to a train station where the brother waited with a loaded gun. The Ghazala Khan case was followed very closely by legal experts in Germany, Sweden, and other countries because it marked the first time that accomplices were found guilty in an honour killing. Discuss the lessons that can be learned from this case.

Source: *The Copenhagen Post* (2006).

The Great Debate

Reread the section "Police Response to Family Violence." Divide the class into two groups. Have one group argue for the practical view and the second group argue for the patriarchal view.

CHAPTER 10

Policing Mental Illness

CHAPTER OBJECTIVES

After completing this chapter, you should be able to:

- Describe the scope of mental illness and its symptoms.

- Identify various medications used to treat mental illness.

- Identify police strategies for responding to mental health calls.

PREVIEW SCENARIO

On October 10, 2000, RCMP officers tried to apprehend an individual pursuant to an Involuntary Examination Order issued under the Ontario *Mental Health Act*. A violent confrontation between the police and the individual ensued but was terminated almost immediately after the mother of the individual arrived on the scene and persuaded her son to surrender to the police. The mother filed a complaint with the Commission for Public Complaints Against the RCMP alleging that the police used excessive force in apprehending her son, failed to inform her son that he was going to be apprehended, and damaged her son's home. An independent investigation of the complaint was conducted.

The complainant's son was born and raised in a small community, was diagnosed in 1997 with schizophrenia, lived in the community, and received support from his mother and psychiatric staff, including a community mental health worker. On the advice of the son's psychiatrist, the son's mental health nurse obtained an order to apprehend the complainant's son and take him to hospital on the grounds that he was suffering from paranoid schizophrenia, that he was refusing to allow family, friends, or community health staff into his home, and that he had been verbally threatening to cause physical harm to others. The attending corporal requested that the mother be informed that her son was going to be apprehended, but, because of a mix-up in communication between police and health officials, she was not. A risk assessment had been conducted prior to the officers' attending the residence of the complainant's son, and the corporal was aware that the son refused to open his door during three previous visits, was passive with two of the constables who had previously taken him to hospital, and had allegedly slit police vehicle tires. The corporal told the two constables who accompanied him to the residence of the complainant's son that the son was going to be problematic, and that the plan was to coax the son out of his home; there was no plan to actually enter the home. At 3:17 p.m. all three police officers arrived at the son's home. The corporal, accompanied by a constable, knocked on the front door while a second constable went to the back door. The corporal called, "Police, open up" but there was no response. The corporal informed the son that he had an order to apprehend him and, when there was no response, threatened that if the door was not opened at the count of five he would break it down. When the officers attempted to gain entry into the son's home, he lunged at them with a six-foot long birch stick that had been sharpened to a point at one end. Police then ripped off the back exterior door and kicked in the interior door. However, they were unable to gain entry because the son continued to lunge at police. At this point, one officer sprayed the son with pepper spray. The son continued to resist, insisting that they leave as they had no authority under God to be in his house, and that they had to shoot him as he would not leave alive. The son also broke the stick in half and began hitting the walls and the door jamb, removed a Swiss army knife from his pocket and threw it on the floor after wiping off the blade. In addition to calling requesting back-up and replenishment of pepper spray, police pulled out a window screen and pulled down curtains to distract the son. Police also encircled the house once additional members arrived to overwhelm the son. At some point the son started to talk about giving up, threw half of his stick on the ground, and repeated several times that he would go with police but did not want to be handcuffed. The stand-off continued, during which the son was repeatedly repelled with pepper spray. The evidence indicated that police pepper sprayed the son an estimated 25 times in approximately 40 minutes. Within 10 minutes of his mother's arrival, the son surrendered. He complied with police instructions, was handcuffed without further resistance, and transported to the psychiatric unit of the hospital. Following the complaint by the mother, the commission issued a report on the incident in which the chair emphasized, "the need for the RCMP members to be trained on how to apprehend someone who is experiencing a mental health crisis." (Commission for Public Complaints Against the RCMP, 2003)

INTRODUCTION

Mental illness is a reality that societies tend to hide or avoid discussing. It is estimated that 20 percent of Canadians are likely to experience mental illness during their lifetime, and that the remaining 80 percent are likely to be affected by a family member, friend, or colleague who is mentally ill (Health Canada, 2002, p. 3). Police contact with people who are mentally ill is common and is on the increase. It is estimated that between 7 and 15 percent of police contacts involve people who are mentally ill (Stedman, Morrissey, Deane, & Borum, 1996, p. 14; Cotton, 2003). One survey showed that, over a one-week period, police responded to a total of 3,596 calls, 509 of which (14 percent) were mental health calls (Kazarian & Persad, 1995). It is estimated that the amount of time police spend on mental health calls has doubled over the last three years (Lawson Health Research Institute, 2000). The advent of new and more effective psychiatric and psychological treatment approaches to mental illness and the goal of deinstitutionalization of inmates in mental health institutions have contributed to the reintegration of the mentally ill in the community. However, shortcomings in community mental health services, including insufficient funding, have led to an increase in the number of mental health calls that police respond to. This chapter examines different types of mental illness, the laws pertaining to mental illness, and strategies that police can use to deal with mentally ill people.

CONCEPT OF MENTAL ILLNESS

Mental illness is a broad term that encompasses a variety of disorders. The Police Executive Research Forum (1997) defines **mental illness** as a group of distinct disabilities marked by disturbances in thinking, feeling, and relating.

mental illness
group of disabilities marked by disturbances in thinking, feeling, and relating

Mental illness is more common than many people think (Keresztes & Kazarian, 1996; Offord et al., 1994; Health Canada, 2002). People with mental illness are criminalized, demonized, and stigmatized. Pejorative terms that are used to refer to them include cuckoo, lunatic, nut, crazy, insane, mental, and psycho. Modern terms used in mental health are psychiatric patient, client, consumer, and survivor (Sharma et al., 2000). A fifth term that may become more popular in the future is psychiatric *thriver*.

Two terms that are used in law enforcement are *mentally ill* and *emotionally disturbed*. A recent survey of 317 police officers in London, Ontario showed that 83.0 percent of them preferred the term "mentally ill," 11.7 percent preferred "emotionally disturbed," and 5.4 percent preferred another term (Kazarian, unpublished data). Other preferred terms included "mentally disturbed," and "mentally challenged." Most frequently, police use the short form "M.I." to describe a person who is mentally ill.

Although mental illness causes disturbances in behaving, feeling, relating, and thinking, such disturbances can also be caused by other factors, including head injury, medical conditions such as diabetes and epilepsy, and substance abuse. For example, people who use cocaine may experience **formication**, a hallucinatory experience in which the users feel that insects or snakes are crawling over or under their skin. As well, people in the aftermath of a cocaine high may become irritable and depressed.

formication
hallucination that involves feeling that insects or snakes are crawling over or under one's skin

Mental illness ranges from mild to severe. Severe mental illness includes schizophrenia, mood disorders, organic brain syndrome, and paranoid and other psychoses.

Mental disturbances can be categorized as *psychotic* and *non-psychotic*. Hallucinations and delusions are the two most common psychotic symptoms. Anxiety and depression are the two most common non-psychotic symptoms. However, a person with mental illness may or may not show psychotic or non-psychotic mental disturbances. For example, six months ago, Joe was taking his prescribed medication and living in a highly supportive social environment. When interviewed, he did not exhibit any noticeable or observable mental disturbances normally associated with his condition. However, when Joe's mother died and he stopped taking his medication, he described feeling that the mafia and police were trying to get him, that he was having impulses to run away from the city to escape them, and that he was hearing voices telling him to harm his sister.

mental disturbance
categorized as either pyschotic or non-psychotic mental illness

MENTAL HEALTH LEGISLATION

On December 17, 1991, the international community recognized the fundamental right of mentally ill people to be protected from discrimination when the UN *Principles for the Protection of Persons with Mental Illness and the Improvement of Mental Health Care* were adopted by resolution of the UN General Assembly (Office of the United Nations High Commissioner for Human Rights, 1991). The Australian *Mental Health Act 1986* is unique in that it specifies that people should not be considered mentally ill on the basis of their diversity characteristics, including race; culture; economic or social status; intellectual disability; philosophy; political activity, belief, or opinion; religion; sexual orientation or preference; sexual promiscuity; antisocial personality; or immoral or illegal conduct. Still, mental health legislation allows the removal of the civil liberties of people with mental illness in certain situations (Persad & Kazarian, 1998). For example, some legislation sets out specific criteria that, if met, permit a mentally ill person to be forcibly confined in a psychiatric hospital. Often, this is done when a person is determined to be a danger to himself or herself or a danger to others, and when the person demonstrates lack of competence to care for himself or herself.

Mental Health Act: Ontario

Ontario's *Mental Health Act* was amended and passed as *Brian's Law* on June 23, 2000. Brian Smith was a popular sportscaster and former National Hockey League player. He was about to drive his car to a nearby town to be the master of ceremonies at a charity event when he was shot and killed by a man with a history of serious mental illness. *Brian's Law* stipulates that a justice of the peace may issue an order authorizing a police officer to take a person in custody to an appropriate place for examination by a physician provided that information grounded on *threat* and *mental disorder* is given under oath. In relation to threat, the statute requires information to the effect that (1) the person has threatened or attempted or is threatening or attempting to cause bodily harm to herself or himself; (2) the person has behaved or is behaving violently toward another person or has caused or is causing another person to fear bodily harm from her or him; or (3) the person has shown or is showing a lack of competence to care for herself or himself. In relation to mental disorder, the statute requires information on reasonable cause or belief that the person is apparently suffering from a mental disorder of a nature or quality that will result in (1) serious bodily harm to the person, (2) serious bodily harm to another person, or (3) serious physical impairment of the person.

Finally, *Brian's Law* stipulates that a police officer may take a person into custody provided the police officer has reasonable and probable grounds to *believe* that disorderly conduct has occurred and has reasonable cause to believe that the person fulfills the conditions of threat and mental disorder described above.

An important feature of *Brian's Law* is that it enables community treatment orders for seriously mentally ill people. These orders allow people to be treated in a community setting that is less restrictive and less intrusive than a psychiatric hospital. Other provinces (for example, Saskatchewan) have similar laws.

Mental Health Provisions in the Criminal Code

Part XX.1 of the *Criminal Code* deals with mental disorders. In particular, section 672.11 describes the circumstances under which a court may order an assessment of the mental condition of an accused to determine

(a) whether the accused is unfit to stand trial;

(b) whether the accused was, at the time of the commission of the alleged offence, suffering from a mental disorder so as to be exempt from criminal responsibility by virtue of subsection 16(1);

(c) whether the balance of the mind of the accused was disturbed at the time of commission of the alleged offence, where the accused is a female person charged with an offence arising out of the death of her newly-born child;

(d) the appropriate disposition to be made, where a verdict of not criminally responsible on account of mental disorder or unfit to stand trial has been rendered in respect of the accused; or

(e) whether an order should be made under section 672.851 for a stay of proceedings, where a verdict of unfit to stand trial has been rendered against the accused.

Sections 672.1-672.63 expand on these points and lay out the powers of the state in these criminal proceedings.

MENTAL DISTURBANCE AND POLICE RESPONSE

Police are most likely to encounter people with substance-related disorders, mood disorders, schizophrenia, and mental retardation. Police are also most likely to have to deal with the mental disturbances of suicidal behaviour; threatening, destructive, assaultive, or violent behaviour; psychotic thinking (losing touch with reality); confusion in thought or action; and strange or unusual behaviours that exceed public tolerance.

Substance-Related Disorders

People with **substance-related disorders** may show mental disturbances of both the **psychotic** and non-psychotic types. For example, consuming alcohol can have such serious effects as blackout and aggression. Angel dust (PCP, Phencyclidine) is known to produce severe anxiety, depression, disorientation, unpredictable aggression, and paranoid thoughts (Levinthal, 1996). Alcohol and drug abuse are also associated with crime and social violence: robbery, burglary, shoplifting, pimping, prostitution, and trafficking and distribution of illicit drugs. For example, police in Orillia, Ontario determined that many of the robberies that occurred there in 2005 and 2006 were committed by drug addicts known to police. These people were stealing to support their addiction to crack, cocaine, and methamphetamine.

In responding to a person with a substance-related disorder, police need to

- ensure their own safety and the safety of others,

- recognize the symptoms the person is displaying,

substance-related disorders
mental disorders caused by substance dependence and abuse, and by substance withdrawal

psychosis
form of serious mental disorder in which an actual break with reality occurs

- expect irrational behaviour,

- decide whether the situation is a medical emergency, and

- make sure that an interim use of physical restraint is safe and unlikely to cause the person added harm.

Mood Disorders and Suicidal Behaviour

mood disorders
mental disorders that affect a person's mood, including depression and bipolar disorder

depression
mood disorder characterized by feelings of despair and hopelessness

bipolar disorder
mood disorder that involves emotional swings between depression and mania; formerly called manic depression

mania
mood disorder characterized by feelings of emotional high, agitation, and impulsivity

suicide
symptom of mood disorder that takes the form of ideation, threat, attempt, gesture, and completed suicide

Mood disorders include depression and bipolar disorder. **Depression** is the common cold of mental illness. No one is immune to depression, which affects children as well as adults. More women are diagnosed with depression than men. Depression is characterized by extended periods of feelings of despair and hopelessness and lack of interest in life. Contrary to popular belief, it is not simply sadness or feeling down. People who suffer from depression may have trouble simply facing each day. They often experience problems with sleeping (either sleeping too much or too little), eating (overeating or loss of appetite), and feeling alienated or separate from the rest of society.

Bipolar disorder, previously called manic depression, is a condition in which a person has emotional swings between depression and mania. **Mania** is a mood state of emotional high, agitation, and impulsivity. Men and women are diagnosed equally with bipolar disorder. Table 10.1 lists the symptoms of depression and mania.

People with mood disorders may exhibit psychotic and non-psychotic symptoms. The psychotic symptoms tend to be *consistent* with their mood state. For example, Nathan's belief that his blood type could cure all the sicknesses in the world was consistent with his state of mania. In his elated mood, Nathan insisted that as much blood as possible be drawn from his arm and taken around the world to cure people of their diseases.

Police knowledge of the type of medication a mentally ill person is on may be useful in responding to a mental health call. Table 10.2 lists drugs frequently used to treat mood disorders. An effective mood stabilizer for bipolar disorder is lithium. Best practices include drug therapy, psychotherapy (cognitive, interpersonal, supportive), psychoeducation to patient and family, and community supports and services.

Suicide is a symptom of mood disorder that takes the form of *ideation* (thinking about it), *threat* (expressing the intention to commit a self-destructive act), *gesture* (a self-destructive act with little or no death intent), *attempt* (a self-destructive act with clear death intent), and *completed suicide*. In 2003, 3,764 people in Canada (2,902 male and 862 female) committed suicide (Statistics Canada, 2002–2006). Suicide is blind to diversity. Men succeed in killing themselves more than women, even though women attempt suicide more often than men. According to Statistics Canada (2006), methods of suicide among men and women are as follows: hanging (46 percent for men vs. 37 percent for women), use of firearms (20 percent for males vs. 3 percent for females), poisoning (20 percent for males vs. 42 percent for women), and other (14 percent for men and 18 percent for women). A person's religious beliefs may serve as a protective factor, but they do not provide complete immunity to suicide. Table 10.3 lists risk factors for suicidal behaviour. It is interesting to note that the media will not report on public suicides such as people jumping in front of trains or jumping off bridges. Even cases with sensational circumstances usually do not make it into the media. The perceived notoriety gained from such an act is seen as encouraging others who might also want to commit a similar act in order to seek attention.

Table 10.1   Symptoms of Depression and Mania

Depression

- Feelings of sadness or emptiness
- Loss of interest or pleasure
- Sleep disturbance (too much or too little sleep)
- Change in eating habits (increase or decrease in appetite)
- Change in weight (loss or gain)
- Psychomotor disturbance (agitation or slowness in movement)
- Loss of energy or fatigue
- Loss of self-esteem
- Feelings of guilt or self-blame
- Cognitive disturbance (poor concentration, indecisiveness)
- Suicidal or homicidal thoughts

Mania

- Inflated self-esteem or grandiosity
- Pressure to keep talking
- Extreme irritability
- Distractibility
- Decreased need for sleep
- Increased sexual, social, school, and work activities
- Increased pleasurable activities (overspending, sexual indiscretion)

Table 10.2   Frequently Prescribed Antidepressant Medications

Class	Trade name	Chemical name
Monoamine oxidase inhibitors	(MAO-I)	Marplan Isocarboxazid
	Nardil	Phenelzine
	Parnate	Tranylcypromine
Selective reuptake inhibitors (SSRIs)	Paxil	Paroxetine
	Prozac	Fluoxetine
	Zoloft	Sentraline hydrochloride
Tricyclic antidepressants (TCA)	Anafranil	Clomipramine
	Elavil, Amitid	Amitriptyline
	Norpramin, Pertofrane	Desipramine
	Pamelor, Aventryl	Nortriptyline
	Sinequan	Doxepin
	Surmontil	Trimipramine
	Tofranil	Imipramine
	Vivactil	Protriptyline
Other	Ascendin	Amoxapine
	Desyrel	Trazodone
	Welbutrin	Buproprion

Table 10.3   Risk Factors for Suicidal Behaviour

- Suicidal plan
- History of suicide attempts
- Absence of community support
- Recent loss (actual, threatened, or imagined)
- Physical illness, including AIDS or other terminal illness
- Change in lifestyle, behaviour, or personality
- Giving away possessions or valuables
- Putting personal affairs in order (for example, making a will)
- Depression, including feelings of hopelessness and helplessness
- Substance abuse
- Recent discharge from psychiatric hospital care
- Anniversaries (birthday, wedding, death of a loved one)

In responding to a depressed and suicidal person, police need to

- avoid telling the person to cheer up or snap out of it;
- assess the risk of suicide by asking direct questions and using the words "kill" or "die" or forms of these words (for example, "Are you thinking of killing yourself?" "Have you made plans to kill yourself?" "Why do you want to die?");
- take suicide threats seriously;
- be empathic (for example, "I would like to help because I know you are in pain");
- avoid swearing themselves to secrecy because officers are required to include relevant details in their report;
- ensure that the person is not left alone;
- draw on the person's social support system (family, friends, counsellor); and
- present the person with two options to choose from (for example, "Would you like to go to the hospital with me or would you rather I call an ambulance?").

In responding to a manic person, police need to

- decrease all extraneous stimulation (for example, noise from a TV);
- avoid arguments;
- allow the person to appropriately discharge energy, such as by pacing;
- be empathic but also firm and direct;
- draw on the person's social support system; and
- present the person with options to choose from.

Schizophrenia

Schizophrenia is a mental illness that causes psychotic mental disturbances. It usually develops in late adolescence to early adulthood and for this reason has been described as the mind cancer of the young. It occurs in both men and women but usually invades men sooner than women. However, in contrast with the symptoms of mood disorders, the symptoms of schizophrenia tend to be *inconsistent* with the person's mood state. For example, the person may break into laughter while discussing the death of a parent rather than feel sad and distressed.

Common symptoms of schizophrenia are thought disorders, hallucinations, and delusions. **Thought disorders** are ideas and speech that make sense to the schizophrenic person but are incoherent to others. **Hallucinations** are sensory experiences that are disturbed and disturbing. Hallucinations can be felt, heard, seen, smelled, or tasted. Hearing voices and seeing things are the more common hallucinations. People who are hallucinating may talk to themselves, show concentration problems, or make head movements toward the source of the voice they hear. A person who is having visual hallucinations may show jerking of the eyes or head. **Delusions** are ideas that are real only to the schizophrenic person. A person with paranoid schizophrenia may believe that he is Jesus and the subject of persecution. Similarly, a person with schizophrenia may believe that dirty thoughts are being inserted into her head or that valuable thoughts are being sucked out of her mind and stolen. A variety of psychotropic drugs are used in the treatment of schizophrenia (for example, clozapine). Table 10.4 lists major symptoms of schizophrenia.

In responding to psychotic symptoms, police need to

- be empathic, reassuring, and helpful, but also firm;

- avoid using deception or humour;

- validate the hallucinatory experience for the person but also communicate that the hallucination does not exist in reality (for example, "I don't see the man, but I understand that you do");

- acknowledge a person's delusion but not agree with, dispute, or attack it, or argue with or try to convince the person that her or his stated belief is not true;

- avoid invading the personal space of a paranoid person or implying special knowledge of the person's paranoid beliefs;

- determine whether the schizophrenic person presents a threat, and, if he or she does, use the least amount of force necessary to control the person in accordance with the use-of-force continuum (Pardy, 2000);

schizophrenia
mental illness described as cancer of the mind that causes psychotic mental disturbances

thought disorder
mental symptom characterized by ideas and speech that are coherent only to the mentally ill person

hallucinations
sensory experiences that are disturbed or disturbing and are real only to the mentally ill person

delusions
ideas that are real only to the mentally ill person

Table 10.4 Positive and Negative Symptoms of Schizophrenia

Positive (excess) symptoms	Negative (deficit) symptoms
- Hallucinations	- Mood disturbances
- Thought disorders	- Impaired interpersonal functioning
- Delusions	- Lack of motivation

- draw on the person's social support system, if necessary; and

- present the person with two options to choose from.

Schizophrenia can be treated with a combination of medication and psychosocial support, such as counselling. However, it is not uncommon for schizophrenics to stop taking their medication because of unpleasant side effects, such as muscle cramps. The symptoms of the disease then return, and may lead the person to engage in activities that prompt a call to police. A recent study that examined the experiences of police officers found that the majority of officers felt that "if the person had stayed on their psychiatric medication, the incident might have been prevented" (McAndrew & Sutton, 2004).

Mental Retardation

Mental retardation is not the same as mental illness. Three criteria are used to establish **mental retardation**: significant subaverage intelligence, significant limitation in adaptive functioning, and onset before the age of 18 years. Terms that have been used in the past for people with mental retardation include feeble-minded, moron, idiot, imbecile, and retard. In many cases, these terms were derogatory; in others, they reflected accepted usage. For example, the Huronia Regional Centre, an institution that assists people with mental disabilities, was once called the Orillia Asylum for Idiots. More recent terms are intellectually challenged, developmentally disabled, or developmentally handicapped.

The communication skills and behavioural development of people with mental retardation are varied but limited. They may have a short attention span, speech impairment, or difficulty with understanding or answering questions. They may act inappropriately with peers or the opposite sex, or be easily frustrated, eager to please, or easily influenced by others. Finally, they may show difficulty in carrying out the activities of daily living, including using the telephone and telling time.

In responding to a person with a developmental disability, police need to

- treat the person with respect and dignity,

- use simple language and short sentences,

- be patient but firm, and

- avoid asking confusing or leading questions.

POLICING MENTAL ILLNESS: POLICE ABILITIES, KNOWLEDGE, AND SKILLS

Policing mental illness is challenging in view of the increasing number of mental health calls received by police services, the importance of a successful response to such calls, and the potential for a tragic outcome. Police encounters with people with mental illness may be violent, and incidents of police shootings of mentally ill people make front-page headlines. In one case, Edmund Wai-Kong Yu, a homeless man with schizophrenia, was shot and killed on a bus by Toronto police when Yu

Table 10.5   Dos and Don'ts of Policing Mental Illness

Dos

- Recognize that mentally ill and homeless people are people with problems, not problem people.
- Recognize the difference between mental illness and mental disturbance.
- Accept police response to mental illness calls as a legitimate police role.
- Treat mentally ill people with respect.
- Be calm, empathic, reassuring, and helpful, but also firm.
- Explain your actions to the person.
- Isolate and contain, if possible.
- Present the person with options to choose from.
- Establish alliances with community services.
- Recognize the potential for mental illness in your own backyard.

Don'ts

- Don't compromise your safety.
- Don't rush.
- Don't deceive the mentally ill person.
- Don't invade his or her personal space.
- Don't touch the person if you don't have to or without permission.
- Don't get into an argument or overreact.

reached inside his coat and withdrew a steel hammer. The police were cleared of any wrongdoing, but a coroner's inquest resulted in 24 specific recommendations for police responses to people with mental illness (Office of the Chief Coroner, 1999).

The Yu case and other cases of police injury and killings of people with apparent mental illness have underscored the need for specialized police training in dealing with people who are mentally ill (Commission for Public Complaints Against the RCMP, 2003). The Ontario Ministry of the Solicitor General's *Policing Standards Manual* (2000) advised chiefs of police to ensure that police services' skills development and learning plans address the training and sharing of information with officers on conflict resolution and the use of force involving persons who may be emotionally disturbed.

The Commission for Public Complaints Against the RCMP (2003) identified several Canadian police services that have implemented training policy guidelines and/or specialized intervention teams, including Ottawa-Carleton, Toronto, Niagara, Guelph, Hamilton, Chatham-Kent, and the Ontario Provincial Police. The specialized approach entails an understanding of mental health legislation and mental disturbances, and specific interventions such as tactical communication, crisis resolution, using containment to diffuse potentially volatile situations (for example, a mentally ill person threatening with a gun), and partnership with available community supports and services (Kazarian & Persad, 1999; Kazarian et al., 1998; Murphy, 1989; Cotton & Coleman, 2003; Commission for Public Complaints Against the RCMP, 2003). These supports and services may include advocacy, consumer and family education, family support, medical and dental services, medication, peer support, police support, and rehabilitation (Fernando & Kazarian, 1995; Kazarian & Joseph, 1994). Community support systems, including crisis response services (crisis lines, mental health teams, hospital emergency wards), require greater funding because the deinstitutionalization of mentally ill people from mental health institutions has resulted in shortages in hospital beds and acute admissions. Dr. Dorothy Cotton (2006), a psychologist with Correctional Service Canada, states,

> [P]ersons experiencing mental illnesses are now more likely to find themselves dealing with the police and the criminal justice system by default, as these individuals and their families, friends and communities find themselves frustrated in their attempts to access mental health services. Police services have gone a long way in developing education and training for their members, as well as trying to coordinate linkages with the mental health system.

Finally, police are human beings and thus are not immune from developing mental illness. It may be difficult for police to accept this reality, because it shatters the image of police invulnerability, formidable emotional strength for dealing with adversity, indestructibility, and emotional impenetrability (Violanti, 1996). Initiatives for promoting the mental well-being of police are consistent with best practices in policing.

CHAPTER SUMMARY

Mentally ill people come from all walks of life. In Canada, the government has made efforts to take mentally ill people out of institutions and reintegrate them into the community. As a result, police involvement with mentally ill people in Canada has increased. Police require specialized training to respond to mental health calls effectively and to minimize the potential for violent confrontations, which can sometimes result in fatalities. They also need to work in partnership with families, professionals, and community services. In addition to responding appropriately to mental health calls, police should be vigilant about their own psychological well-being.

KEY TERMS

mental illness	mania
formication	suicide
mental disturbance	schizophrenia
substance-related disorders	thought disorder
psychosis	hallucinations
mood disorders	delusions
depression	mental retardation
bipolar disorder	

REFERENCES

Brian's Law (Mental Health Legislative Reform), SO 2000, c. 9.

Commission for Public Complaints Against the RCMP. (2003, October 20). Report into a complaint concerning RCMP treatment of a person experiencing a mental health crisis. http://www.cpc-cpp.gc.ca.

Cotton, D. (2003, March). Top ten reasons for mental illness training. *Blue Line Magazine*, p. 28.

Cotton, D., & T. Coleman. (2003). Ten years of suggestions: A review of inquest recommendations related to deaths of mentally ill individuals from 1992-2002. Unpublished research. Moose Jaw Police Service, SK.

Fernando, M.L.D., & S.S. Kazarian. (1995, April). Patient education in the drug treatment of psychiatric disorders: Effect on compliance and outcome. *CNS Drugs* 3: 291–304.

Health Canada. (2002, October). *A report on mental illnesses in Canada*. Health Canada.

Heafey, S. (2002, September 30). The relationship between police and the mentally ill. Speech delivered to the First national Conference on Police/Mental Health System Liaison. http://www.cpc-cpp.gc.ca.

Kazarian, S.S., & L.W. Joseph. (1994). A brief scale to help identify outpatients' level of need for community support services. *Hospital and Community Psychiatry* 45: 935–37.

Kazarian, S.S., & E. Persad. (1995). Training of police in community-oriented psychiatric support: Needs assessment. London, ON: London Psychiatric Hospital.

Kazarian, S.S., & E. Persad. (1999). Mental health plan and police response to a crisis situation involving a mentally ill person: Yu inquest debriefing. Unpublished manuscript. London, Ontario.

Kazarian, S.S., E. Persad, R. Silverson, & J. O'Flaherty. (1998). Police perceptions of their training and their interactions with mental health institutional supports. Unpublished manuscript. London, ON.

Keresztes, C., & S.S. Kazarian. (1996). Mental health: A developmental perspective. In R. Adler, E. Vingilis, & V. Mai (Eds.), *Community health and well-being in southwestern Ontario: Resource for planning* (pp. 207–16). London, ON: Middlesex Health Unit and Faculty of Medicine.

Lawson Health Research Institute. (2000, September 24). *Trends in police contact with persons with serious mental illness*. London, ON: Lawson Health Research Institute.

Levinthal, C.F. (1996). *Drugs, behavior, and modern society*. Needham Heights, MA: Allyn and Bacon.

McAndrew, A., & E. Sutton. (2004). Searching for solutions: The front line police perspective on mental health interventions in Simcoe County. Paper for the Research Analyst Program, Georgian College, Barrie, ON.

Mental Health Act, RSO 1990, c. M.7, as amended. Amended and passed as *Brian's Law* on June 23, 2000.

Murphy, G.R. (1989). *Managing persons with mental disabilities: A curriculum guide for police trainers.* Washington, DC: Police Executive Research Forum.

Office of the Chief Coroner. (1999). Inquest into the death of Edmund Wai-Kong Yu. File no. Q99015. Toronto: Office of the Chief Coroner.

Office of the United Nations High Commissioner for Human Rights. (1991, December 17). *Principles for the protection of persons with mental illness and the improvement of mental health care.* http://www.ohchr.org/english/law/principles.htm.

Offord, D., M. Boyle, D. Campbell, J. Cochrane, P. Goering, E. Lin, A. Rhodes, & M. Wong. (1994). *Mental health in Ontario: Selected findings from the Ontario Health Survey.* Toronto: Queen's Printer for Ontario.

Ontario Ministry of the Solicitor General. (February, 2000). Police response to persons who are emotionally disturbed or have a mental illness or a developmental disability. *Policing standards manual,* s. 29.

Persad, E., & S.S. Kazarian. (1998, November). Physician satisfaction with review boards: The provincial psychiatric hospital perspective. *Canadian Journal of Psychiatry* 43(9): 905–9.

Pardy, J. (2000). *Conflict management in law enforcement.* Toronto: Emond Montgomery.

Police Executive Research Forum. (1997). *The police response to people with mental illnesses.* Washington, DC: Police Executive Research Forum.

Sharma, V., D. Whitney, S.S. Kazarian, & R. Manchanda. (2000, February). Preferred terms for users of mental health services among service providers and recipients. *Psychiatric Services* 51(2): 203–9.

Statistics Canada. (2002–2006). Causes of death 1999, 2002, 2003 and death by causes 2000 and 2001. Ottawa, ON: Statistics Canada.

Statistics Canada. (2006). *Causes of death 2003.* Ottawa, ON: Statistics Canada catalogue no. 84-208-XIE.

Stedman, H., J. Morrissey, M.W. Deane, & R. Borum. (1996). *Police response to emotionally disturbed persons: Analyzing new models of police interactions with the mental health system.* Washington, DC: National Institute of Justice.

Violanti, J.M. (1996). *Police suicide: Epidemic in blue.* Springfield, IL: C. Thomas.

EXERCISES AND REVIEW

Personal Reflections

Read each statement below and circle whether you agree or disagree with it.

1. Mentally ill people take away from real police work.

    AGREE   DISAGREE

2. Police should treat mentally ill people the way they treat all criminals.

    AGREE   DISAGREE

3. Police training in mental health issues helps police officers handle calls more effectively and safely.

    AGREE   DISAGREE

4. People with mental illness are no more dangerous or violent than the average person.

    AGREE   DISAGREE

5. Most police encounters with mentally ill people involve referring people to mental health professionals and other community resources.

    AGREE   DISAGREE

6. Police training in mental health issues just turns police officers into mental health professionals.

    AGREE   DISAGREE

7. Mentally ill and homeless people are major sources of crime.

    AGREE   DISAGREE

8. Responding to mental health calls is an appropriate part of police work.

    AGREE   DISAGREE

9. The proper place for mentally ill people is a mental hospital.

    AGREE   DISAGREE

10. Police play a valuable role in ensuring that mentally ill people receive appropriate and needed care.

    AGREE   DISAGREE

SCORING: Give yourself one point for agreeing with the following statements: 3, 4, 5, 8, and 10. Give yourself one point each for disagreeing with the remaining statements. Higher scores reflect higher acceptance of the role of police in responding to mental health calls. Compare your score with a classmate's. Try to reconcile the differences in opinions.

Diversity IQ: Multiple Choice

Circle the best answer.

1. Which of the following options are available to police in dealing with a person who is mentally ill?

   a. invoking psychiatric assessment under mental health legislation

   b. arresting the person for a criminal offence

   c. assisting the person to see a mental health professional

   d. all of the above

2. Which of the following is true about people with mental illness?

   a. they are all criminals

   b. they are all psychotic

   c. they are people with problems rather than problem people

   d. all of the above

3. Which of the following is a psychotic mental disturbance?

   a. hallucination

   b. delusion

   c. paranoia

   d. all of the above

4. Under mental health statutes, police officers may take a person into custody for psychiatric assessment on the grounds of

   a. threat

   b. mental disorder

   c. lack of competence to care for self

   d. all of the above

5. The right of mentally ill people to be protected from discrimination is recognized

   a. in many countries around the world

   b. by psychiatrists only

   c. by psychologists only

   d. by police only

6. Which of the following is an appropriate police response to delusion?

    a. agreement

    b. disputation

    c. argument

    d. none of the above

7. Which group has the highest risk for completed suicide?

    a. men

    b. women

    c. young people under 18 years of age

    d. none of the above

8. People with schizophrenia

    a. develop the condition at a young age

    b. have psychotic symptoms

    c. a and b

    d. none of the above

9. Which of the following is a risk factor for suicide?

    a. anniversaries

    b. recent loss

    c. depression

    d. all of the above

10. Which of the following is a symptom of bipolar disorder?

    a. depression

    b. mania

    c. a and b

    d. none of the above

Diversity IQ: True or False?

____ 1. Police officers are immune to mental illness.

____ 2. Police need to provide assistance that meets the unique needs of people with mental illness.

____ 3. Effectively responding to people with mental illness requires police knowledge of community supports and services.

____ 4. More women have schizophrenia than men.

_____   5. It is best to refer to people with mental retardation as morons, idiots, imbeciles, or retards.

_____   6. Prozac is an antidepressant medication.

_____   7. Pressure to keep talking is a symptom of depression.

_____   8. Men attempt suicide more often than women.

_____   9. Feelings of sadness and loss of interest in life are symptoms of depression.

Application Now

1. You receive a call from a family from the aboriginal community that a 17-year-old male has committed suicide by shooting himself with a gun. The surviving family members consist of a father, mother, and 7-year-old sister. What would you do to assist the surviving family members in the short and long term?

    Short term

    Long term

2. Imagine that you are a police officer. Read each of the following situations and indicate the course of action you would take. Options you should consider include asking the person to go with you voluntarily to a hospital for assessment; laying a charge and taking the person to hospital; taking the person to hospital without laying a charge; laying a charge and bringing the person before a justice of the peace; diverting the person to a home (family, relatives), a community program, or a community agency for care and safety; and referring the person to a diversion program that involves the criminal justice system and mental health agencies.

    A mentally ill man has committed a serious crime and is clearly showing debilitating symptoms of mental illness.

A homeless man has committed a violent crime and is clearly showing debilitating symptoms of a mental disorder.

A mentally ill woman has committed a serious crime but has been functioning adequately.

A mentally ill refugee has committed a minor offence and is clearly showing signs of a serious mental disorder.

A mentally ill woman has committed a minor offence but poses no threat to public safety.

Food for Thought

Identify strategies that enable police to work in partnership with the mental health system and diverse groups in the community to deal with mental health calls.

From Thought to Action

1. Analyze each of the following scenarios by answering the questions below and then role-play them. Consider reversing roles and re-enacting the scenes.

a. A 24-year-old mentally ill man is threatening his mother with his fists. Your assessment of the situation is that he is unlikely to physically act out his anger and there is no real possibility that anyone will get hurt accidentally. You say, "If you don't stop threatening your mother you're going to have a battle on your hands. Now what's it going to be?"

What is the problem?

What are the issues?

What are the solutions?

b. A 28-year-old homeless woman has been drinking and is now threatening passersby with a knife. You decide that she is unlikely to attack anyone or hurt anyone accidentally. You say, "All you homeless people are drunk. What are we going to do with you people?"

What is the problem?

What are the issues?

What are the solutions?

c. A teenager tells you that the dentist put a microchip in his mouth when he went for a filling so now everyone can hear his private thoughts all the time. You say, "You believe that people are spying on you. That must be very scary for you."

What is the problem?

What are the issues?

What are the solutions?

d. A 65-year-old mentally ill woman tells you that her husband and children are trying to get rid of her by poisoning her food. You tell the family that the woman is a "psycho" and you have to take her to a "nut house."

What is the problem?

What are the issues?

What are the solutions?

2. Read the list of dos and don'ts in table 10.5 (on p. 285). What do you think should be deleted from the list and what should be added?

Lessons from History

Invite mentally ill people and their families, activists, and service providers to provide historical perspectives on homeless or mentally ill people. Make sure topics such as the police–mental health system relationship or police response to homelessness calls are discussed, as well as unique needs and system improvements.

The Great Debate

There are two major views regarding the effect of police culture on the mental health of police officers. One is that the collectivist culture plays a positive role in officers' mental health; the other is that the collectivist culture plays a negative role. Have half the class support one view and the other half support the other view. The goal for each group is to promote health in police services and prevent mental health issues.

Glossary

aboriginal peoples' rights
rights of Canada's aboriginal peoples to preserve their culture, identity, customs, traditions, and languages, and any special rights that they have currently or may acquire in the future

acculturation
process of acquiring cultural attributes of an ethnic community to which one does not belong

achievement culture
culture that focuses on work

assimilation
rejection of one's culture of origin in favour of absorption into the host culture

assimilation ideology
ideology that expects people of diversity to relinquish their cultural and linguistic identity and adopt the culture of the host state

assimilationist
intolerant of immigrants' heritage culture, demanding that they relinquish that culture and adopt the host culture

asynchrony
state of two (or more) communication styles being out of step with each other as a result of cultural differences

authoritarianism
conduct that demands obedience to authority

bipolar disorder
mood disorder that involves emotional swings between depression and mania; formerly called manic depression

bullying
open or subtle acts or remarks that tease, frighten, threaten, hurt, or disempower people

Canadian Charter of Rights and Freedoms
part of the Canadian constitution that establishes the protection of nine basic rights and freedoms deemed essential to the maintenance of a free democratic society and a united country

Canadian Human Rights Act
law that prohibits discrimination based on race, national or ethnic origin, colour, age, sex, marital status, disability, sexual orientation, or conviction for an offence for which a pardon has been granted

Canadian Human Rights Commission
federal body responsible for investigating and adjudicating complaints of violations of the *Canadian Human Rights Act*

Canadianism
national Canadian identity that cuts across age, income, and gender differences and goes beyond regional, ethnic, and linguistic lines

child abuse
physical and psychological maltreatment of children by adults

child sexual abuse
sexual exploitation and maltreatment of dependent and developmentally immature children and adolescents

civic ideology
ideology that shares the principles of multiculturalism ideology but does not support state funding to maintain and promote ethnocultural diversity

civil liberty policing model
law enforcement model that places civil liberties at the forefront of police services

civil order policing model
law enforcement model that places national security at the forefront of police services

code of silence
core value of withholding information from anyone who is not a member of the police culture

collectivist culture
"we"-oriented culture that values family, group harmony, and conformity

community policing principles
principles associated with the police services approach that provide for identifying and solving problems, resolving the underlying causes of disputes, preventing future recurrences, and finding alternatives to arrest and conviction whenever possible

constructive discrimination
discrimination that results from a requirement, qualification, or factor that seems reasonable but effectively excludes, restricts, or favours some people contrary to human rights laws

core values
values of self-control, cynicism, respect for authority, hypervigilance, and a code of silence associated with the collectivist police culture

cross-cultural communication
understanding the verbal and non-verbal communicative patterns of people from diverse cultures for the purpose of effective intercultural interchange

cross-cultural criminal investigation
application of diversity principles in crime investigation

cross-cultural training
training in how to deal with other cultures, whether in another country or within one's own country

cultural awareness training
training in how to deal more effectively with cultural issues, either in general or in terms of a particular culture

culture
pattern of behaviour and results of behaviour that are shared and transmitted among members of a particular society

cynicism
belief that the primary motivation behind human behaviour is selfishness

delusions
ideas that are real only to the mentally ill person

democratic rights
rights to vote or run in an election and the assurance that no government has the right to continue to hold power indefinitely without seeking a new mandate from the electorate

depression
mood disorder characterized by feelings of despair and hopelessness

discrimination
illegal and negative behaviour that deprives a group or its members of their civil rights

diversity
socially constructed characteristics on the basis of which individuals and groups define themselves and/or are defined by others

diversity acculturation orientation model
concept that suggests interplay between orientations of host communities and those of people of diversity

diversity equity
equity based on belief that there are no superior or inferior cultural groups

diversity-motivated beliefs and practices
negative views of and activities against people of diversity

diversity policing framework
policing framework that affirms and values people of diversity; assumes a police–community climate that validates diversity; empowers voices of diversity within and outside the police force in goal setting, problem solving, and decision making; and promotes a police–community culture that is respectful of police safety and police personhood

diversity training
a holistic approach to preparing police and police organizations to become culturally competent

ego forcing
use of unnecessary force to boost a macho self-image

elder abuse
physical, sexual, emotional, or psychological abuse or neglect, or financial exploitation, of an older person by a caregiver

employment equity
strategy designed to make workplaces reflect society's diversity by encouraging the full participation of people of all diversities

equality rights
rights of all Canadians, regardless of race, national or ethnic origin, colour, sex, age, or mental or physical disability, to be equal before the law and to enjoy equal protection and benefit of the law

ethnic identity
attachment to, or feeling of pride in, one's cultural heritage

ethnicity
individual or group identification with a culture of origin

ethnist ideology
ideology that expects people of diversity to assimilate, but the state defines which groups should assimilate and thus which ones will not enjoy the same legal rights as other members of the state

ethnocentrism
tendency to view one's ethnocultural group more positively than others, and to view other groups as inferior

exclusionary
intolerant of immigrants' heritage culture and of immigration in general

family violence
behaviour that causes one partner in a relationship to be afraid of and controlled by the other, or that is caregiver abuse of children or abuse of caregiver by children

formication
hallucination that involves feeling that insects or snakes are crawling over or under one's skin

freedom from discrimination
under part I of the Ontario *Human Rights Code*, freedom from discrimination with respect to services, goods, facilities, accommodation, contracts, employment, and occupational associations, and freedom from sexual solicitation in the workplace and by those in a position of power

fundamental freedoms
freedom of conscience and religion; freedom of thought, belief, opinion, and expression, including freedom of the press and other media of communication; freedom of peaceful assembly; and freedom of association

gendered apartheid
viewpoint that considers women unequal to men and treats women as a subordinate class

ghettoization
process in which members of a particular ethnic, religious, or national group live in high concentration in poverty stricken areas either by choice or by force

hallucinations
sensory experiences that are disturbed or disturbing and are real only to the mentally ill person

harassment
comments or conduct toward another person that is unwelcome

hate crime
criminal offence against a person or an entire group of people that is motivated in whole or in part by hatred of or bias or prejudice against the victim's race, national or ethnic origin, language, colour, religion, sex, age, mental or physical ability, sexual orientation, or any other similar factor

hate propaganda
any writing, sign, or visible representation that advocates or promotes genocide

high-context culture
culture that relies on context to convey the meaning of a message

host community
comprises groups of people who have the power and influence to shape societal attitudes toward the remaining groups in society

hypervigilance
belief that survival of police and of others depends on police ability to view everything in the environment as potentially life-threatening and dangerous

ideology
belief system or world view of an individual, a group, or a society

independent self-construal
view of the self as independent and self-reliant for its well-being

individualist culture
"me"-oriented culture that values the pursuit of personal goals, self-reliance, non-conformity, and competition

integration
embracement of the host culture of settlement and continued maintenance of the culture of origin

integrationist
supportive of immigrants adopting features of the host culture while maintaining aspects of their heritage culture

interactive acculturation model
concept that suggests interplay between orientations of host communities and those of settlement groups

interdependent self-construal
view of the self as interdependent and reliant on family, kin, or the in-group for its well-being

kinesics
physical communication, including look and appearance, eye contact, facial expressions, posture, body movements, and touching

legal rights
basic legal protection to safeguard Canadian citizens in their dealings with the state and the justice system

loose culture
culture that tolerates deviation from established norms and expectations

low-context culture
culture that relies on words to convey most of the message being sent

male white culture
culture in which whiteness, masculinity, and hierarchy are emphasized and diversity, women, and gays and lesbians are devalued

mandatory arrest policy
a policy to lay criminal charges in family violence cases; arrest must take place whenever probable cause exists, even for less serious offences

mania
mood disorder characterized by feelings of emotional high, agitation, and impulsivity

marginalization
simultaneous rejection of the culture of origin and the host culture

mediative police response
aims to avoid the arrest of the abuser; police officers responding to family violence calls take a hands-off approach

mental disturbance
categorized as either pyschotic or non-psychotic mental illness

mental illness
group of disabilities marked by disturbances in thinking, feeling, and relating

mental retardation
significant subaverage intelligence, significant limitation in adaptive functioning, and onset before the age of 18 years

misattribution
misinterpretation of a message or behaviour

mobility rights
freedom to enter, remain in, or leave the country, and to live and seek employment anywhere in Canada

mood disorders
mental disorders that affect a person's mood, including depression and bipolar disorder

multicultural heritage
the unique and constitutionally enshrined multicultural character of Canadian society

multiculturalism ideology
ideology that recognizes and supports people of diversity in maintaining or promoting their diversity, provided that their practices do not clash with the laws of the nation

multiculturalism policy
Canadian policy that recognizes, values, and promotes the cultural and racial diversity of its people by allowing them the freedom to preserve, enhance, and share their cultural heritage

official languages
English and French as confirmed by the Charter, which guarantees that the federal government can serve members of the public in the official language of their choice

Ontario *Human Rights Code*
Ontario statute that protects the dignity and worth of every person and provides for "equal rights and opportunities without discrimination that is contrary to law"

Ontario *Police Services Act*
law that stipulates that police services shall be provided throughout Ontario in accordance with the safeguards that guarantee the fundamental rights enshrined in the Charter and the Ontario *Human Rights Code*

Ontario Human Rights Commission
provincial body responsible for investigating and adjudicating complaints of violations of the Ontario *Human Rights Code*

paralanguage
features of speech, such as tone, loudness, speed, and use of silence

persuasive disclosure
approaches people use to persuade others

pluralism
state of having many cultural groups in one country

police–community interface
represented by the motto "to serve and protect," the principle that police functions are to be afforded to all community residents regardless of their culture, race, ethnic origin, religion, sex, age, sexual orientation, or physical or mental ability

police culture
attitudes, values, and beliefs of police and police organizations that influence police reactions and behaviours within the police services and on the street

police force approach
approach to policing that emphasizes a reactive, crime control mandate; measures police effectiveness by such indicators as number of random patrols to deter criminal activity, response rate to police calls, number of arrests and convictions, and citizen satisfaction surveys

police services approach
approach to policing that emphasizes problem solving, crime prevention, and partnerships between police and communities

preference hierarchy for cultural groups
expressed feeling of comfort with particular cultures, suggesting that Aboriginal peoples and European cultural groups evoke feelings of comfort more so than groups of non-European origin, particularly those considered visible minorities

prejudice
bias against a person or group, without justification, because of presumed objectionable qualities ascribed to the person or group

private values
personal attitudes and activities of individuals in the domains of domestic and interpersonal relations

pro-arrest policy
encourages arrest in family violence cases but the decision to arrest is at the discretion of the officer

proxemics
use of space, in terms of physical distance between people, as a form of non-verbal communication

psychosis
form of serious mental disorder in which an actual break with reality occurs

public values
democratic ideals, constitutional and human rights provisions, and civil and criminal codes of the state

race
classification based on biological or cultural traits

race relations training
training in how to deal more effectively with race-related issues, from the perspective that racism is a social disease that can be eliminated with education

racial profiling
police detention or other treatment that singles out any person on the basis of race

racism
predictions, decisions, and actions based on the belief that some races are superior or inferior to others

recidivism
relapse into criminal activity

relationship culture
culture that focuses on social relations

religion
a spiritual belief system

religious beliefs
tenets of particular faiths

religious practices
concrete expressions of religious beliefs

respect for authority
core value stemming from the prevailing paramilitary organizational structure of police services, which provides simplicity, clarity, and comfort for police in fulfilling their role and executing their duties

restorative justice approach
involvement of offender, victim, and community to repair material and psychological damage to victim and community reintegration of offender by use of shaming and invoking remorse for wrongful action

schizophrenia
mental illness described as cancer of the mind that causes psychotic mental disturbances

segregationist
opposed to immigrants and other cultures, preferring that immigrants return to their countries of origin

self-control
overcontrol of emotions by suppression of verbal and non-verbal expressions of emotion

separation
individual rejection of the host culture and maintenance of the culture of origin

settlement patterns
the variety of ways that people establish themselves in a country, whether born there or as immigrants

spousal abuse
violence or mistreatment experienced by a man or a woman at the hands of a marital, common-law, or same-sex partner

stereotyping
making generalizations that are usually derogatory about individuals or groups

substance-related disorders
mental disorders caused by substance dependence and abuse, and by substance withdrawal

suicide
symptom of mood disorder that takes the form of ideation, threat, attempt, gesture, and completed suicide

systemic racism
racism at the social or organizational level that is supported by policies and procedures that discriminate

thought disorder
mental symptom characterized by ideas and speech that are coherent only to the mentally ill person

tight culture
culture that values predictability, certainty, and security

visible minority
an individual, other than an aboriginal person, who is non-Caucasian in race or non-white in colour

Answers to Diversity IQ: Multiple Choice and True or False

CHAPTER 1

Multiple Choice

1. b	6. c
2. d	7. c
3. d	8. b
4. d	9. a
5. d	10. d

True or False?

1. T	6. T
2. F	7. T
3. F	8. F
4. T	9. F
5. F	10. T

CHAPTER 2

Multiple Choice

1. d	6. b
2. d	7. d
3. d	8. b
4. a	9. a
5. a	10. a

True or False?

1. F	6. F
2. F	7. F
3. T	8. T
4. T	9. F
5. T	10. T

CHAPTER 3

Multiple Choice

1. c	6. a
2. d	7. d
3. d	8. d
4. a	9. b
5. c	10. d

True or False?

1. T	6. T
2. F	7. F
3. F	8. T
4. T	9. T
5. T	10. F

CHAPTER 4

Multiple Choice

1. b	6. c
2. d	7. c
3. c	8. b
4. e	9. c
5. c	10. c

True or False?

1. T	6. F
2. F	7. T
3. F	8. T
4. T	9. T
5. T	10. F

CHAPTER 5

Multiple Choice

1.	a	6.	b
2.	b	7.	a
3.	d	8.	b
4.	d	9.	c
5.	b	10.	a

True or False?

1.	F	6.	T
2.	T	7.	T
3.	T	8.	F
4.	T	9.	F
5.	F	10.	T

CHAPTER 6

Multiple Choice

1.	b	6.	b
2.	c	7.	a
3.	b	8.	b
4.	a	9.	c
5.	a	10.	b

True or False?

1.	F	6.	T
2.	F	7.	F
3.	F	8.	F
4.	T	9.	F
5.	F	10.	T

CHAPTER 7

Multiple Choice

1.	b	6.	b
2.	d	7.	d
3.	d	8.	a
4.	b	9.	a
5.	d	10.	d

True or False?

1.	T	6.	F
2.	T	7.	F
3.	T	8.	T
4.	T	9.	F
5.	T	10.	T

CHAPTER 8

Multiple Choice

1.	a	6.	d
2.	c	7.	a
3.	d	8.	d
4.	c	9.	d
5.	d	10.	c

True or False?

1.	T	6.	F
2.	F	7.	F
3.	T	8.	T
4.	T	9.	T
5.	T	10.	T

CHAPTER 9

Multiple Choice

1.	a	6.	b
2.	d	7.	c
3.	d	8.	b
4.	a	9.	b
5.	d	10.	c

True or False?

1.	F	6.	F
2.	T	7.	T
3.	T	8.	T
4.	F	9.	F
5.	T	10.	T

CHAPTER 10

Multiple Choice

1.	d	6.	d
2.	c	7.	a
3.	d	8.	c
4.	d	9.	d
5.	a	10.	c

True or False?

1.	F	6.	T
2.	T	7.	F
3.	T	8.	F
4.	F	9.	F
5.	F	10.	T

Index

equality rights, 69
ethnic identity, 46
ethnicity, 137
ethnist ideology, 39
ethnocentrism, 45
exclusionary, 106

family violence
    barriers to leaving violent relationships, 262
    cost of, 257
    defined, 254
    diversity, and, 258-61
    explanations for, 261
    immigrants and refugees, and, 259-61
    law, and, 255
    myths about, 259
    police responses to, 264
    sexual orientation, and, 259
    size of problem, 256-57
    social responses to, 262-63
First Nations peoples, 142-44
formication, 277
freedom from discrimination, 72
fundamental freedoms, 66

gendered apartheid, 261
ghettoization, 40

hallucinations, 283
harassment, 73
hate crime, 198-202
hate propaganda, 198
high-context culture, 140
Hinduism, 171
host community
    acculturation orientations of, 106
    cultural pluralism and, 105
    defined, 105
    policing, and, 119-21
human rights
    Canada, 65-72
    international, 65
    law enforcement, and, 79, 80
    Ontario, 72-79
    post-9/11, 79
hypervigilance, 11

ideology
    assimilation ideology, 39
    civic ideology, 39
    defined, 38

ethnist ideology, 39
    multiculturalism ideology, 38-39
immigration policies (Canada)
    1900 to 1945, 110-12
    1946 to 1961, 112-13
    1962 to 1992, 113
    1993 to 2001, 113-14
    evaluation, 116
    family reunification, 117
    post-9/11, 117
    pre-Confederation to 1899, 108-10
    refugees, pre-9/11, 114-16
    skilled workers, 118
independent self-construal, 141
individualist culture, 140
integration, 107
integrationist, 106
interactive acculturation model, 107
interdependent self-construal, 141
international human rights and freedoms, 65
Islam, 172-73

Jehovah's Witnesses, 174
Judaism, 174-76

kinesics, 235

legal rights, 67
linguistic ethnocentrism, 106
loose culture, 139
low-context culture, 139

male white culture, 6
mandatory arrest policy, 264
mania, 280
marginalization, 107
mediative police response, 264
mental disturbance, 277
Mental Health Act, 278
mental illness
    concept of, 277
    defined, 277
    mental health legislation, 278
    police response to mental disturbance, 279-84
mental retardation, 284
minority, 138
misattribution, 235
mobility rights, 67
mood disorders, 280
multicultural heritage, 72
multiculturalism ideology, 38

Credits

Table 1.1: Criminal Code Incidents Reported by Police in Canada, 2003. Adapted from Statistics Canada publication *The Daily*, Catalogue 11-001, July 28, 2004, online at http://www.statcan.ca/Daily/English/040728/d040728a.htm.

Table 1.6: Visible Minority Shares of the Population, Ontario Metropolitan Areas from 2005 to 2030. © 2005. Reproduced with the permission of The Centre for Spatial Economics.

Appendix 1.1: Canada's Population Growth, 1921 to 2031. © 2005. Reproduced with the permission of The Centre for Spatial Economics.

Appendix 1.2: Ontario's Births and Deaths, 1971 to 2031. © 2005. Reproduced with the permission of The Centre for Spatial Economics.

Appendix 1.3: Ontario's Population Growth Sources, 1971 to 2031. © 2005. Reproduced with the permission of The Centre for Spatial Economics.

Appendix 1.4: Canada's Immigration by Source, 1956 to 2001. © 2005. Reproduced with the permission of The Centre for Spatial Economics.

Table 4.2: Canadian Immigration Point System, 1993-2001. Office of the Auditor General of Canada (2000).

Table 4.3: Skilled Worker Selection Grid. Citizenship and Immigration Canada (2002). Bill C-11: Immigration and Refugee Protection Act. http://www.cic.gc.ca/english/irpac/c11-overview.html. Reprinted with the permission of the Minister of Public Works and Government Services Canada 2007.

Table 5.2: Top 10 Ethnic Groups in Canada, 2001. Adapted from Statistics Canada publication *Canada's ethnocultural portrait: The changing mosaic, 2001 census*, Catalogue 96F0030XIE2001008, released January 21, 2003, online at http://www.statcan.ca/bsolc/english/bsolc?catno=96F0030XIE2001008.

Table 5.3: Brant, C.C. Native ethics and rules of behaviour. 1990. 35:6 *The Canadian Journal of Psychiatry* 534-39. Reproduced with permission of The Canadian Journal of Psychiatry.

Table 7.1: Hate Crimes in 12 Major Police Forces, 2001-2002. Adapted from Statistics Canada publication *JURISTAT*, Catalogue 85-002, Hate Crime in Canada, 2004, vol. 24, no. 4, released June 1, 2004, at 17.

Table 8.1: Perceptions of bias and racism within the Ontario criminal justice system: Results from a public opinion survey. 1994. Toronto: Commission on Systemic Racism in the Ontario Criminal Justice System. Reproduced by permission of Scot Wortley.

Table 8.5: Based on Laws, J. 2005. *Durham Regional Police Services: 2005-2010 diversity strategic plan*. Graybridge Malkam. Reproduced by permission of Durham Regional Police Services.

Table 9.2: *Isolated, afraid, and forgotten: The service delivery needs and realities of immigrant and refuge women who are battered. National Clearinghouse on Family Violence*, Public Health Agency of Canada (1990). Reproduced with the permission of the Minister of Public Works and Government Services Canada, 2007.